Law as Civic Education

If a civic education is the essential foundation for a functioning, discursive democracy, how should it be taught? This book offers an innovative solution, arguing that far from abandoning the often-grand promise of civic education as a means of cultivating reasoning skills and democratic character, we should embrace it, and proposes a reimagined civic education based on teaching students in primary and secondary school law and legal reasoning.

Drawing on a range of theoretical disciplines—law, philosophy, ethics, sociology, psychology, and moral educational and child development theory—this monograph justifies the benefits of law learning as a form of character and civic education and offers historical and comparative educational examples to show what is possible. It demonstrates how legal teaching can be incorporated into a K-12 curriculum and argues that such training can be transformative, guiding students to become citizens capable of meeting the demands of democracy: citizens with stronger reasoning skills, a motivation to self-examine their values and beliefs and bring them into conversation with social values, and an ability to effectively navigate political institutions and participate in public discourse.

This compelling and deeply original work will be of interest to scholars and educators in the fields of civic education, character and virtue education, legal studies, and philosophy of education.

Ariel J. Liberman is Assistant Professor of Law and Legal Studies in the Department of Political Science at Auburn University, USA.

Routledge Research in Character and Virtue Education

This series provides a forum for established and emerging scholars to discuss the latest debates, research and theory relating to virtue education, character education and value education.

Historical and Contemporary Foundations of Social Studies Education
Unpacking Implications for Civic Education and Contemporary Life
James E. Schul

Ubuntu Virtue Theory and Moral Character Formation
Critically Reconstructing Ubuntu for the African Educational Context
Grivas Muchineripi Kayange

Civic Education at Crossroads
The Christian Nationalist Threat to Public Schools
Bryan J. Henry

The Pedagogy of the Community of Philosophical Enquiry as Citizenship Education
Global Perspectives on Talking Democracy into Action
Edited by Joshua Forstenzer, Fufy Demissie and Vachararutai Boontinand

Educating for Care and Virtue Development in Young Children
Research Approaches in Ethics Education from the MelArete Project
Edited by Luigina Mortari

Law as Civic Education
Reimagining a K-12 Curriculum for Democratic Citizenship and Individual Character
Ariel J. Liberman

For more information about this series, please visit: www.routledge.com/Routledge-Research-in-Character-and-Virtue-Education/book-series/RRCVE

Law as Civic Education

Reimagining a K-12 Curriculum for Democratic Citizenship and Individual Character

Ariel J. Liberman

Routledge
Taylor & Francis Group
NEW YORK AND LONDON

First published 2025
by Routledge
605 Third Avenue, New York, NY 10158

and by Routledge
4 Park Square, Milton Park, Abingdon, Oxon, OX14 4RN

Routledge is an imprint of the Taylor & Francis Group, an informa business

ISBN: 9781032975825 (hbk)
ISBN: 9781032979861 (pbk)
ISBN: 9781003596523 (ebk)

DOI: 10.4324/9781003596523

Typeset in Times New Roman
by Newgen Publishing UK

To my wife and son, who have my whole heart.

Contents

About the Author

Ariel J. Liberman is Assistant Professor of Law and Legal Studies at Auburn University in Auburn, Alabama. As an interdisciplinary scholar of law, religion, and education, his published works have explored subjects of schooling and learning through legal, political, historical, philosophical, comparative, religious, and ethical perspectives. He also researches more broadly in legal and political theory, legal education, and comparative law. He gained his doctorate in 2023 from Emory University School of Law, where he was named Randolph W. Thrower Scholar in Law and Religion. He also holds an L.L.M. (2022) from Emory University, a J.D. (2018) from Boston University School of Law, and a B.A. (2015) from New York University.

Preface

The following contributes to scholarship offering law-solutions to problems facing the educational project in the United States on both practical and philosophical levels. Endeavoring to tackle concerns held by many over child-rearing in today's complicated socio-political climate is a subject large in scope—inculpating questions of community and family, law and children, character formation and values, democratic survival, schooling policy and administration. Each of these is very near to my heart, yet, in the following, I offer only something small. I trust, however, that it touches on all these issues and will initiate a conversation.

I had another project in mind originally, asking: how can the public education governance paradigm—faced with challenges and fraught with controversy, berated for being "bland" and ineffective,[1] out-of-touch, consistently subject to misguided reform and revision[2]—be reconceptualized to better partner with, in my view, our most fundamental and influential apparatuses for raising children and young citizens: the family and the community.[3] This, of course, is far from the current situation, with the "family and community" often blamed for impeding the public educational mission.[4] Yet, despite undertaking a thoughtful intellectual exercise to place the "community" at the center of educational administration, I ran into a big problem: even *if* afforded the authority to innovate their community public schools, *why* would communities—and, more specifically, the members—rise to meet a new governance charge? Sure, if you exist in a middle-or-upper class neighborhood where parents send their kids to the local public school, where folks have the time to spare to think about their community's educational needs, I understand seizing upon a more elaborate role in how resources are received, where it goes, and who decides. But others? One need not strain to think of communities where the bulk of children are already enrolled in external parochial school options or, still others, where parents send their children out of district. Still more, there are disenfranchised communities where, though the bulk of students might avail themselves of public schools, members could hardly spare a second to involve themselves in education administration. Even with assured personal impact, there is no sense that people (communities) would step up and prioritize their involvement in the educational project. Really, there is no incentive for communities to involve themselves in *anything* related to self-controlled public education; I mean, I can hardly get my neighbor to pick up a parcel off my doorstep unless there is something in it for them!

While I firmly believe that grassroots, community-involvement is a key to more successful public schools,[5] acknowledging the specter of poor participation means that a newly modeled public-school paradigm, in today's socio-cultural milieu, would be of little help. It is a technical solution to a complex, adaptive challenge. Indeed, it is one that could even exacerbate social division, adding to the girth of tasks already on overcrammed schedules of parents and community leaders who exclusively avail themselves of the public system—many of which constitute the most economically and socially vulnerable communities in our country. It would offer no incentive for parents to pull children from parochial schools, who already see themselves as investing time and money in *their* children's education. The argument is no more effective than arguments for voucher programs or school choice. In short, it only exacerbates difference and also reveals our inherent self-preoccupation.

Further, considering this reveals a deeper, more concerning phenomenon: existing apathy and jadedness when it comes to believing that we—citizens—can do anything to better our educational paradigm. This is emblematic of a deeper problem: lack of connectedness with our system, unity, belief, and buy-in in our civic institutions *until it affects them*, an at-best fragile social "overlapping consensus"[6] of what is important for us, individuals, in terms of national civic and social justice. Put broadly, our democracy is failing in part, at least, because *we are not producing citizens who care*. The problem, as I conceive of it is an educational one—though not exclusively. Apathy is compounded by a flat, non-character-and-civic-focused (which I view as intertwined, as you will see) public-school education in a more diverse and divergent society. A mentality that is *civic*—relating to the duties one has toward the collective—connotes an impulse toward involvement, interest. But education, by and large, or really any project part and parcel to the civic enterprise (think: equality, healthcare access, etc.) is simply not a part of our collective *ethos* today. There is nothing to push us, or, in turn, our children, or children's children to change their minds to convince them that they can effect change. The collapse of any civic infrastructure is, indeed, "not my problem" … until it is.

Taken to its logical extreme, our failure to bridge pluralities through a harmonious construction of what matters to us in terms of our institutions makes us all "vulnerable to those who would instrumentalize and exacerbate our ethical and social differences for the purposes of commercial or political gain."[7] This, I found, is a scary prospect owing to much of the divisiveness we currently experience. My idea for community-centered education paradigms is a project that, I think, has merit, but not until we engage in the work of getting our citizens *invested*. Lest we simply "trust" all individuals in each community to take an interest, and, more than that, to actively volunteer themselves to better their schools, the paradigm fails. But they wouldn't (and why would they!). This project, I believe, can be framed as a question of character formation in education. Thus, and in the spirit of, again, offering law-solutions to education problems, I arrive at the topic of this book: a theoretical argument for *better* educating children for civic aims and for ethical aims (and against apathy!) in school by incorporating law learning—which I conceive of as an empowering, inspiring, and a potential jolting tool to public discourse—into the elementary and secondary school citizen education experience.

Defending the merit, value, and urgency of this addition is the subject of these many pages. As a matter of background, however, it might help the reader to know that, in doing so, I am also offering a solution to some of the core attacks levied against the public-school system by its opponents. For instance, where some argue that public school's prioritization of neutrality over encouraging the development of children's autonomous sense of self, identity, morality is antithetical to the civic mission,[8] I want to show that law learning in public-school context is a way to introduce those conversations on individual values *and* respect plurality by couching them within universal systems that offer a common institutional rhetoric for addressing values-conflicts. To others who contend the opposite, that many public schools and communities around the nation are *too* concerned with some values over others, that they can foster bigotry, that they alienate minority groups, and ineffectively educate around civics, diversity, tolerance, compromise, and commitment,[9] I want to show that universal law learning curricula can be an efficient and effective remedy. The subject brings children together to discuss mutually important issues, critique the system, contend with differing perspectives, and resolve disputes. Law learning offers occasion to discuss different moral viewpoints, contend with difficult political topics, and address systemic concerns without promoting any one of them. In short, my project is still of the same theoretical category as before—how do we make public school better—but taken from a different angle. This direction, on the surface, however, and the disposition of this book will be about applying law learning to *all* elementary and secondary school curricula as a matter of policy (though public schools and their constituencies will, in my view, particularly benefit).

So, what will I and what won't I be doing here? Let us start with the former. I will discuss the way law learning uniquely impacts and develops the character of the citizen (not just the lawyer), serves toward civic goals (and the greater educational project), endows them with certain capacities and perspectives (and, by extension, skills), and why this is important for children in America today. To support an argument for the legitimate benefits of a law learning program, I will contextualize the proposal within a larger landscape of philosophy of education discourse and show its consistency with our historic national educational mission. Focusing on the way law learning empowers and teaches, this book will articulate how a versatility with the law unites citizens, serves as starting point for producing future leaders for our legal-political-social system, intentionally reforms responsive civic institutions, and, when inserted into the curriculum of diverse classrooms with students embracing differing political, religious, cultural, and social identities, as those that exist already in public schools,[10] leads to important identity-building and relationship-strengthening through respectful, tolerant, and discursive discussions *we need to be having*. It teaches calculative and reflective temperament, appreciation for tradition, and respect for others; it is the sort of education, when properly conceived, that empowers students to connect with systems, see their worth and value as changemakers, to *want to act*, and build relationships with that in mind. In turn, beneficiaries of this education in the next generation might be more inclined to care and effectively improve civic projects, to put stock in conversations that are now seen as "not one's problem."

Now, I turn to what I *won't* be doing in this piece. The benefits of a legal education have been, in the main, relegated to lawyers and law students, those who seek out the benefits and skills of law-think. And to be sure, much scholarship has been penned concerning how important it must be—and, indeed, it is[11]—or the everyman to know their rights and the law, a *public legal education*.[12] But this is not what I talk about when I talk about law learning. For our purposes, law learning has just about as much to do with *why* the law is as *what* the law is. More than studying what, constitutionally, an officer can do at a traffic stop (the "what"), for instance, empowerment is found through exploring *with* children issues of fairness and justice. Lessons might include therefore the reasons *why* the scope of their search is limited—what values are inculpated—discourses on the weighing of privacy, autonomy, and examining principles behind the consequences of this violation. What do you believe as informed by your community and relational experience? How do we prioritize interests to build a system that is just? What is and is not right about a case's outcome? And where should the changes be made? It is an education in critical thinking and higher reasoning!

Empowerment, for our purposes, takes the form of presenting a difficult question, expressing differing views, and dialoguing critically with the expectation that the results will not be stringently enshrined beliefs or ideas, right or wrong dispositions, but yield a respectable myriad of dispositions and roundtable discussion. Law learning *informs* perspectives rather than indoctrinates; indeed, one studies the system from without rather than from within. We combat, in turn, superficial understanding that leaves one vulnerable to political sway[13]; we develop the individual to a place of true *autonomy*, above manipulation.[14]

Notes

1 This description comes from Charles Glenn's critique of the present state of public-school education. "Civic Norms and Distinctive Convictions: Finding the Right Balance," in Pickard et al. (eds.), *The Impact of Education on Character Formation, Ethics, and the Communication of Values in Late Modern Pluralistic Societies* (Leipzig: Evangelische Verlagsanstalt, 2022). He articulates that:

> [public] schools today love to talk about differences of color, of sexual identities and preferences, and of trivial customs, but not convictions—these must remain unexpressed in the public-school contexts of the bland leading the bland, and thus youth are often persuaded that deep-rooted beliefs play no part in defining a worthy life.
>
> (Glenn, "Civic Norms," at 68)

As a matter of background, the purpose of the public school, at its inception and into today, is the formation of adjusted, loyal citizens out of diverse populations capable of participating within and strengthening the nation. The inability to educate in the matter of conviction, Glenn maintains, is a major failure for the public school seeking to educate students toward this goal. Indeed, outside of imparting on children generally agreeable social civic behavior norms—which Glenn takes no issue with—public schools today overstep the family, "presume[ing] to provide [children] with a distinctive worldview" that is superficial and contingent, that avoids, in the interest of "social unity and progress," conversations on controversies, even insofar as an account of the nature of a "flourishing life". *See also* John Coons, "Populism and Parental Choice," *First Things*, November. 2000, 16; Charles L. Glenn, *The Myth of the Common School* (Amherst: University of Massachusetts Press, 1988). The "tolerance" that is being propped up in the public school is, to Glenn, simply "nonjudgmental relativism," and not genuine respect or understanding. A failure to reinforce belief, conviction, character-building, depth of ideas of self, all contribute to youth vulnerability and toward "self-definition through impulse and unbridled consumption." Indeed, the fear of fostering division among students by talking about controversial convictions or beliefs leaves students unprepared for real-world encounters with others espousing different ideas. Charles L. Glenn, *The Myth of the Common School* (Amherst: University of Massachusetts Press, 1988), 67–68; *see also* James Davison Hunter, *Culture Wars* (New York: Basic Books, 1991). Thus, the "civic republican" supporter of the modern form of public education "risks negating or at best minimizing the benefits that children gain from becoming self-fulfilled individuals who can choose from among various visions of the good life under the guidance of their family and cultural community." James Davison Hunter, *Culture Wars* (New York: Basic Books, 1991) 65. And to be sure, democratic citizenship suffers. *See also* Rosemary C. Salamone, *Visions of Schooling: Conscience, Community and Common Education* (New Haven: Yale University Press, 2000).

2 For further reading on the issue of school reform history, *see* Charles L. Glenn and Jan De Groof (Eds.), *Balancing Freedom, Autonomy, and Accountability in Education*, Vols. 1–4 (Oisterwijk, The Netherlands: Wolf Legal Publishers, 2012); Diane Ravitch, *Left Back: A Century of Battles Over School Reform* (New York: Simon & Schuster,

2001); James Davidson Hunter, *The Death of Character: Moral Education in an Age without Good or Evil* (New York: Basic Books, 2000).

3 Glenn shares similar views, but with a mind toward advocating for school choice. He articulates that:

> the insistence that government-operated schools are the unique source of social unity and civic virtue, has today, in consequence, only a negative function as the leading political argument for opposing schools that promote alternative sources of meaning and loyalty … the positive content of an educational program centered on developing patriotic commitment and citizen solidarity has long since been replaced by incoherence.
>
> (Glenn, "Civic Norms," at 68)

My project's conception would have contended with reinvigorating the public-school schema itself to rectify some of the issues with this type of educational experience on a theoretical level. This would be something novel for the American milieu, but not necessarily internationally. Indeed, it can be likened to a pluralistic model of an educational school system, like those in the Netherlands, England, Belgium, and other nations, but the diversification and support would be centered on public schools. *See* Ashley Berner, "Public Education and Moral Formation in the United States: A View from the Early Twenty-First Century," in Pickard et al. (eds.), *The Impact of Education on Character Formation, Ethics, and the Communication of Values in Late Modern Pluralistic Societies* (Leipzig: Evangelische Verlagsanstalt, 2022); *see also* Charles Glenn, "What the United States Can Learn from other Countries," in James Tooley and David Salisbury (eds.), *What Americans Can Learn from School Choice in Other Countries* (Washington, DC: Cato Institute, 2005), 79–90. Of course, my model would have had some nuance from other national systems given the unique nature of our educational administrative paradigm—involving, for instance, the question of making every school magnet schools, balancing charter school options, resourcing, and more.

4 *See, e.g.,* Elmer John Thiessen, *Defense of Religious Schools and Colleges* (Canada: McGill-Queens University Press, 2001); Robert Pondiscio, *How the Other Half Learns: Equality, Excellence, and the Battle over School Choice* (New York: Avery Publishing Group, 2019).

5 "Civic Norms and Distinctive Convictions: Finding the Right Balance," in Pickard et al. (eds.), *The Impact of Education on Character Formation Ethics, and the Communication of Values in Late Modern Pluralistic Societies* (Leipzig: Evangelische Verlagsanstalt, 2022), 63. Harkening back to an earlier time in our nation's history where "local schools, established and funded by local citizens, [taught] as much literacy and numeracy as was judged necessary to meet local needs and, along with those skills, a common morality reflecting that of the sponsoring community."

6 This is a highly developed idea in the field of political science and associated fields. Charles Taylor, "How to Define Secularism," in Alfred Stephan and Charles Taylor (eds.), *Boundaries of Toleration* (New York: Columbia University Press, 2014), 59–78. *See also*, John Rawls, *Political Liberalism* (New York: Columbia University Press, 2005); Michael G. Barnhart, "An Overlapping Consensus: A Critique of Two Approaches," 66 *Rev. Polit.* 257–83 (2004).

7 Robert W. Hefner, "Character Socialization and Diversity in Modern Democracies Today," in Pickard et al. (eds.), *The Impact of Education on Character Formation, Ethics, and the Communication of Values in Late Modern Pluralistic Societies* (Leipzig: Evangelische Verlagsanstalt, 2022).

8 "Civic Norms and Distinctive Convictions: Finding the Right Balance," in Pickard et al. (eds.), *The Impact of Education on Character Formation Ethics, and the Communication of Values in Late Modern Pluralistic Societies* (Leipzig: Evangelische Verlagsanstalt, 2022), 72–77. *See also* Stephen Macedo, *Liberal Virtues: Citizenship, Virtues, and Community in Liberal Constitutionalism* (Oxford, England: Clarendon Press, 1990).

9 *See, e.g.*, Linda C. McClain, "Bigotry, Civility, and Reinvigorating Civic Education: Government's Formative Task amid Polarization," in Witte Jr., et al. (eds.), *The Impact of Law on Character Formation, Ethics, and the Communication of Values in Late Modern Pluralistic Societies* (Leipzig: Evangelische Verlagsanstalt, 2022).

10 Linda C. McClain, *The Place of Families: Fostering Capacity, Equality and Responsibility* (Cambridge, MA: Harvard University Press, 2006), 50–84.

11 For other studies on the monopolization of "law-think" skills by the legal academy, *see, e.g.*, W. Bradley Wendell, "Lawyers, Citizens, and the Internal Point of View," 75 *Fordham L. Rev.* 1473 (2006); Amita Dhanda et al., eds., *Decolonization of Legal Knowledge* (London: Routledge, 2009).

12 For more on the subject of public legal education, *see, e.g.*, Richard Grimes, *Public Legal Education—The Role of Law Schools in Building a More Legally Literate Society* (London: Routledge, 2021). For more on "ignorance of the law," *see, e.g.*, Bruce Grace, "Ignorance of the Law as an Excuse," 86 *Columbia L. Rev.* 1392 (1986).

13 *See* Robert W. Hefner, "Character Socialization and Diversity in Modern Democracies Today," in Pickard et al. (eds.), *The Impact of Education on Character Formation, Ethics, and the Communication of Values in Late Modern Pluralistic Societies* (*referencing* Michael Sandel, "The Procedural Republic and the Unencumbered Self," 12 *Pol. Theor.*, No. 1, 81–96 (1984)) in arguing that actors in all societies are "encumbered by the attachments and identifications constitutive of their social beings." Meaning, in other words, that when one is a part of a group, by virtue of being entrenched one can be mobilized in a way antagonistic to the democratic values.

14 *See* Cathleen Kaveny, "Autonomy, Solidarity, and Law's Pedagogy," 27 *Louvain Stud.*, 339–357 (2002) (discussing Joseph Raz, *The Morality of Freedom* (Oxford: Oxford University Press, 1986), 410). Here, she notes that "autonomy on the part of the individual cannot exist without significant social commitment," that Raz argues for three fundamental attributes to individual autonomy, including "1) the raw mental capacity to make and carry out our choices; 2) freedom from attempts at both manipulation and coercion; and 3) a range of morally worthwhile choice." Kaveny then articulates that "a society committed to raising autonomous citizens will ensure they grow up in a stable and nurturing environment … [it will] refrain from manipulating them but also give them tools to recognize their manipulation." As we shall see, learning law helps accomplish this goal.

Acknowledgments

Early iterations of the ideas discussed in *Law as Civic Education* were presented as a part of my doctoral thesis at Emory University School of Law. Accordingly, I am indebted to three incredible mentors who helped guide my research as a part of my committee, Professors John Witte, Jr., Michael Broyde, and Alexander Volokh. A special thanks to Professor Broyde for inspiring me to even undertake the doctoral program at Emory in the first place, and for first guiding me fervently through the fascinating world of law and religion. Likewise, I want to express my deepest gratitude to all my colleagues and friends at Emory's Center for the Study of Law and Religion who helped to support and nurture my research interests as both a student and, later, a post-doctoral fellow. To Dr. Alexa Windsor, a long-term colleague and close friend, thank you for your comments on earlier versions of this book, and for the many long conversations refining these ideas. I would like to also thank two exceptional undergraduate students who have served diligently as research assistants on this project, Ms. Mica Einhorn and Ms. Natalie Garcia-Ramos. They will surely go on to do exceptional things.

To my colleagues and friends at Auburn University, who I have only known for a short while, thank you for supporting me throughout this process of putting ideas to paper. To Professors Steven Brown, Jacqueline Smoke, and Debra Armstrong-Wright, especially, I cannot tell you how excited I am to continue innovating—perhaps with the aid of some of the ideas presented in this book—our exceptional program in Law and Justice. Here's to many more years together!

Finally, the bulk of my gratitude must always go to my family. To my parents, Natasha and Harry, I love you and could not be more grateful to you both for all that you have done (and continue to do) for us. To my siblings, Bryan and Sydney, I love you beyond words. And, above all, to my wife, Michelle, and my son, Asher, thank you a million times over for your love and support.

Introduction

In 2018, Dr. Kim Lane Scheppele penned a formidable piece on what she terms "autocratic legalism" and the destruction of democracy by law.[1] This is a process by which "charismatic new leaders are elected by democratic publics and use their electoral mandates to dismantle by law the constitutional systems they inherited."[2] Eventually, these leaders—as she evinced through case studies (among them, the United States)—eliminate citizens' ability to exercise their democratic rights and to hold institutions accountable. There is a point of no return in these processes, but she proffers a source of hope. The predictable method to their madness can be anticipated; institutional bulwarks can be arranged to prevent the ascension of the poisonous leader.

But though Scheppele expounds on *how* to observe and prevent "autocratic legalism," the question of *who* should be charged with doing so remains open. The "highly technical" nature of the "de-liberalization of constitutional systems" often prevents most people from seeing the issues as they arise, "most people see only that there is a constitution still proclaim[ing] 'we the people.'"[3] So, *who* then? Well, Scheppele made an interesting call out to the lawyers. She avers that "those of us who work in the field of constitutional law [must] stare into the face of the new autocracy to track in detail how it works … to recognize the new signs of danger."[4] She goes even further to say the citizens themselves ought to be empowered to join the fray that "law is too important to leave only to the lawyers."[5] To her mind, a "citizenry trained to resist the legalistic autocrats must be educating in the tools of law themselves … democratic constitutionalism cannot remain an elite ideal that has no resonance in the general public."[6] In other words, "citizens need to be trained as constitutionalists—to understand the point of constitutionalism, to recognize threats to self-sustaining democracy, and *to care about defending liberal values*."[7]

I quite agree, becoming a nation of constitutionalists, especially in an era as civically divisive and derisive as we are presently experiencing, is necessary and pressing. But the means of doing so she proposes—*teaching citizens "the tools of law"*; to *care* about defending liberal values—demands much,

DOI: 10.4324/9781003596523-1

much more attention. Scheppele calls (albeit briefly) for a civics education that "teaches people to recognize new signs of danger" the way lawyers, ostensibly, are already predisposed to doing.[8] It is not a new proposal.[9] However, a question that ought to be posed is as follows: *how* can the citizen be trained as constitutionalist when they otherwise lack the undergirding critical thinking skills with which constitutional lawyers are specifically trained? Moreover, what good would it do to educate citizens in the "signs of danger" when generally the public is experiencing the greatest levels of apathy toward (and, parallelly, ignorance of) our institutions and civic processes in memory?

Thus, we arrive at the thesis of this book, which these next chapters offer and defend: the first step to producing a more civically minded American populace and assuring the maintenance of uncorrupted, responsive civic institutions in perpetuity is to begin teaching law to younger generations of students—especially, legal reasoning skills—for the purposes of developing civic temperament, institutional awareness, civic values, and critical-mindedness in the next generation. To learn law and legal reasoning is an empowering education for children, one that occupies an important theoretical position at the nexus of emphasizing the acquisition of political capabilities *and* democratic virtues.

Before commencing this conversation, we must elaborate on four important pieces to this thesis at the outset.

The first is to state overtly the more robust problem that this piece seeks to address. Scheppele offers one dimension to the larger issue that I see as tripartite. Yes, the devolution of our democratic institutions is owed to systemic ignorance, lack of citizen engagement, and unawareness or inability to identify the problem. But, So too, is the fact that when we *do* civically engage, we often do so poorly, inconsistently, and in ways altogether representative of an utter lack of skill, strategy, or understanding of the system we are endeavoring to move.[10] And yet a third aspect of this problem is institutional and systemic—that our political system, though historically predicated on principles of responsiveness to the public, does not *really* favor receptivity; that our public education system especially favors and breeds complacency, political impotence, and apathy.[11] To teach children law young, in ways we shall see, addresses all these concerns.

A second question that merits upfront discussion is *why children especially*? The answer, in my view, is self-evident. We live in a time of greatly contested civics, of extremist tendencies, of megalomania, and of disheartening jadedness. Voting-age adult citizens today are wholly unequipped to *understand*, let alone deal with a contemporary political scene. This ignorance ultimately favors polarization and hate, shortsightedness, and an inability to see the "full picture" on a given issue (e.g., the values-balancing implicated, counterarguments, etc.). It's a sad reality; my position, at least for the purposes of this project, is that fixing the issue of adult ignorance is also a lost cause. Proposals for mandatory citizenship and law training for voting adults, continuing life-long education courses in law learning, or even any other trainings are excellent, but, in my view, difficult to realize and the adults too difficult to access. This is not the case with the younger generation, however. Engaging *this* demography with law learning promises, as we shall see, better reception to its virtues in terms of not only institutional awareness and skills versatility but also character formation.

The book's subject concerns the construction of a more aware, caring, and vested public citizenry and, by association, more responsive civic institutions *in the long term*. To invest in our children in this way can better prepare students to live in the present time of contested civics, of corruption and abuse, of derision and dissension. In other words, to educate 6-year-olds in kindergarten in law, to let them wrestle—in intentional ways in the classroom—with the important texts, values, and ideas that make up our constitutional democratic system, will breed a generation more capable of resolving our divisive issues in 25 years as well as to see and to prevent abuse of power systematically in our government.

Furthermore, as to individual impact, law learning can serve as a conduit by which children can learn to relate to each other, respect one another, and—along with complimentary education in social, emotional, and ethical learning—begin fostering healthier relationships than can lead people to better, more empowering lives.[12] I say this because law *is*, in the United States, how many of us relate to one another, *the* mechanism by which community identity is often forged, and by which we begin to conceive of and judge one another in this country. For this reason, the below will focus exclusively on the United States. Unlike other countries—some of which might place with primacy national culture or religion or ideology at the fore of its governmental and citizen model, with "law and order" as a secondary tool reflective of the former and changing with the winds—America has decided, for better or worse, that law is essential to our constitution, to our spirit as a nation, and to our operational capacity. Law dictates grouping; law not only epitomizes national values but dictates them. Indeed, our laws and legal classifications—those beyond the technical—change rarely and slowly, and the imbued values that they serve on a broader level are even rarer and slower. Thus, it is beneficial politically and in our personal relationships for the citizen to be equipped to consider how law treats us all in our capacity as autonomous individuals, distinguishes us, divides us, and indeed serves as a collective memory of how we relate to one another—is helpful politically and even personally in framing our relationships. Thurgood Marshall captures the impact law has on this highly personal conversation in his remarks to the Supreme Court in the *Brown v. Board of Education* case:

> So whichever way it is done, the only way that this Court can decide this case in opposition to our position, is that there must be some reason which gives the state the right to make a classification that they can make in regard to nothing else in regard to Negroes, and we submit the only way to arrive at that decision is to find that for some reason Negroes are inferior to all other

> human beings… . The only thing can be is an inherent determination that the people who were formerly in slavery, regardless of anything else, shall be kept as near that stage as is possible, and now is the time, we submit, that this Court should make it clear that that is not what our Constitution stands for.[13]

For Marshall, the law served a symbol of the American view of a specific disenfranchised community; the codification in law of *Plessy* was a collective, national indictment on the inferiority of the Black population. This is despite the passage of 13th and 14th Amendments nearly a century prior. It offered license and tacit endorsement to those who would hate, and an obstacle for those who sought understanding and equality. It represented a dissonance between a law—which held values of equality and anti-discrimination—and a culture of hate. Thus, the only way to make a change societally would be for the law (*Plessy*, a manifestation of a racist cultural reaction) to change and reflect American values enshrined in the amendments, not to protest or riot or write.[14]

Still, protesting, rioting, and writing help to bridge the dissonance between culture and law if they work on higher levels and aspire specifically to legal change. Understanding this, a civic education in legal reasoning and law knowledge is, therefore, about individual, community, and national empowerment. The call in this piece is, therefore, a complete reorientation from our current civic structure which, as we shall see, fails to do these things. While civic education now might promote volunteerism, it does so with little results or impact on student behaviors; when it promotes protest, it does not teach them how to make lasting change; while it tells you your rights, it does not show you what values they are to you or why you ought to care to defend them.

A third point that requires upfront discussion is more a disclaimer concerning teachers and teaching: this is not an attempt to tell educators how to educate better, but rather a theoretical discussion of improving the quality of the educational project *writ large*. This book's historical sections situate the prospect of teaching children law as a piece of the long-held systemic philosophies on public education, treats the subject itself as independently important, empowering in terms of substance and methodology, and as an option for a civics education that is both helpful and has mass-appeal in our democratic system. It is not, however, a comment on the strength, passion, or devotion that teachers currently afford students in their civics classrooms, nor is it an attempt for an outsider to tell anyone how to teach children better. I cannot and will not argue as such.

And finally, a fourth point concerns the broader applicability of this seemingly America-centered argument. What, indeed, does a volume about *American* civics and the role that law learning might play in strengthening an *American* democratic citizenry concern an international audience? While the specific defense of the instant argument to incorporate law learning in our national citizenship education indeed finds strength in American history and this country's unique democratic challenges, allow me to recommend that the "theory" of law learning is not itself *only* viable in America. The broader argument here—that law, both as a subject and in how we study it, is especially poised as both a value and a civic education to cultivate empowered citizens—can be co-opted in a myriad of national contexts that feature high legalist faith, where values find voice in law and legal change, and where interpersonal and inter-community relationships are often legalistic in nature.[15] And indeed, one need not look far to find such cultures, as the intersection of law, values, and culture is observably a major phenomenon in the history of the Western legal tradition and finds manifestation across all nations touched by its development.[16]

It can be said, therefore, that to learn law—across hundreds of nations—empowers citizens to connect with *their* national systems and, in doing so, to see *their* worth and value as change-makers within *their* society. Where Scheppele warns of the dangers of "autocratic legalism" at home in the United States, she also offers comparisons to concerning situations in Hungary under the authority of the government of Prime Minister Viktor Orbán, in Russia under the elected government of President Vladimir Putin, and in Turkey under the government of Recep Tayyip Erdoğan. Her (partial) antidote to all is the same: law learning. The following discussion, therefore, though focused on the American context, should be considered merely exemplary by international readers. I leave, in turn, an examination of the viability of law learning as a civic tool across different countries and contexts to future writers abroad passionate about addressing pressing democratic challenges in their places and spaces by means of education.

Now, with these four points disclaimed, I offer a brief outline of the structure of this piece. The first three chapters are designed to review the contemporary, historical, and philosophical background pertinent to my central proposal. I explore, in Chapter 1, a story of problematic civic educational trends, of unrealized ambitions, and lost purpose to which my interjection is designed to ameliorate. Chapters 2 and 3 contextualize my proposal for learning law and legal reasoning as inspired by moral education and social justice philosophy and as a natural outgrowth of a historic national education project. Thereafter, in Chapter 4, I dive more deeply into the mechanics of this proposal, highlighting the particularly important ways in which such an education can help in human development, civic development, and character development. Chapter 5 is then devoted to defending against anticipated criticisms and counterpoints. I will then conclude with Chapter 6, focused on re-asserting the value that law learning can have for young students, the potential benefits this proposal poses for our democracy, and the temperament of our citizenry.

Notes

1 Kim Lane Scheppele, "Autocratic Legalism," 85 *Univ. Chicago L. Rev.* 545 (2018).
2 Kim Lane Scheppele, "Autocratic Legalism," 85 *Univ. Chicago L. Rev.* 545 (2018).
3 Kim Lane Scheppele, "Autocratic Legalism," 85 *Univ. Chicago L. Rev.* 582–583 (2018).

4 Kim Lane Scheppele, "Autocratic Legalism," 85 *Univ. Chicago L. Rev.* 518–583 (2018). Such signs of danger include attacking "liberal constitutionalism with constitutional amendments," or "preserv[ing] the shell of the prior liberal state—the same institutions, the same ceremonies, an overall appearance of rights protection—but in the meantime [hollowing out] its moral core."

5 Kim Lane Scheppele, "Autocratic Legalism," 85 *Univ. Chicago L. Rev.* 518–583 (2018).

6 Kim Lane Scheppele, "Autocratic Legalism," 85 *Univ. Chicago L. Rev.* 518–583 (2018).

7 Kim Lane Scheppele, "Autocratic Legalism," 85 *Univ. Chicago L. Rev.* 518–583 (2018).

8 Kim Lane Scheppele, "Autocratic Legalism," 85 *Univ. Chicago L. Rev.* 518–583 (2018)

> Civic education needs to teach people to recognize the new signs of danger. Under what circumstances is it safe to trust the appointment of judges to a political process? When is presidentialism a sign of danger? How can the discretionary use of public power for economic intimidation be curbed? Why is the call to draft a new constitution alarming? People beyond the educated elite need to know why these questions matter, and they need to learn how to think about answering them.

9 *See, e.g.*, Harold Berman, "Law in the University," 10 *Leg. Stud.* 53 (1986) (a more philosophical perspective on the need to teach non-law students the law); *see also* many articles on "street law" programming, i.e., Sean Arthurs, "Street Law: Creating Tomorrow's Citizens Today," 19 *Lewis and Clark L. Rev.* 926 (2015).

10 To consider both the phenomenon of lack of youth engagement *and* lack of skills in engaging, consider, on the one hand, the protester who seeks to "tear the system down" given its frustrating treatment of the LGBT experience, and, on the other hand, the protester that seeks to placate by advocating for a "Don't Say Gay Bill." Both are attempting to answer the issues posed by our system in different ways, both are missing the point of the conversation entirely. With this said, I do want to refer to the extensive body of protest literature produced, much of which argues that the youth are, in fact, organizing effectively. *See, e.g.*, Edison Lanza, *Protest and Human Rights*, Inter-American Commission on Human Rights (2019). However, though they might have the right stratagem and slogans, protesting lacks long-term impact precisely because there is no conception of how to move the system integrally.

11 Arguments for reform are myriad both from within the school system and by way of external institutions. *See, e.g.*, Michael Rebell, *Flunking Democracy: Schools, Courts and Civic Participation* (University of Chicago Press, 2018).

12 Such programs are incredible, and I am deeply familiar with them. *See, e.g.*, Center for Contemplative Science, Emory University, Atlanta, Georgia SEE Learning. https://seelearning.emory.edu/. They do not, however, educate for citizenship or for versatility with democracy but are approaches to compassionate dispositions and perspectives on the world. We need the pair.

13 Thurgood Marshall, "Argument before the U.S. Supreme Court in Brown v. Board of Education," *in* Josh Gottheimer ed., Ripples of Hope Great American Civil Rights Speeches (New York: Basic Civitas Books, 2003).

14 Another complimentary illustration of dissonance between law and culture—how law can move culture, or culture should move law (but often fails to do so)—might be the current debate over abortion. While at least 61% of the population culturally accepts abortion as a medical option and an inherent right, legally we are at best neutral and at worse hostile to a right to privacy *writ large*. This was made ever apparent in *Dobbs* where constitutional rhetoric was mobilized to say that America does not stand for abortion or even privacy. What is the solution? It is not necessarily to just protest; protesting has little effect *unless* we start working with higher aims. Many have appreciated the role of law and legal pronouncements in vindicating socially held beliefs, including abortion. In order to let the law reflect our values, we must work on higher levels: arguing using the rhetoric of rights is the only sustainable solution. This, of course, requires a substantive change to the Constitution, which, again, is not something we have seen for over a century.

15 The study of such legalistic subcultures, especially in comparative perspectives, has been highly fascinating to socio-legal scholars for some time. *See, e.g.*, Gibson and Caldeira, "The Legal Cultures of Europe," 30 *Law Soc. Rev.* 36 (1996) Cambridge University Press, Cambridge, England.

16 One authoritative work on this is, of course, Harold Berman, *Law and Language: Effective Symbols of Community* (John Witte, Jr., ed.) (Cambridge University Press, 2016). For a shorter article on the intersection of law and culture, *see* Tamar Frankel and Tomasz Braun, "Law and Culture," 101 *B.U. L. Rev. Online* 157 (Boston, Massachusetts, 2021). Of course, this argument may have less of an impact where the intersection of law with values is less emphasized, as is the case of Japan or China with alternate emphases.

Part I

Background, Context, and Guiding Lights

"Build the wall! Build the wall!" Three young boys chanted the familiar slogan as they began constructing a wall of blocks across the length of their first-grade classroom during unstructured playtime.[1] Their teacher, not normally one to interfere during this period in the day, called a time-out. She approached the boys, mindful of the many other children gradually succumbing to discomfort. When she asked the students what they were doing, the boys proudly responded, "we're building a wall to keep the Mexicans out!"[2] Unsure of what to do—herself also disquieted—the teacher posed a question to the whole of the class: "why do some people want to keep other people out?"[3] One child responded as follows: "because sometimes you just want to be alone or with your best friends, and so you have to say no to some people." Another said, "because you have to stay safe, and you don't know if strangers could be dangerous." And finally, one of the boys building the wall offered, "because the Mexicans will take our jobs."[4]

The above encapsulates the current problem in civic education, as well as my proposed answer to those issues, for two reasons. First, to say that when one speaks of civic education—the broader project, its goals, and, indeed, the objectives of any democratic citizen education—it begins at the earliest of ages. Just consider how political rhetoric finds its way even to first graders! This is helpful to note because when most of us consider civic education and its issues, we tend to envision a classroom of secondary school students—many of whom are already about to drive, some of whom are even able to vote—certainly capable of abstract thought and critical analysis to certain degrees. But any solution proffered for civic education's reorientation must also address how teachers in the above contexts might be able to turn an experience like the above into teachable moments. If effectively directed, the altercation above could have resulted in a proper conversation about law, our system, and our treatment of people—a lesson that could have helped shape how these students think about such issues as immigration or even free speech, going forward. Yet, more on this later; for now, suffice to say that politics, beyond the shadow of a doubt, has entered our collective conscience

DOI: 10.4324/9781003596523-2

at all ages. Politics is in *every* classroom, furthermore. And this should be so! Civic classes are—or at least should be—spaces to contend with this reality.

The above case study also obviates the myriad of ways not just the students, but other constituencies might respond to *how* the teacher resolves this conversation.[5] At a later meeting of the Jersey City K–8's School Culture Committee, composed largely of elementary school parents, teachers, and administrators, there were many differing opinions offered on how to transform that moment into a learning opportunity. One parent shared that she would have gotten political, "talk about the issue to correct the thought process behind the behavior." Indeed, the teacher could have "taken the time to explain to them the difference between legal and illegal immigration."[6] Another offered that "first graders have different developmental needs ... a more nuanced and critical response is needed." Such a response should be contemplated in a developed, standardized curriculum. Still another offered:

> [the boys displayed] a partisan move ... creatively engineered a way, and they were drawing on current events in the process. That should have been celebrated by the teacher, but instead [we propose] their entire innovation [ought to be] discouraged.[7]

There is no resolution, only discordance.

Should schools be neutral on politics and values? What are the capacities we need to engender, and how can we do so in spontaneous political situations in the classroom? What is the role of the school in arbitrating these discussions? How do we conceive of a civic education that is singular in purpose and unified in philosophy, but not indoctrinating, censoring, or obliterative of diverse opinion? These are open questions—posing great issues for our now lackluster civic paradigm. As Martha Nussbaum comments, "until it is clear what we are striving for [in a democratic education], it is difficult to figure out how to get it to those who need it."[8] To be sure, civic education requires an overhaul; the paradigm begs a deep reorientation in its educational philosophy. And, because of the unique importance this type of education is receiving today,[9] as well as the massive amounts of federal attention, it is positioned well to be reconsidered. In this monograph, we will reconfigure a working view of civics as a character education supported by a robust educational philosophy, as well as one rooted deeply in the historic purposes of public education. But, first, let us dive into the maelstrom of confused motivations and unrealized ambitions that dot the contemporary civic education landscape.

Notes

1 This case study is borrowed from Meira Levinson and Jacob Faye, *Democratic Discord in Schools: Cases and Commentaries in Educational Ethics* (Cambridge, MA: Harvard Education Press, 2019), 13–17.

2 Meira Levinson and Jacob Faye, *Democratic Discord in Schools: Cases and Commentaries in Educational Ethics* (Cambridge, MA: Harvard Education Press, 2019), 13–17.
3 Meira Levinson and Jacob Faye, *Democratic Discord in Schools: Cases and Commentaries in Educational Ethics* (Cambridge, MA: Harvard Education Press, 2019), 13–17.
4 Meira Levinson and Jacob Faye, *Democratic Discord in Schools: Cases and Commentaries in Educational Ethics* (Cambridge, MA: Harvard Education Press, 2019), 13–17.
5 Meira Levinson and Jacob Faye, *Democratic Discord in Schools: Cases and Commentaries in Educational Ethics* (Cambridge, MA: Harvard Education Press, 2019), 13–17. (In the actual case study, Elena, the teacher, responds by focusing on the response about the threat of Mexicans taking our jobs, by offering the following syllogism: "a student's job is to learn, be kind, caring and respectful. Nobody can take this job away from you. Therefore, nobody can take your job.")
6 Meira Levinson and Jacob Faye, *Democratic Discord in Schools: Cases and Commentaries in Educational Ethics* (Cambridge, MA: Harvard Education Press, 2019), 13–17.
7 Meira Levinson and Jacob Faye, *Democratic Discord in Schools: Cases and Commentaries in Educational Ethics* (Cambridge, MA: Harvard Education Press, 2019), 13–17.
8 Martha Nussbaum, *Not for Profit: Why Democracy Needs the Humanities* (Princeton, NJ: Princeton University Press, 2016), 12.
9 Consider, for instance, Carl Smith, "Civic Education Is Having a Moment and Here Is What It Means," in *Governing: For the People Making Government Work* (March 2023), available at www.governing.com/now/civic-education-is-having-a-moment-this-is-what-that-means

1 The Current Conundrum in the Citizen Education Project

As much as politics has entered the classroom—our fundamental values as a nation being raised, critiqued, explored, and interrogated in little conversations and little moments across the country at all times—we are still reputed as the chief-most apathetic, civically illiterate generation.[1] We are at extremes: it seems to me that either we accept political ideas blindly from our immediate communities that tout them, or we know nothing and care not. Contemporary iterations of civic education face problems at definitional levels. What are key attributes of the citizen we are trying to cultivate? How can civic education promote those attributes? To explore both aspects, specifically emphasizing the confused education models—a problem persistent not just in the previous decades, but for centuries[2]—is the central preoccupation of this chapter. Highlighting the uncertainty and variance between definitions of adequate civic education, as well as the problem-riddled projects on the ground, will obviate the need for reorienting ourselves theoretically and promote interest in corresponding substantive reform.

1.1 On Defining and Theorizing Civic Education: In Search of Commonalities

To be sure, the notion that a robust civics education prepares citizens for political participation is hardly contested.[3] However, definitions for what constitutes this learning elude us to some extent. What are the bounds and goals of a civics education? What skills should students walk away with? Is this just a one-and-done classroom experience or something more? As we shall see, there is little consistency from merely surveying definitions.

The Center for Civic Education provides a modern phraseology as a start, describing this sort of learning as that which cultivates "informed, responsible participation in political life by competent citizens" who are "committed to the fundamental values" of America's democracy.[4] This commitment is necessarily predicated on acquiring a "body of knowledge" consisting of "intellectual

DOI: 10.4324/9781003596523-3

and participatory skills" and the "development of certain dispositions or traits of character" that enhance political participation, which "contribute[s] to [a] healthy functioning [political system]."[5] Under this approach, civics instruction is both within and beyond the classroom, institutional and personal, and the instruction raises questions for students about their history, position with the government, their obligations and personal responsibilities, their value-sets, and what skills they need to hold the office of citizens in increasingly tumultuous times. Civics education does the important work of blending democratic knowledge, behaviors, and values needed to participate in our political society.

While this articulation is generally comprehensive, it is important to note that other definitions—just as widely mobilized and circulated—are just as prevalent and yet laden with ideological partisanship. Consider that, on the federal level, the definitions (and objectives) put forward by the last three administrations were competing, to say the least, and demonstrate a one-dimensional consideration of the topic of civics. For instance, the Bush administration offered civics education to strengthen "the public's knowledge of American history values, and civic traditions." To teach civics was to teach "a love of democratic principles,"[6] or, in other words, the "right" citizen is a patriotic, obedient, and reverent one. In the Obama administration, the position changed: civics education was refocused on outcome-based characterizations, like "increas[ing] civic knowledge, voter participation, and volunteerism."[7] In the administration's words, "civics learning puts students at the center. It includes both learning and practice—not just rote memorization of names, dates, and processes."[8] For the Obama administration, civics had a dual focus of informing the democratic life as well as helping raise student achievement generally. Finally, under the Trump administration, the definition of civics saw further shift; civics was oriented toward indoctrinating ideology, a tool against what the administration termed "cancel culture," an extension of "Make America Great Again."[9]

And to be sure, civics can be *all* these things. It is not, however, just one of those things. The diverse reconceptualization of "civics"—and, thereby, the discordant views on the right type of "citizen"—depending on the political power of the day presents problems, confusion, and ultimately inertness.

In the academy, the project of defining civics shows equal variability; there are chasms between conceptions about civics' educational goals. One can find definitions about changing attitudes,[10] resistance and activism, and still others about embracing communities, connecting on local levels, simple participation.[11] The jumble of rationales, definitions, and objectives has caused great confusion and has hindered the educational project in recent decades. So, in thinking about situating this new civics argument amid the existing theoretical literature, I ask the following: what are the commonalities across definitions upon which this "new civics" builds? What specific ideas, behaviors, instructional content, values should civics education impart in the project of building an involved body politic?

One central commonality between definitions and approaches is to develop reasoning traits and good behaviors for good citizens based off an as-yet unfound formula of blending foundational knowledge, values, and social commitment.[12] Implicit in this formula is a view of the *comprehensive* education of the student—in terms of subject-matter as well as education in the diversity of values in the American zeitgeist—toward competently participating in citizenship. This is certainly not novel in the discourse. In 2003, one report on the civic enterprise in American schools argued that the civics paradigm ought not only to "help young people acquire and learn to use the skills, knowledge, and attitudes that will prepare them to be competent and responsible citizens" but also ensure that "students are generally informed and thoughtful, act politically and are [morally and civically] virtuous."[13] As such, one gleans that a civics course trains the student to stay current on civic discourse and empower them with the ability to obtain information, in addition to teaching students the information itself. To favor this view of civics as educating the *whole* of the person is to place attention less on the descriptive substance of the education and more on the skills, abilities, and habits one develops as part of the process.

On the ground, however, civics classes place little thought on this aspect. Instead, these classes tend to pacify the learner with descriptive historical or technical information. They thereby engender a citizen who is obedient, yet distant; historically aware but uninvested. Of course, knowing history is no bad thing, but alone those qualities are insufficient to meet the demands of the American citizens as envisioned by the founders. Consider, for instance, how one Washington State Civics Textbook boils the civics experience down to a lesson in "obey[ing] rules and laws, helping others, voting in elections, telling an adult if someone is in danger to themselves or others, and being responsible for your own actions and how they affect others."[14] These platitudes offer little to the student seeking to be empowered, through civics learning, toward social mobility, activism, or government participation. Another Kansas program goes a little farther, urging that these duties also extend to "community involvement, staying informed, practicing tolerance, and 'pass[ing] along the importance of good citizenship to future generations.'"[15] While this approach is a bit better, it remains vague. Similar curricula do little to tell us about the character and thinking of the good citizen. One yearns for instruction in more profound virtues like personal responsibility, participation, and justice,[16] perhaps, "enlightened political engagement," and so much more.[17] Teaching students *what* the law is—which is what these curricula do—is exactly what we do *not* want. We want to teach students *how to think about law*. But this gets ahead of ourselves.

Of course, it is hazardous to play the game of determining "what should or should not be a profound trait," or "what sort of civic character we want to see instilled in students."[18] Given the dynamic nature of our current political landscape—the great schisms that exist—articulating any discrete sets of values for civic learning is foolhardy; freedom, tolerance, the value of labor, and patriotism itself are the subject of scrutiny.[19] While the conservative would maintain that schools ought to teach burgeoning citizens respect for constitutional machinery, liberals are less inclined to the project of venerating institutions. Whereas liberals advocate for equipping students as agents of change, conservatives would maintain that activist-civics distract from in-classroom-learning. That said, let us consider another commonality between partisan approaches: civic solidarity.[20] Civic solidarity connotes a process of *deliberation*. In other words, the citizen must understand others, make an active effort to listen, and appreciate the differing values that make up an American melting pot.[21] This might involve practicing moderating claims to find common ground upon which to build political decisions, which, in turn, orients citizens to the common good. The essence of the civic nation is the development of such an inclusive natural culture that benefits from a dynamic, challenging environment.[22] Civic solidarity, and even one's political identity, is not "defined according to a concrete content," but "by the fact that everybody is attached to that identity in his or her own fashion, that everybody wants to continue that history and proposes to make that community progress."[23] It is the project of civics education therefore to help produce dispositions conducive to participation in the social experiment of deliberation: "autonomy and open-mindedness"; "social engineering"; "non-participative and participative citizenship"; "doing justice to diversity"; "service learning"; "political efficacy"; and "voting." Indeed, even more radical believers articulate that "dissent" ought to be the great project of civics education.[24]

Based on the above two commonalities, our civics proposal aims to build an "American character" that is dissenting, critical, and imaginative, while being discerning, and deliberative and informed in that dissent. This has always found expression in our histories. This may not be the *only* goal of civics, but it is arguably a universally approved one.

Of course, we have yet to figure out how to do just that. Nussbaum argues that our "teach-to-test" mentality, an issue since the No Child Left Behind Era,[25] has been especially detrimental to the democratic educational project *writ large*. In her words:

> critical thinking and sympathetic imagining are not testable by quantitative multiple-choice exams … [teach-to-test] produces an atmosphere of student passivity and teacher routinization. The creativity and individuality that mark the best humanistic teaching and learning has a hard time finding room to unfold.[26]

Further,

> curricular content has shifted away from material that focuses on enlivening imagination and training critical faculties toward material that is directly

> relevant to test preparation. Along with the shift in content has come an even more baneful shift in pedagogy: away from teaching that seeks to promote questioning and individual responsibility toward force-feeding for good exam results.[27]

Though Nussbaum wrote this a decade ago, we see this still reflected in contemporary iterations of civic learning.[28] Nussbaum warns ultimately that this is not only an American problem, and that "nations all over the world will soon be producing useful machines, rather than complete citizens who can think for themselves, criticize tradition, and understand the significance of another person's sufferings and achievements."[29]

Yet, there are innovative voices and initiatives out there that offer a source of light and hope. These are worth exploring before we add our ideas to the conversation. Scholars have recently turned their attention to whether civic behavior should be treated as an individualistic or a communal project. To be communal in nature is to express that "knowledge [ought] to be passed on [in] reference [to] facts regarding the larger national entity."[30] Courses that embrace this line of thinking stress communal values such as obedience, nationalism, and adherence to existing structure. While this is important, and indeed seems to undergird traditional civics curricula to date, a more progressive contingent has begun considering the benefits of individual-centric civics, touting the following conception:

> knowledge that will be passed on will include the ways in which the individual can act in the social sphere and in the same manner, the values to be instilled will stress the importance of the acts of the individual.[31]

In the individualistic approach, the student is empowered to think of themselves as having the ability to change their surroundings and to be an integral part of the system. From this, one might derive the phenomenon of action-civics, an emphasis on volunteerism, and protest.

Of course, as I will argue, civics is both a communal and individual project; I agree, furthermore, that theoretical civics is a balance of values, a values education. Three specific value categories are important for young citizens to learn. Students must be educated in (1) "values that relate to self," (2) "values that relate to the encounter with the others," and (3) "values that relate to society."[32] However, we acknowledge that to balance these values in a civics education context is an arduous task. The teacher must educate students, therefore, in all the processes that affect people's beliefs, commitments, and actions as members of the community. These can "be processes and institutions that both empower and obscure values, norms, and rights."[33] Students ought to be confronted—and should be able to contend—with questions as profound as "what makes a good citizen?" They should, as well, be exposed to descriptive information like "what rights are guaranteed under the Constitution," though alongside questions like "what does justice mean to me?" Yet, very few, if any, civics classrooms do this work of melding the approaches.[34]

1.2 Civic Education on the Ground

In 2008, theorists proffered five categories of civics curricula in the United States: "national democracy," "cross-national comparisons," "discussion and decision-making," "service learning," and "multicultural education."[35] In terms of creating a national uniformity for education, the differing approaches promise only piecemeal education for our students; each focuses on only one fraction of the total conversation concerning the behaviors of the good citizen. More recent reform efforts have, at best, doubled down in their commitment to one perspective. As of 2018, curricula across states "largely reflect an approach to civics knowledge that emphasizes structures and functions rather than critical analysis and active civic participation."[36] This, in my estimation, yields only a complacent and apathetic culture; inaction at best and, at worst, susceptibility to misinformation. Our younger generation *must* feel responsible for what is being conducted through our system, how it operates, and what its future looks like. However, the descriptive course requires that students merely mechanically recall information, yielding a generation of students who often do not even take an interest in major issues.

Unfortunately, while there has undoubtedly been great attention turned toward civic learning initiatives on the federal level[37] and on the state level[38]—many of which feature a more comprehensive, skills-focused curriculum—paths forward for sustainable entrenchment of these programs are vague, results are still bleak, and the future is unclear. Consider, Illinois which, in 2015, adopted a high school civics course requirement embedded with evidence-based practices. Through a public–private partnership, Illinois built a statewide system of support that ensured fidelity of implementation among schools and districts, improved dispositions among teachers, and accelerated discernable shifts in pro-civic behaviors among students taking the class. A 2017 survey[39] showed that students who completed the course were more likely to serve as leaders in a group or organizations, discuss politics, or help make their city a better place to live. However, later research demonstrates gaps in civic empowerment across race lines,[40] continuously vague course objectives for teachers, and disparate outcomes across schools.[41]

On the national level, there has been innovation that also warrants discussion. In 2010, the National Council for the Social Studies created a common core curricular structure for "informed and engaged citizenship." They were to be directly implemented and adopted by state education departments. The curriculum aspires to develop critical thinking, participation, and problem-solving skills as part of students' civics learning.[42] Courses do so by way of "active engagement components," for instance, opportunities for "working with news-media fluency," "frequent current events discussions," "community service," "attending school board meetings," "simulations of democratic processes and procedures," and action-civics programming.[43] Philosophically, these skill-focused experiences may inspire students to develop "civic behaviors," or the "civic agency and confidence to vote, volunteer, attend public meetings, and engage with their communities."[44] While this is certainly a more effective form of civic learning,[45] sadly, as of 2018, only 23 states[46] have properly adopted these proposed standards,[47] *no* states have "local problem-solving components in their civics requirements,"[48] and community service is only required for one state for graduation.[49]

But even if there were a more widespread reception of a common civics structure, or other practical skills circular reforms, is this enough? Perhaps not. There are some resounding critiques of the above model. For instance, it is merely a standard rather than a framework; states are still able to create their own content. While its emphasis on skills rather than specific content can be seen in a positive light, many maintain that the flexibility afforded states betrays the creators' attempts to "fend off fights about both the politics of content and the potential for federal overreach into states 'rights'" which weakens the program's impact. If there is a "presumption that the United States really does operate on democratic values, when that presumption often depends on which [state,] community or economic class one hails from?"[50]

Furthermore, this combination of increased deference, low levels of formal structure, and increased skills-and-experience focus also predisposes curricula to aggrandize singular visions of civic behavior at the expense of multi-dimensional approaches. In other words, in trying to identify concrete, universally necessary-to-learn values, policymakers and educators in fact ignore others. One example of this could be the prioritization of social protest and demonstration in civic classes, rather than, say law obedience, or civic solidarity, or really any other important citizen quality. As scholars have highlighted:

> young people are engaged and enraged by the problems that surround them. They may feel overwhelmed and powerless to impact change or may organize walkouts and protests because these are the only tactics that they know about from bring about positive social change.[51]

There is an increasingly frequent debate about the question of how "schools and districts should respond to youth civic actions when they disrupt formal instruction and place students' safety, civil liberties, and social cohesion in tension."[52] And, to be sure, civic classes that focus squarely on protest history and protest power have had a hand in increasing the levels of those walkouts and on-site student demonstrations.[53] Of course, having had a conversation about protest is uniformly regarded as important.[54] Young people are, after all, not just citizens-in-the-making but have the "right and capacity to contribute in real time to policies that shape and constrain everyday choices."[55]

Yet, the conversation about responding to protests, especially in school, is far from uniform. There are those administrators that "student tactics of initiating walkouts from classes and joining public protests put them at risk," and that their oft lack of expertise "muddles social justice goal, interrupts instructional time, and further divides the community."[56] Others dismiss this concern, arguing that parents and teachers are often "more discomforted by protest than engaged with the authentic concerns of the youth involved, who may have carefully and collectively thought through their rational for employing these tactics."[57] To be sure, students might (or might not) be strengthening civic skills when they protest, but these actions—and responses that promote them—may also be contributing to the deterioration of school climate,[58] the cultivation of a "with us or against us" mentality,[59] and, rather than foster dialogue within the classroom, walkouts and protests in schools could effectively preclude conversations from taking place.

Some suggest that if we are not teaching students to protest, then we are not teaching them civics. But, while protest skills and rights are important, both to learn and to exercise, they are not the only end goal of civic education. The all-important question—how much should young people be positioned as compliant subjects versus critical, autonomous agents who might challenge the structures that govern their society?—can be answered in more ways than just teaching people how to "take matters into their own hands." For, after all, in the opinion of many scholars:

> protest is usually ineffective. Protesters assume that decision makers have the capacity to solve the problem, which is often not the case. They believe that the best way to move authorities to action is through confrontation, which in fact may simply deepen intransigence.[60]

Therefore, civic education must harken for more. Therefore, it remains a concern when schools, districts, states maintain myopic one-dimensional views of civics, even when new standards promise important pivots in the landscape with aptitudes-and-abilities rhetoric.[61]

A better approach is a civic education proposal that promises quality and not just facts, a mindset-change, new perspectives, and a new orientation. It can be anchored, moreover, simply in the two broad objectives—"civic character" and "civic solidarity"—gleaned from definitional commonalities above. To its core, civic learning is an education preparing one to live in a diverse democracy and making decisions in an informed and thoughtful way. Decisions require knowledge: not just the "facts," but also an understanding of how other people see the issue and how they will be affected. They require deliberation and discussion.[62] To be sure, "few public issues are matters of right and wrong; they are complicated arguments about decisions that will have disparate impacts on people."[63] An education in civics, I posit, should open the door for students in many ways. What do I mean by this? They should be *empowered* to engage with the complex values, structures, and ideas of policy. Their ideas, gradually over time, should become more nuanced when it comes to criticizing the government. Students, furthermore, should acquire the tools to question their own value-sets and those of their country. A civics education should build communication skills—both expressing and understanding facts and opinions—as well as intellectual skills that allow youth to critically describe, explain, and analyze political and social issues, including multiple viewpoints. This means, in turn, that they should develop skills of participation necessary for active civic life, such as respectful public dialogue, civic planning, and coalition-building. It should instill characteristics and engender dispositions, including tolerance, appreciation of diversity, and concern for the common good.

1.3 What Type of Citizen Are We Building, Anyway?

We must proffer a firmer, reoriented definition of the capacities of the citizen. Martha Nussbaum proposes that a suitably educated citizen is one who has "cultivated capacities for critical thinking and reflection [crucial] for keeping democracies alive and wide awake. [They] can think well about a wide range of cultures [and] groups … and the ability to imagine the experience of another."[64] Indeed, for her, the following capabilities seem essential to the work of the citizen:

- The ability to think well about political issues affecting the nation, to examine, reflect, argue, and debate, deferring to neither tradition nor authority.
- The ability to recognize fellow citizens as people with equal rights, even though they may be different in race, religion, gender, and sexuality: to look at them with respect, as ends, not just tools to be manipulated for one's own profit.
- The ability to have concern for the lives of others, to grasp what policies of many types mean for the opportunities and experiences of one's fellow citizens, of many types, and for people outside one's own nation.
- The ability to imagine well a variety of complex issues affecting the story of human life as it unfolds: to think about childhood, adolescence, family relationships, illness, death, and much more in a way informed by an understanding of a wide range of human stories, not just by aggregate data.
- The ability to judge political leaders critically, but with an informed and realistic sense of the possibilities available to them. The ability to think about the good of the nation, not just one's own local group.[65]

For the most part, these attributes are concordant with my view of the citizen for the purposes of this proposal. Like Nussbaum, my argument is for cultivating intellectual disposition as opposed to an outcome-orientation; a citizen is not one who protests louder, or one who votes more liberally or conservatively, or one who knows their "rights" technically. The suitably educated "citizen" is one with certain abilities, capacities, and attitudes that best compliment a democratic milieu. They are, for all intents and purposes, especially prepared for the political and legal unknown; capable of appreciating, understanding, and even resolving novel constitutional and political problems by way of sophisticated intellectual discourse with others of like- and opposing-mind and the balancing of interests.[66] On this last idea—the idea of discourse—I would also add another definition provided by Jurgen Habermas, whose discourse theory of law and democracy is something I will explore further soon. Habermas offers, in a way that dovetails neatly with Nussbaum, that "the view of the citizen [especially for the work of citizenship education] should be that of an *active, competent, ethical* participant in reasoned conversations about issues of common concern."[67]

To be balanced and appreciative of all perspectives, however, does not mean that the citizen is intrinsically moderate. Indeed, they can be extreme in their political direction, even "civilly disobedient where there is a cause, [so long as they] manifests a calculatedness and reflectiveness, as well as an appreciation for the varied interests, diverse values, and voices that are inculpated in decisions to act, protest, or disobey."[68] They must, however, tolerate counterarguments, building perspectives off the basis of reason rather than social pressure. To our mind, the citizen is both obedient to law and skeptical, eager for change but also mindful of the need for deliberateness and legitimacy, interested in forgoing short-term resolutions in favor of potentially more impactful long-term maneuvers. They can have these conversations with peers and are savvy enough with institutional knowledge to conceive of ways of reforming within the system.

With that said, a citizen must still be "encouraged to be curious about the different groups that compose [their nation and democracy] and their varied histories and differential life opportunities. An adequate education for living in a pluralistic democracy must be multi-cultural."[69] Just as importantly, "part of a civic mindset means talking about the big ideas that people living in democracies grapple with all the time, like how to balance individuals rights against the common good."[70] Even very young children, as we saw at the outset of this chapter, can engage in deep conversations about when it's okay to vote on something, let the majority rule, or not "because it's taking away someone's rights or endangering them."[71] The foundation is there; the question is the method by which we instruct students in these important, mindset-inspiring characteristics.

Learning law, legal reasoning, and approaching critically problematic law questions is just such a broader education. This type of learning, and *how we learn it*, presents a marriage of understanding, dissent, practical skills-building, and empowering know-how. It provides the "rules of the game to all interested in playing in the same court"—even if you disagree in how to play the game. In the following chapter, I begin couching the proposal in a governing educational philosophy and, later, as a consistent product of the historic national civic education project.

Notes

1 The Atlantic, "When it comes to Politics, Do Millennials Care About Anything?" (2019) www.theatlantic.com/sponsored/allstate/when-it-comes-to-politics-do-millennials-care-about-anything/255/. Citing various polls in support of this contention.

2 The complicated landscape surrounding civics education could be owed, at least in part, to the confused history with which the ideas have been developed. In the early republic, the primary objective of civics education was to cultivate citizens able to self-rule. Civics education eventually evolved to become more engendering of patriotism and loyalty. This might include, for instance, "obedience to the law," "respect for government and public officials," "individuals' recognition of their political obligations," "a minimum degree of self-control," "responsiveness to community needs in stressful times," "knowledge of and agreement with the legitimating national ideology," and a "recognition of the special qualities of people within one's country compared to those of other nations." By contrast, toward the onset of the Cold War, civics education in turn had the goal of promoting a more uniform American culture predicated on pro-social and democratic values. It was only by the 1980s that researchers advocated for increasing civic competence and promoting enlightened political engagement with a goal of preparing the next generation for political activity in the community. However, even this new branding of civics, being built on shaky and unsure foundation, is not entirely accepted across the nation. *See* Diana Owen, "Public Attitudes about Civic Education," Political Science Association Annual Meeting (2013).

3 *See* Walter Parker "Knowing and Doing in Democratic Citizenship Education," in L. S. Levstik and C. A. Tyson (eds.), *Handbook of Research in Social Studies Education* (New York: Routledge, 2008), 65, 68; *see also* Frederick Hess and Matthew Rice, "Where Left and Right Agree on Civics Education, and Where They Don't," *Educ. Next.* (March. 25, 2020), www.educationnext.org/where-left-right-agree-civics-educationwhere-they-dont/

4 Center for Civic Education. www.civiced.org/campaign-to-promote-civic-education/rationale

5 Center for Civic Education, www.civiced.org/campaign-to-promote-civic-education/rationale

6 The White House of President George W. Bush Archives, Speech from The Rose Garden, "President Introduces History and Civic Education Initiatives (CEIs)," September 17, 2002, accessed at https://georgewbush-whitehouse.archives.gov/news/releases/2002/09/20020917-1.html (emphasis added).

7 Secretary Arne Duncan's Remarks at "For Democracy's Future" *Forum at the White House*, January 10, 2012, accessed at https://democracyu.wordpress.com/2012/01/20/secretary-arne-duncans-remarks-at-for-democracys-future-forum-at-the-white-house/

8 Secretary Arne Duncan's Remarks at "For Democracy's Future" *Forum at the White House*, January 10, 2012, accessed at https://democracyu.wordpress.com/2012/01/20/secretary-arne-duncans-remarks-at-for-democracys-future-forum-at-the-white-house/

9 For a robust discussion on this, *see, e.g.*, Eleni M. Mantas-Kourounis, *The Politics of Civic Education* (Rowman & Littlefield, London, England, 2024).

10 Walter Parker, for instance, puts forward that the educational landscape sets about the task of changing people's attitudes, knowledge, and behaviors regarding the relationships between the state and its citizens. Walter Parker "Knowing and Doing in Democratic Citizenship Education," in L. S. Levstik and C. A. Tyson (eds.), *Handbook of Research in Social Studies Education* (New York: Routledge, 2008), 65, 68.

11 Crittenden, Jack and Levine, Peter "Civic Education," *The Stanford Encyclopedia of Philosophy* (2018); Still further, Jack Crittenden, in his entry in the Stanford Encyclopedia of Philosophy, states that civics education need only inform of "the processes that affect people's beliefs, commitments, capabilities, and actions as members or prospective members of communities."

12 Walter Parker "Knowing and Doing in Democratic Citizenship Education," in L. S. Levstik and C. A. Tyson (eds.), *Handbook of Research in Social Studies Education* (New York: Routledge, 2008), 65, 68 ("political engagement refers to the action or participation dimension of democratic citizenship … Democratic enlightenment refers to knowledge and commitments that inform this engagement"). There is a popular clamor—from the political right and left—that civics classrooms try and promote a certain type of "good citizen." Consider, as one example, the robust debate around action-civics as "protest civics" as featured in Sara O'Brien's and Meira Levinson's short piece, "Taking the Action Out of Civics?: Polarized Debates over Civic Education," Harvard Graduate School of Education, *Just. Sch.* www.justiceinschools.org. The proposal here does not purport to take a side on this debate.

13 2003 Civic Mission of Schools Report.

14 Teaching Elections in Washington State: Lesson Plans & Classroom Activities, (Office of the Secretary of State, Jan. 2023) www.sos.wa.gov/_assets/elections/civics/whats%20a%20good%20citizen.pdf

15 "Rights and Responsibilities of the Citizen," Kansas State Government, available at https://www.kansascouncilss.org/civics

16 This was the barometer established by Westheimer and Kahne, Westheimer, Joel, and Kahne, Joseph, "What Kind of Citizen? The Politics of Educating for Democracy," 41 *Am. Educ. Res. J.* 237–269 (2004).

17 Walter Parker "Knowing and Doing in Democratic Citizenship Education," in L. S. Levstik and C. A. Tyson (eds.), *Handbook of Research in Social Studies Education* (New York: Routledge, 2008), 65, 68 ("political engagement refers to the action or participation dimension of democratic citizenship … Democratic enlightenment refers to knowledge and commitments that inform this engagement").

18 Civic education has not been a high priority at the federal level for this reason. The primary tensions of reform agenda lie in the conflicting conceptions of citizenship: progressive democrats favor the development of critical thought and citizenship for social reconstruction, while the conservative voices favor the "cultural heritage of the dominant society and citizenship for social reproduction." Kathleen H. Jamieson, "The Challenges Facing Civic Education in the 21st Century," 142 *Daedelus* 65–83 (2013).

19 Frederick Hess and Matthew Rice, "Where Left and Right Agree on Civics Education, and Where They Don't," *Educ. Next.* (March. 25, 2020), www.educationnext.org/where-left-right-agree-civics-educationwhere-they-dont/

20 Susan Song, "What Does It Mean to Be an American?," 138 *Daedelus* 31 (2009).

21 Susan Song, "What Does It Mean to Be an American?," 138 *Daedelus* 31 (2009).

22 Susan Song, "What Does It Mean to Be an American?," 138 *Daedelus* 31 (2009). (noting that this is a mirage in many ways. Indeed, modern "civic" nations have not in practice really transcended ethnicity. As she explains:

> transcended ethnicity or ethnic sentiments. This is a Western mirage, reality-as-wish; closer examination always reveals the ethnic core of civic nations, in practice, even in immigrant societies with their early pioneering and dominant (English and Spanish) culture in America, Australia, or Argentina, a culture that provided the myths and language of the would-be nation.)

23 Susan Song, "What Does It Mean to Be an American?," 138 *Daedelus* 31 (2009).

24 *See, e.g.*, Michael S Merry, "Can Schools Teach Citizenship?," 41 *Discourse: Stud. Cult. Pol. Educ.* 124 (2020).

25 The No Child Left Behind Act of 2001 ("NCLB") ushered in a new century of federal education initiatives. The NCLB primed schools to prioritize standardized achievement goals over students' advancement, increased falsification of reporting, failed to encourage an accounting for individual student needs, and impacted teaching quality. While the NCLB tried to give some *purpose* to the educational mission—to close the achievement gap by increasing the accountability of schools toward federal standards—the means of attaining this purpose was so fraught with polarization, the methodology so disconnected from the reality of the schooling process, that its lofty goals were little realized. For more background, s*ee, e.g.*, Daniel Koretz, "Moving Past No Child Left Behind" 326 Science 803 (Journal of the American Academy of Science, 2009); Michael Heise, "From No Child Left behind to Every Student Succeeds: Back to the Future for Education Federalism," 117 *Colum. L. Rev.* 1859–1896 (2017).

26 Martha Nussbaum, *Not for Profit: Why Democracy Needs the Humanities* (Princeton, NJ: Princeton University Press, 2016), 134–135.

27 Martha Nussbaum, *Not for Profit: Why Democracy Needs the Humanities* (Princeton, NJ: Princeton University Press, 2016), 134–135.

28 "Should Students Have to Passa. Civics Test to Graduate? The New York times: Upfront (April 25, 2022) https://scetl.asu.edu/sites/default/files/2022-05/12-UPF-042522-Debate-CivicsTest%5B13%5D_0.pdf

29 Martha Nussbaum, *Not for Profit: Why Democracy Needs the Humanities* (Princeton, NJ: Princeton University Press, 2016), 134–135.

30 Aviv Cohen, "Four Aspects of Civic Education: Teaching the History and Geography of the Land of Israel as a Case Study," CUFA 2009 Conference.

31 Aviv Cohen, "Four Aspects of Civic Education: Teaching the History and Geography of the Land of Israel as a Case Study," CUFA 2009 Conference.

32 *See* Michael Bottery, "Values Education," in R. Bailey (ed.), *Teaching Values and Citizenship across the Curriculum: Educating Children for the World* (London: Kogan Page), 3–13.

33 Michael Bottery, "Values Education," in R. Bailey (ed.), *Teaching Values and Citizenship across the Curriculum: Educating Children for the World* (London: Kogan Page), 3–13.

34 *A.C. v. Raimondo*, C.A. No. 18-645 WES 1, 2 (D. R.I. Oct. 13, 2020) (now *A.C. v. McKee*, No. 20-2082 (1st Cir. 2022). The case was ultimately dismissed. Yet, it serves as an exceptional example of folks—young folks—calling for change. The

action took place in Providence, Rhode Island, where, in 2019, students asserted that their state education program failed to require and provide a robust enough civic education *so much so* as to raise constitutional concerns. Plaintiffs had argued that the government of Rhode Island did not offer them "an education that is adequate to prepare them to function productively as civic participants capable of voting, serving on a jury, understanding economic, social and political systems sufficiently to make informed choices, and to participate effectively in civic activities." A *strong* civics education, to their minds, is not just "about the mechanisms of our democratic system, but its spirit; about what it means to be an American and even what America means." They hoped not just for discrete information alone, but a civics education that promoted skills enough to be able to criticize and assess issues that are endemic within political prioritization, legal and institutional dynamics, and the values-structure in America. This is a rare case of activist students "knowing what they don't know" but also reflects how little their education prepares them to accomplish their duties as a citizen.

35 *See generally* L. S. Levstik and C. A. Tyson (eds.), "Introduction," in *Handbook of Research in Social Studies Education* (New York: Routledge, 2004).

36 Michael Rebell, *Flunking Democracy: Schools, Courts and Civic Participation* (University of Chicago Press, 2018).

37 In 2019, the National Endowment for the Humanities and the U.S. Department of Education (ED) funded the Educating for American Democracy (EAD) initiative. The EAD's report and a detailed road map to improve civic education were published in 2021. The U.S. House and Senate introduced the "Civics Secures Democracy Act" in 2021, a "bipartisan effort to provide $1 billion a year over a period of five years to support innovative and engaging civics and history programs." The "Every Student Succeeds Act," introduced in the Senate in 2015, calls for a well-rounded education that includes civics and government, history, geography, and economics.

38 Non-legislative initiatives taken in states include things like (1) a mandated task force (Massachusetts, Illinois, Alaska, and Oregon, among others, have appointed task forces to study and make recommendations for potential improvements in civic education), (2) accountability metrics (Florida and Tennessee have "attached consequences for students and schools for poor performance outcomes on standardized civics assessments"), (3) statewide initiatives (Illinois and Florida have developed "networks of academic institutions committed to civics education." For instance, Illinois' Democracy Schools are high schools recognized by the Illinois Civic Mission Coalition for their commitment to civic learning. The Florida College System Civics Literacy Initiative provides civics education opportunities for postsecondary students and the communities in which they live), (4) administrative directives (some state officials have used their authority to push civic education agendas and initiatives), and (5) initiatives of secretaries of state (because of their role in elections, Secretaries of State in Idaho, Mississippi, Ohio, Oregon, and Washington have provided civics resources and educational tools for teachers to educate about the political system and encourage voting behaviors). On the legislative level, there is equal diversity in action: From 1981 to 2020, 76 bills and resolutions were introduced in the U.S. Congress that referenced in some way civic education. Of these, only eight became law; of those eight only the following three did so after 2000: the No Child Left Behind Act of 2001, the American History and Civics Education Act of 2004, and the 2015 Every Student Succeeds Act. Some of note include College, Career, and Civic Life Framework for Social Studies

(C3) (to establish a Framework that would incentivize state departments of education to develop social studies standards "that support students in learning to be actively engaged in civic life") and CEI (incentivizing state legislatures to enact legislation that make the U.S. Citizenship and Immigration Services exam for naturalization the barometric civics requirement for high school graduation). Brady Delander and Maria Millard, "Education Commission of the States, Different paths to a Common Goal: Preparing Students for Civic Life" (2014).

39 Conducted by Center for Information Research on Civic Learning and Engagement.

40 Shawn P. healy, "Illinois Semocracy Schools Largely Embracing Lived Civics Principles, but Civic Empowerment Gap Persists," (October 31, 2019) http://illinoiscivics.blogspot.com/2019/10/illinois-democracy-schools-largely.html

41 Noah Shaar, "New Study Gives Illinois an 'F' for Civics and History Education Standards," Illinois Policy (July 2021) www.illinoispolicy.org/new-study-gives-illinois-an-f-for-civics-and-history-education-standards/

42 National Council for Social Studies, "College, Career, and Civic Life (C3) Framework for Social Studies State Standards: Guidance for Enhancing the Rigor of K-12 Civics, Economics, Geography, and History," www.socialstudies.org/standards/c3

43 Michael Hansen, et al., "2018 Brown Center Report On American Education: An Inventory Of State Civics Requirements," (June 2018) www.brookings.edu/research/2018-brown-center-report-on-american-education-an-inventory-of-state-civics-requirements/

44 Rebecca Winthrop, "The Need for Civic Education in 21st Century Schools" (June 2020) www.brookings.edu/policy2020/bigideas/the-need-for-civic-education-in-21st-century-schools/

45 A total of 14 states have adopted this approach. Amanda Litvinov, "Forgotten Purpose: Civics Education in Public Schools,"(National Education Association; NEAToday) (March 2017) www.nea.org/advocating-for-change/new-from-nea/forgotten-purpose-civics-education-public-schools. Sadly, the current paradigm doesn't even do rogue memorization well. *See* Amanda Robert, "Americans are divided by age and race on the fairness of the justice system, ABA civics survey finds" (April 2021), www.abajournal.com/web/article/2021-civics-survey (noting that less than half of participants could name the current Chief Justice of the Supreme Court, and one in five demonstrated confusion as to the rights guaranteed under the First Amendment to the Constitution. Still more, the survey showed considerable differences of opinion when it came to defining items like the meaning of "defund the police," or the consequences of "aggressive prosecution," or even agreeing with the notion that "the nation's judicial system adheres to the rule of law, under which all individuals are treated equally in the eyes of the law.")

46 There are around 20 states, among them Michigan and Illinois, that have updated their educational programming on government and social studies in line with the C3 framework. The guide to upgrading these standards is framed around an "inquiry arc," which "supports student-centered, engaged learning by guiding students to develop questions and plan inquiries, apply disciplinary tools and concepts, evaluate sources and use evidence, and communicate conclusions and take informed action." *See* Paul Baumann and Jan Brennan, "State Civic Education Policy: Framework and Gap Analysis Tool," Education Commission of the States (December 2017) www.ecs.org/wp-content/uploads/State-Civics-Education-Policy-Framework-and-gap-analysis-tool.pdf

47 Report, 2018 Brown Report on American Education, www.brookings.edu/wp-content/uploads/2018/06/2018-Brown-Center-Report-on-American-Education_FINAL1.pdf, p. 20.
48 Sarah Shapiro and Catherine Brown, "The State of Civic Education," Center for American Progress (February 2018) https://files.eric.ed.gov/fulltext/ED586237.pdf
49 Sarah Shapiro and Catherine Brown, "The State of Civic Education," Center for American Progress (February 2018) https://files.eric.ed.gov/fulltext/ED586237.pdf
50 Au, Wayne. (2013). "Coring Social Studies within Corporate Education Reform: The Common Core State Standards, Social Justice, and the Politics of Knowledge in U.S. Schools." 4 *Crit. Educ.* No. 5, 1–13.
51 Meira Levinson and Jacob Faye, *Democratic Discord in Schools: Cases and Commentaries in Educational Ethics* (Cambridge, MA: Harvard Education Press, 2019), 60 (referencing Roderick Watts, "Critical Consciousness: Current Status and Future Directions," in *Youth Civic Development: Working at the Cutting Edge: New Directions for the Child and Adolescent Development* (Jossey-Bass, San Francisco, 2011)).
52 Meira Levinson and Jacob Faye, *Democratic Discord in Schools: Cases and Commentaries in Educational Ethics* (Cambridge, MA: Harvard Education Press, 2019), 57.
53 *See, e.g.*, Mark Rodeghier, "How Education Affects Attitude to Protest: A Further Test," 32 *Soc. Q.* 277–288 (1991).
54 Meira Levinson and Jacob Faye, *Democratic Discord in Schools: Cases and Commentaries in Educational Ethics* (Cambridge, MA: Harvard Education Press, 2019), 58. Furthermore, "few people seem to question the value of the local, national, and global issues around which students are rallying."
55 Meira Levinson and Jacob Faye, *Democratic Discord in Schools: Cases and Commentaries in Educational Ethics* (Cambridge, MA: Harvard Education Press, 2019), 57.
56 Meira Levinson and Jacob Faye, *Democratic Discord in Schools: Cases and Commentaries in Educational Ethics* (Cambridge, MA: Harvard Education Press, 2019), 57.
57 Meira Levinson and Jacob Faye, *Democratic Discord in Schools: Cases and Commentaries in Educational Ethics* (Cambridge, MA: Harvard Education Press, 2019), 57.
58 Meira Levinson and Jacob Faye, *Democratic Discord in Schools: Cases and Commentaries in Educational Ethics* (Cambridge, MA: Harvard Education Press, 2019), 57.
59 Meira Levinson and Jacob Faye, *Democratic Discord in Schools: Cases and Commentaries in Educational Ethics* (Cambridge, MA: Harvard Education Press, 2019), 57.
60 Meira Levinson and Jacob Faye, *Democratic Discord in Schools: Cases and Commentaries in Educational Ethics* (Cambridge, MA: Harvard Education Press, 2019), 67.
61 Diana Owen, "Unification and Identity in Civic Culture and Civic Education" (2009).

> Students' opportunities to participate in high-quality, school-based civic learning are largely determined by students' socioeconomic status and ethnicity/race. Students in poorer communities and students of color have fewer opportunities to

develop the skills and dispositions necessary for full participation in democratic life. Children with fewer home civic opportunities receive unequal civic learning opportunities through their schools (defined as opportunities provided by the school to participate in student government, service clubs, newspaper/yearbook, or community service). Students of lower socioeconomic background are less likely to attend schools where community service opportunities are offered. Higher socio-economic status youth are likely to be exposed to peers who perform service who in turn may introduce them to new civic opportunities.

62 Meira Levinson and Jacob Faye, *Democratic Discord in Schools: Cases and Commentaries in Educational Ethics* (Cambridge, MA: Harvard Education Press, 2019), 20.

63 Meira Levinson and Jacob Faye, *Democratic Discord in Schools: Cases and Commentaries in Educational Ethics* (Cambridge, MA: Harvard Education Press, 2019), 20.

64 Martha Nussbaum, *Not for Profit: Why Democracy Needs the Humanities* (Princeton, NJ: Princeton University Press, 2016), 10.

65 Martha Nussbaum, *Not for Profit: Why Democracy Needs the Humanities* (Princeton, NJ: Princeton University Press, 2016), 26.

66 Martha Nussbaum, *Not for Profit: Why Democracy Needs the Humanities* (Princeton, NJ: Princeton University Press, 2016), 10. A suitably educated citizen is one who has "cultivated capacities for critical thinking and reflection [crucial] for keeping democracies alive and wide awake. [They] can think well about a wide range of cultures [and] groups … and the ability to imagine the experience of another."

67 Habermas, Jürgen. "Citizenship and National Identity: Some Reflections on the Future of Europe," in Ronald Beiner (ed.), *Theorizing Citizenship* (State University of New York Press, New York, 1995), 255–282.

68 Martha Nussbaum, *Not for Profit: Why Democracy Needs the Humanities* (Princeton, NJ: Princeton University Press, 2016), 26. This attribute of the citizen is also called for by protest scholars and even abolitionist-thinkers who might disagree with other aspects of this definition of the citizen. *See, e.g.*, Michael Lipsky, "Protest as a Political Resource," 62 *Am. Pol. Sci. Rev.*1144–1158 (2014) concerning how protest leaders and activist-citizens are obligated to develop certain aptitudes:

> [They] must nurture and sustain an organization comprised of people with whom they may or may not share common values. They must articulate goals and choose strategies so as to maximize their public exposure through communications media. They must maximize the impact of third parties in the political conflict. Finally, they must try to maximize chances of success among those capable of granting goals.)

69 Martha Nussbaum, *Not for Profit: Why Democracy Needs the Humanities* (Princeton, NJ: Princeton University Press, 2016), 91.

70 Meira Levinson and Jacob Faye, *Democratic Discord in Schools: Cases and Commentaries in Educational Ethics* (Cambridge, MA: Harvard Education Press, 2019), 20.

71 Meira Levinson and Jacob Faye, *Democratic Discord in Schools: Cases and Commentaries in Educational Ethics* (Cambridge, MA: Harvard Education Press, 2019), 20.

2 Building a Cogent Educational Philosophy for a New Civic Education

With the problem of a lost and confused civic education paradigm in sight, we can now begin circling around a proposed solution. As a first point of contact, it is important to contextualize the idea of teaching children law in a grounding educational philosophy. In this chapter, I focus on two fields: commentaries on moral education (or the development of moral character) and commentaries on the capabilities approach philosophy (especially regarding education). The former draws chiefly from the ideas of John Dewey and Lawrence Kohlberg; the latter explores the capabilities approach of Martha Nussbaum. To my mind, the normative capabilities approach to education is a way of thinking about the goals of this civic educational innovation *writ large*, while the moral educational component can serve more subordinately, expounding on the sorts of values-learning we already see in educational projects of this sort. For, as Nussbaum rightly says, "there is no values-free form of education in the world."[1]

Now these disparate philosophers and philosophical camps have historically been in conversation to varying degrees; Dewey especially is a grounding force for Nussbaum, as we shall see. Still, they are, for the most part, independently operating, each relying on their own forbearers and scarcely overlapping outside a general interest in education for democracy and autonomy. These thinkers help support the following proposal from two angles I see as essential to a civic education: serving the moral and character development of citizens, and strengthening skills, abilities, and capacities to take on the arduous task of citizenship. With that said, though these philosophical discussions are not always put in conversation, we will see that they are by no means incongruous; indeed, they reveal quite a lot about the current landscape of the discussion surrounding education for democratic means.

However, there is of course one elephant left in the room: where is the "law" background in this purportedly "law solution" to civic education policy? The grounding theory behind this proposal is one of education policy and philosophy, not law directly. It is worth discussing why this is the case, briefly, at the outset. To do so, I want to first assume, without defending, a view of law consistent with the jurisprudence of Jürgen Habermas (1929–present), one helpful in elucidating how "law" fits into the larger arc of this proposal.

DOI: 10.4324/9781003596523-4

2.1 Looking to Law as a Reflection of Values, Not as a Solution to Problems

To Habermas, law properly conceived is an institutionalization of practical discourse on social norms.[2] In other words, the law is a conduit for social integration and reflection of social values, with these values differing dependent on the community.[3] Distinct from his contemporaries in schools of critical legal theory,[4] political theory,[5] or even sociology of law,[6] Habermas takes the position that "law must be [and is] legitimated by the intersubjective agreement of all affected."[7] Law is, indeed, a "self-referential system, that, because of its 'facticity' in the eyes of the citizenry, can evoke respect for the law beyond sheer compliance."[8] "All practical questions can be judged impartially and decided rationally, including law, morality, and politics."[9] While this does not excuse the fact that law is also a "social fact that draws upon the state's monopoly on power to compel citizens to align their conduct to the prescriptions of law,"[10] Habermas stops short of agreeing with critical theorists that suggest law is majorly coercive and exclusively accessible to the domain of powerful elites,[11] and also the positivists who aver that the sheer act of going through a formal procedure makes law legitimate.[12]

Law is "communicatively mediated" through "intentional social relations," implying that autonomous,[13] thoughtful " 'flesh-and-blood' individuals are in a regular dialogue with their laws and legal systems to best reflect their values."[14] Ethical–political reasoning by those of us in the democracy influence the consensus of the affected that contribute to democratic law formation[15]; *all* actors are empowered to take yes or no positions on "various claims pertaining to propositional truth, normative rightness, and subjective truthfulness" in a given matter.[16] Participants argue about validity claims, and, according to Habermas, are swayed by the "peculiarly constraint-free force of the better argument."[17] To persuade, rather than to coerce, becomes the *modus operandi* of the functioning democracy; law represents the output of peek persuasion, collective influence, and self-determination.[18]

A Habermasian jurisprudential view—however naïve, as some critics might say[19]—lends itself well to the larger project of instructing younger students in law, an active experience in which burgeoning citizens develop tools for intelligent criticism, a robust understanding of competing values and legal processes, and awareness of larger ideas. In a sense, it is an education *of* and *for* the autonomist view of citizens and society. By the same token, if the law is self-referential and reflective of larger social norms and agreement, consistency would dictate that a solution to the perceived ills of our democracy today does not lie in treating law or passing a law or top-down change, but its citizens from the bottom-up.

To elucidate this, consider, for instance, the abortion-debate post-*Roe* and *Dobbs*. The widespread impact, principled stances, and dramatic declarations fueled change in some of the best ways. But there is no denying that these were stances and judgments passed through law at the highest level in divisive climates beyond the consensus of the affected. In other words, technical pronouncements were dissonant with social consensus—it was forced before its time. Former Justice Ruth Bader-Ginsberg admonished *Roe v. Wade* for this very reason; its sweeping nature—couched as a medical decision rather than in the preferable light of a women's rights case—materialized too soon for our collective consciousness.[20] She remarked in 2013, "now all the doors [were] open, but we [hadn't] come all the way."[21] Prior to *Roe*, anti-abortion activists were operating on a state level. The Supreme Court's ruling turned the movement into a national one,[22] a formerly bipartisan political issue into a partisan target until *Dobbs* unilaterally dismantled 50 years of precedent to add *even more* fuel to the public debate fire. The manipulation of law, in other words, without the commensurate, rational agreement of the citizenry (as revealed through public debate and expression) is damaging.

As another, school-related example, consider the public attention now being afforded critical race theory in schools, recently (and wrongly) also enlarged to include anti-sexuality and gender studies sentiment. In such cases, lawmakers mobilize power, politics, and law to change or impose values without credence to the affected. DeSantis' Parental Rights in Education Act (the "Don't Say Gay Bill") was promulgated as a political ploy which has since had chilling effects on teachers' ability to educate children (even connect with students, many who have same-sex parents, for fear of violating the bill against discussing sexuality), stifled dialog on the basis of faulty reasoning, and become a political rallying-cry attracting white supremacists seeking to defend "tradition."[23] In no way was the instruction of critical studies ever conceived of as threatened to democracy, until then-President Trump indicated as much in 2020 and promised to defend against the threat through the use of law.[24] Now, it is a demon and Rick DeSantis emboldens the fear by fiat, mobilizing law to coerce values and ideas, rather than reflect citizen debate and discussion, lending to disastrously divisive consequences. Circularly, this attack by law is met with short-sighted protests and reactionary backlash which accomplish little, negate further dialog, and increase partisan politics. In turn, we have reached our present milieu, one where the public is against the lawmaker, distrust is at a high, and our civic education—and indeed, all our education—is suffering from pushes for neutrality, unmooring from principles, and external pressure.

Laws are important exemplifiers and tools for normalizing and strengthening, but reform needs to come from a new angle. Legal change needs to be bottom-up, by people, reforming toward the highest levels of change (legal change and operation). The law learning project proposed in this piece, achieves this by teaching legal reasoning and institutional awareness to the citizen but is *not* about teaching law itself.[25] In other words, my proposal is an education philosophy-centered solution designed to offer tools to the citizen to succesfully speak America's language of law.

So, let us begin the argument for creating "law learning" at the lowest levels (young children) and why it is imperative. In creating a philosophical framework for this idea, let us start with our moral education thinkers, and situating law learning as, in a word, a character education (in a similar way in which civic education is often currently considered).[26] What do I mean by this? Character education fosters—to varying degrees—core ethical values, develops perspectives on thinking, feeling, and behavior, and a curriculum that provides students the opportunity to practice morality. In other words, this education develops moral character by strengthening "the enduring aspects of personality that are tied to an ethical normative orientation."[27] It is already deeply rooted in the public school system;[28] *all education involves, intentionally or unintentionally*, moral and character education—either in discrete classes (maybe like a civics class, or spread out in other, typically liberal arts courses, curricula). As our first philosopher, John Dewey suggested, moral values are a part of a hidden and unstudied curriculum, even when they are not highly objectified.[29] Law learning is one such strengthening character education, as we shall see. The question is, *how* will it develop character? And, for this, we need to devise a rhetoric using inspiring moral education theory. In the following, I discuss the theorists that really inspire this proposal.

2.2 "Growth," Moral Deliberation, and Perpetual Learning

John Dewey (1859–1952) was perturbed, as I am, with apathy; his whole moral educational philosophy was predicated on combatting indifference.[30] For our purposes, we might trace his fear and frustration to one important phenomenon of the educational disposition of his day, inspiring (at least in part) his moral democratic education philosophy: that "[a student's] growth [was] regarded as having an end [or goal], instead of being an end [unto itself]."[31] Dewey's critique of this notion, his counter-conception of "growth," and his proposal for a priming education in perpetual "moral deliberation" will be the focus of this section (and indeed a guide-post for our new civics).

Dewey observes that an educational project fixated upon training children to become adults (as if adulthood is a fixed, perfect standard), or citizens, or to achieve X or Y purpose is fallacious and venomous.[32] Indeed, "we may [even] say that the adult should be growing in childlikeness," for doing so would at least take into account the natural instinct of "sympathetic curiosity, unbiased responsiveness and openness of mind" that are instinctive to the child.[33] Fixing goals to education involving "growing" to adulthood—whatever that entails in terms of temperament, disposition, skillset—puts forward a desire for "conformity"[34] which, when drilled into children through rote memorization of commonly perceived "good works," recitations, and bland lessons, Dewey observes, yields "lack of interest in the novel, aversion to progress, and dread of the uncertain and the unknown."[35] This is not to say that Dewey took issue with the conception of being "adult," but rather that growth was something done *to* the student, that the student was somehow lacking until they reached adulthood, rather than something they *do*, something in which they active and involved. This, in many ways, promotes passiveness.

This passiveness in education yielded a "tragedy of the lost individual"[36]—a byproduct, he saw, of the "rugged individualism of capitalism and the mass culture of standardization" that produced, on the largest level a "debased form of democracy."[37] For survival, he argued for a reconfiguration of the school away from the "hollow" place "stuffing children full of facts and asking them to regurgitate them,"[38] where all learning was reduced to "one dead level"[39] to achieve some goal of creating adults and workers. The status quo, as he articulates:

> would not have the children learn to govern themselves and one another, but would have the masters rule them, ignoring the fact that this common practice in childhood may be a foundation for that evil condition in adult society where the citizens are arbitrarily ruled by political bosses.[40]

Indeed, the "lost individual" denoted a "burgeoning spiritual degeneration" amidst a modern culture of material affluence and political freedom; "the student fails to reconfirm their sense of existence,"[41] or find their own voice which, incidentally, is central to self-reliance and the foundational notion of citizenship upon which this country is predicated.[42] In turn, this "this loss of intensity among life among young people darkens our [democratic] culture as a whole."[43]

To fix this, Dewey begins by abandoning the notion of "growth" as educating toward the goal of maturity and reaching adulthood—we "surrender our habit of thinking of instruction as a method of supplying this lack by pouring knowledge into a mental and moral whole which awaits filling."[44] All stages and ages of childhood development become equally valuable, and, indeed, education becomes about "the enterprise of supplying the conditions which ensure growth." More specifically, Dewey argues that school ought to foster "a continuous reorganization of a child's experience in his or her interaction with the adult world."[45] Creative imagination, reflective thought, and experimentation, Dewey postures, are key to developing character. Moreover, Dewey argues that the contributions and ideas of the younger are just as important as the institutions and pronouncements of the older. Indeed, "growth is an ongoing interaction between the innovation of the younger generation, on the one hand, and the wisdom and cultural heritage of the older."[46] Learning denotes the development of criticality and plasticity—already inherent in children—which in turn form habits, which are more helpful as tools for the citizen and the adult than any reproduction of information or recitation as takes place in school.[47] These "habits involving thought, invention, and initiative in applying capacities to new aims" are essential for the citizen.[48] "They are opposed to routine which marks an arrest of growth";[49] they cultivate a "social spirit" that is now being "atrophied for lack of use"[50]; they are the blocks upon which we can construct free citizens.

Importantly, again, this is a *growth without fixed ends*. The process is ongoing throughout the whole life, and, indeed, is a sustaining lifeblood of a healthy democracy. Dewey thought about training thinkers rather than mass-producing "adults" according to a one-dimensional ethic or ideal. This needs emphasizing: Dewey's educational philosophy is without focus on imparting *particular* moral values, precepts, or principles.[51] While Dewey did maintain that the school holds an essentially ethical and moral responsibility to the student (and served an indelible social function), he believed that the "moral work and worth" of the school is often too rigidly construed: for example, "training for citizenship, and then citizenship is then interpreted in a narrow sense as meaning capacity to vote intelligently, disposition to obey laws."[52] Instead, to Dewey, the moral purview of the school ought to be as a facilitator for "moving ideas, motive forces in the guidance of conduct."[53] While a child should have virtues and values, more importantly, is that they know how to "evaluate" those ideas over time and prevent complacency in a singular ideology.[54] There is a singular set of good values, so long as the arc of one's judgment bends toward the common good.

How can one learn to have an evaluative and critical mind? For Dewey, the moral education of the child can always be integrated fully by way of "making the methods of learning, of acquiring intellectual power, and of assimilating subject-matter, such that they will render behavior more enlightened, more consistent, more vigorous than it otherwise would be."[55] In other words, emphasizing process as much as substance; *how* we teach is as valuable as what we teach. This education could be promoted in many subjects that are conducive to moral and ethical conversations.[56] Dewey observed: "[where] the child approaches the book without intellectual hunger, without alertness, without a questioning attitude, and the result is the one so deplorably common: such abject dependence upon books as weakens [one's] vigor of thought and inquiry."[57] The subservient attitude is fatal! Instead, argues Dewey, growth should take place by doing, figuring things out, thinking about them, and raising questions. The change he wanted was, he said "the change from or less passive and inert recipiency and restraint to one of buoyant outgoing energy."[58] Educators should help students acquire knowledge through intelligent study of historical and existing forces and conditions; they should teach students to use their minds well—to think critically, to examine competing perspectives and accounts, and to value and use democratic deliberations and scientific inquiry to sort them out and reach decisions. And, of course, educators should *not* tell students to what end they should use these competencies or what to value; students are not to be indoctrinated, but left to use their minds as they see fit. It is up to them—intelligent, democratic citizens—to engage in the ongoing work of government of, by, and for the people.

This all falls under Dewey's heading of developing a *morally deliberative* citizen—teaching children to consider values and ideas within specific contexts and with critical perspectives constantly, rather than predisposing them to rigidly hold to an ethical belief or value-set. "Moral Deliberation" is an individual's "dramatic rehearsal of various competing possible action."[59] It is a counter-position to the notion that a strong character education requires teaching specific virtues to students. For Dewey, indeed, new problems require new solutions, one ought not to rely on stale conceptions of values and ideas to meet brave new challenges.[60] As one writer reflects:

> Dewey's conception of moral deliberation is consistent with his pragmatism. First, Dewey believes that moral inquiry is the same as intelligent inquiry; both are meant to serve human interests. Second, Dewey believes that there is no single universal principle that could apply in every moral problem; the general principle only exists in the continual investigation. Third, Dewey insists that moral judgment depends on the problematic situation. We must understand the situation to decide among the many possible actions.[61]

The philosophy reflects fluidity in the way we perceive problems throughout life, ingratiates students to the notion that there is a "gray" area in which we operate morally, and generally predisposes "us to reflect on the established social order and encourages them to develop a new social order." Perhaps more importantly (and certainly more practically) this educational focus promotes, among other skills,[62] the power of "good judgment."[63] To Dewey, "judgement is the sense of relative values involves ability to select, to discriminate."[64] In acquiring information alone, one cannot develop this skill; indeed, "development of judgment is in spite of, not because of, methods of instruction that emphasize simple learning."[65] Importantly, Dewey writes:

> the one who has judgment is the one who has ability to size up a situation. He the one who can grasp the scene or situation before him, ignoring what is irrelevant, or what for the time being is unimportant, who can seize up the factors which demand attention, and grade them according to their respective claims.[66]

These ideas—from cultivating morally deliberative citizens un-indoctrinated to a single set of moral values, to exercising skills of good judgment, to active learning in the way of fostering dialog—all in the interest of producing the most self-reliant citizen—will be a major focus of this proposal, and, indeed, a primary tool of the American citizen's toolbox.

2.3 At the Crux of Individual and Society: Process, "Development," and Moral Judgment

Dewey offers us a guiding theory, as well as some suggestions, about *why* and *how* to pivot learning to foster greater democratic citizenship. However, it is highly individualized. Even where Dewey discusses active learning and the role of the teacher, he neglects to really venture into how others—peers, community, family, etc.—impact the learning process. Furthermore, he ascribes no real benchmarks for students as they undertake his new-fangled learning—how do we know (and measure) whether we are succeeding in producing the citizens needed for our thriving democracy?

For these questions of socialization and process, we can consider a complimentary thinker, Lawrence Kohlberg (1927–1987). Kohlberg took up Dewey's mantle in many ways—notably embracing his value-relativist stance in education, rejecting traditional core ethical standards, and adopting the belief that students can aim to ascend to higher levels of moral functioning. Kohlberg is especially renowned for pioneering a formula of moral education based on developing *moral judgment.* This education includes cultivating in students a (already universally held) pre-disposition for ethical reasoning by leading them through his "six stages of moral development"[67] *and* nurturing them within morally upright communities. His socialization-developmental approach to moral education was about both the classroom and the individual child; he was all about process, substance, *and* surroundings.

Kohlberg himself represents a squaring away of two moral education theory camps. The first was led by Emile Durkheim,[68] and known as the socialization perspective on moral education whereby it was argued that students came to understand morals through group affiliation and solidarity. The second, and by far the more influential of the two on Kohlberg, was the developmental school of Jean Piaget.[69] Piaget, like Dewey in his preoccupation with the individualistic nature of moral education and the belief in the internal potentiality of the child to morally ascend, criticized traditional character education, which only focused on training of "good habits"—i.e., honesty, responsibility. Piaget saw this as, essentially, indoctrination of a way of thinking. His approach, therefore, had students "actively construct universalizable moral principles rather than a teacher actively indoctrinating conventional social norms."[70] But, unlike Dewey, Piaget (and Kohlberg) focused on the act of educating to support students' development of autonomous *inner standards of justice*[71] (note: this is distinguishable from Dewey's interest in the common good or educating for the base principle of conscience) that overcome the dependence on external authorities. For Kohlberg, though the process of moralization is content-free (defined by patterns in terms of the moral stages), the end to which it strives has a definite shape and character: *just* citizens; justice as the overarching ethical principle.

Kohlberg channeled Piaget deeply in his "six stages"—the preconventional, the conventional, and the post-conventional. Indeed, the "universal nature of Kohlberg's theory rested upon the idea of the potentiality of the stages, the fact that we all have it within ourselves to reach the highest stages of moral growth."[72] Furthermore, it relied on process, on the notion that the instructor guides them through each stage in sequence—each laden with its own value benchmarks—through activities that promote a method of progression called "disequilibrium," where "the tension aroused by the discrepancy between the moral compasses of the person and the events he is confronted with leads to a sense of imbalance" pushing them to higher stages of reasoning. To be sure, one can conceive of Kohlberg as more a mechanist than Dewey: unpreoccupied with the emotional nature of moral deliberation, and heavily considerate of the steps and technical metrics of such an education, whereas Dewey was more interested in the cognitive evolution naturally.

One way in which this technicality manifests—helpfully, for our purposes in contriving of a "model for teaching children law"—is in his 'dilemma discussion' activities, where Kohlberg posed complicated moral problems to children to determine more judgment. These discussions rested on three assumptions: (1) that moral and democratic behavior depends on a person's ability to apply moral skills in a conflict before them and in conversation with opponents, (2) these competencies are fostered throughout one's life, and (3) that "moral competency is best fostered in an environment where children feel safe."[73] Within the discussion, students reacted colorfully, answered thoughtfully, and problematized the issue in ways that were foundational to moral development. Regularly conducting these activities allowed children to wrestle with values through development stages, bending ultimately toward a character in line with the "arc of justice," and creating measurements for student advancement. Just as importantly, contriving of practical activities for students allowed Kohlberg to properly theorize the role of facilitator in such a moral education. Kohlberg affirmed Dewey in that the teachers[74] in the classroom *do not* need to be role models of morality.[75] The teacher does not even need to operate at the highest level of morality (the "post-conventional") to guide students toward "just" moral decision-making through critical reflection. They work only to "foster the moral development of his students by different methodologies: clarifying dialogues, discussing real moral dilemmas, role-playing, procedures for active neutrality, simulations, conflict resolution."[76] The teacher helps each student issue more judgments that approximate a universal principle of justice.[77]

But, of course, Kohlberg needed to answer for an obvious critique: with little to no connection to real-world experience, how can developing one's reasoning through mere "dilemma-mongering" guarantee that individuals will act in consistently moral ways in practical settings?[78] In other words, students are not learning about the relationship between moral reflections in "dilemma discussions and their normally noncritical approach to daily affairs."[79] Indeed, in reality, as Kohlberg concedes, "the individual uncovers the 'moral stages' through his interactions with his society"; "justice as the highest moral virtue is realizable only in the social milieu."[80] "In this sense moral education must address itself to the issues of both competence and performance."[81] It entails taking into account the social context in which individuals make decisions, and to Kohlberg's mind, could only be fostered by the creation of a moral society.

Enter inspiration from Durkheim's socialization theory.[82] Kohlberg's "just community" in the classroom[83] represents his next-most important contribution to moral education and will help us conceive of the classroom environment best conducive to instructing young children in law. Kohlberg urged the augmentation of moral education with a moral environment providing a space for dialog, "consensus, acceptance of personal responsibilities, and universal human rights within the framework of collective collaboration."[84] There were five main objectives to his "just community" schools and classrooms:

> creating creativity and adaptation to the rules of all children; stimulating children's moral reasoning abilities; maintaining a balance between reasoning and action; training moral empathy and encourage pro-social commitment; and developing a solid value system based on forbearance and openness.[85]

From this, Kohlberg's moral education approach deviates further from Dewey, straddling the line between a student's internal reasoning and a school's solidarity. Durkheim's socialization perspective acknowledges the following:

> students must first learn to obey society's rules before they can reasonably understand when it is ethically required not to be obedient; from a developmental perspective, it acknowledges that there are better and worse reasons for students to follow the rules.[86]

The confluence of these two dimensions, the individual and the social in the classroom, is highly instructive for the modern civic classroom. A program might be "restructured to promote student participation for them to reconcile their interests with society's interests."[87] Indeed, "the strength of the just community approach lies on the fact that self-criticism and self-reflexive conduct must accompany moral education."[88] In this way, moral reasoning is developed in the just community but based on moral responsibility.

To my mind, this manner of moral education in the classroom compliments well even the intellectual aspects of the class. When learning about values (or really a lack of concrete values but encouraging a plethora of options to which one can turn based on their internal compass), ideas, and critiquing institutions, we bear Kohlberg and Dewey in mind in conceiving of effective pedagogical and theoretical educational innovations toward fostering a new, intrinsic civic orientation in students. But we keep Nussbaum—our final thinker—in mind when we consider articulating the larger goals and perspectives students must acquire to be functional citizens navigating a robust, complicated political environment.

2.4 Fulfillment, Flourishing, and Control: A Foundation in the Capabilities-Approach

By way of two dimensions: a discursive community of learners and an open values model of learning which favors emphasis on active learning and participation, the child's ability to inquire and question—Dewey, Kohlberg, and a long line of others in the field of moral education (think: Rousseau, Alcott, Montessori), and, onto Nussbaum are setting us up well so far for our law interjection into re-conceiving of a moral-and-practical civic education. Martha Nussbaum (1947–present), however, is worth a greater nod. Her philosophy offers an important contribution to the contemporary fight against mere "passive assimilation of facts and cultural traditions [in education], [toward] challenging the mind to become active, competent, and thoughtfully critical in a complex world."[89]

Her approach is distinctive from the other moralists. Whereas Dewey's moral education philosophy contemplated the self-reliant citizen for the purpose of *engendering the common-good*, and Kohlberg's with individuals of sound moral judgment, an *intrinsic sense of justice*, and a "just community" of learners, Nussbaum cares for, among other things, cultivating the critical-thinker[90] *capable* of practical reason, deliberation, choice for the purposes of *exercising freedom*, *executing social justice*, and holding accountable (even control over) a political society that ought to protect such freedoms as to promote human dignity and flourishing.[91] All this—and indeed her view of education—is enshrined in the capabilities approach, a normative approach to assessing human development and welfare that concentrates on the "actual capability of persons to achieve lives they value rather than solely have a right or freedom to do so."[92] This is an education at the intersection of "capabilities" and "functionings." "Capabilities" are the answers to Nussbaum's question "what is this person able to do and to be."[93] She is preoccupied with three types of capabilities: there are the *basic capabilities*, internal abilities—"innate equipment"—naturally contrived in the person (i.e., imagination, basic reasoning), the *internal capabilities*, "states of the person herself that are, so far as the person herself is concerned, sufficient conditions for the exercise of the requisite functions" (i.e., to speak and to think in accordance with your own consciousness),[94] and *combined capabilities* or "internal capabilities combined with suitable external conditions for the exercise of the function."[95] Indeed, she explores ten central *combined capabilities* needed by the human to flourish; for "a life that is deprived of any of the capabilities is not a good human life."[96] Notably, the ascendancy that takes place between the different levels of capabilities makes intuitive sense and is tied into her notion of "functioning," or an "active realization or more capabilities," "beings and doings that are outgrowths of realizations of capabilities."[97] In other words, Nussbaum's theory of education *for* capabilities therefore operates on two levels: what are we priming students to accomplish X; how much is our society letting us apply those primed skills.

An education, to her mind, forms peoples' *basic capabilities* into developed *internal capabilities* of many kinds.[98] Nussbaum focuses on "fertile functioning" and argues that even a basic education can mean the difference in questions of disadvantage and inequality. So too can it mean the difference in oppression, governmental abuse, and societal divisiveness. A *true* education for human development, however, requires more than just basic literacy and numeracy; it needs rather "critical thinking, the ability to imagine and to understand another person's situation from within, and a grasp of world history and the current global economy."[99] This is reminiscent of both Dewey and Kohlberg in many ways. Adherents to the capabilities approach must attend to *pedagogy* and *content*, asking how both the substantive of studies and the nature of classroom interactions fulfill the following aim: "acquiring knowledge, skills, values and understanding which enables children to think in new ways, to 'be', to develop agency in society and make decisions."[100] I will discuss more precisely her view of the classroom environment soon but suffice to say that Nussbaum's education is intrinsically civic in its criticality and promotion of self-agency.

The realization of *combined capabilities*—of which, again, she cites ten central ones—is a much loftier discussion, inculpating responsibilities for government, public policy, and resources. To the minds of capabilities theorists like Nussbaum, the aim of public policy is the production of these combined capabilities. In other words, public policy must "promote the states of the person by providing the necessary education and care, as well as preparing the environment so that it is favorable for the exercise of practical reason and the other major functions." [101] Importantly, Nussbaum does *not* say that "public policy should rest content with internal capabilities, but remain indifferent to the struggles of individuals who have to try to exercise these capabilities in hostile environments."[102] Her view on capabilities, therefore, has as much to do with what students *learn* as consistently ensuring that the government is *empowering them to mobilize* that learning. A perfect view of education carries both interests at heart.

We might consider two of her ten central combined capabilities to help us understand this idea and its relation to this piece's larger proposition. Consider, first, the "practical reasoning capability"—where one is "able to come up with a conception of good and think critically about life plans." It is of a "combined" nature—where the society and individual implicitly come together within the capability: one might be able to reason (individual) of their own accord, but "practically reason" promises versatility within an existing socio-cultural milieu, and awareness of surroundings, and political control is achieved through an education (society). Yet, practical reason is *essential* to the flourishing of the individual. Nussbaum emphasizes especially "practical reason" as *architectonic* and pervasive across all other capabilities.[103] Good policy, therefore, is to promote the development of practical reasoning skills,[104] as well as for society to ensure opportunities for people to orient themselves in the social order' so that they can best exercise choice and decision-making.[105]

Another relevant combined capability is "having control of one's political environment"—where one can effectively participate in "political elections controlling their life."[106] To be sure, the act of voting, for instance, is a "functioning," but the notion of deliberating intelligent, criticizing values and ideas, and ultimately choosing between political candidates is "capability." This ladder aspect is central to the educational project. By the same token, one might have the capability to discern between political groups, to understand the values at stake, but the "combined" element might be lacking: "citizens of repressive non-democratic regimes have the internal but not the combined capability to exercise thought and speech in accordance with their conscience."[107] In other words, some people might learn to have a voice but have no way to use it. In this way, Nussbaum appropriates moral philosophy into development economics.[108] The normative version of the capabilities approach asks people to consider "what makes for a minimally just society." It forces critical thinking and develops specific arguments against other social justice theories in a process of political justification.[109] The capabilities approach is therefore a good basis for political principles in a pluralistic society—can citizens *think* and can citizens *act.* Eventually, this can become the basis for "overlapping consensus among holder of the main religious and secular views … [manifesting as a] form of political liberalism showing respect for citizens by not asking them to endorse a political doctrine built on any religious or metaphysical view."[110] Nevertheless, the nation *still* has a moral role securely grounded in the central importance placed on people's freedom and self-definition.[111]

Nussbaum points out that democratic nations are better positioned than others to ensure both functioning and capabilities. However, as is the case of the United States, it is not a guarantee. I posit, indeed, that a person might live in our political environment where they *could* bring a capability—practical reason or control over one's political environment—to function, but they are not educated well toward that capability.[112] In other words, the system is set up to be used and bettered by civically inclined, thoughtful citizens. But we have few; we therefore have not realized the combined capability. My main conception of *law learning* addresses the failure to develop capabilities despite having the infrastructure for "functionings." And this is highly cogent with Nussbaum's philosophy! She prioritizes "capabilities" over "functionings";[113] voting is not the goal, the goal is rather to achieve the higher order reasoning skills needed to cast the vote.[114] Just so for us: the outcome is not the goal—students knowing technical law or voting a certain way—but only providing them with notion of being able to discern values, make choices, consider counterarguments and participate in political processes intelligently.

In the broadest strokes, Nussbaum offers an idea as to how to improve access to the *tools* people use to live fulfilling lives. She assesses societies for their "basic decency and justice"; indeed, she asks: "what is each person able to do and to be?"[115] This mentality is focused on *choice* or *freedom*; the hallmark of good societies is promoting for their people a set of opportunities or "substantial freedoms" which people then may or may not exercise: the choice is theirs. This is thus a respect for people's powers of self-definition.[116] Her list of ten capabilities, indeed, is thus a precursor to the exercise of choice. Furthermore, the capabilities approach is entrenched in conversations about social justice and inequality, viewing failure to promote in people these discrete capabilities as a result of discrimination and marginalization.[117] She pushes on government and public policy responsibility—namely, to "improve the quality for life for all people, as defined by their capabilities."[118] In this way, she diverges from Dewey and from Kohlberg: she may be preoccupied with the "common good" or even with intrinsic senses of justice, but that's not her end-goal. Rather, Nussbaum is (1) purpose-oriented and firmly practical in her approach—with a social justice end steeped in an appreciation of the problems of the present day; (2) focused not just on the school, but the government, in her educational philosophy saddling the highest echelons of society with a duty and burden to educate. This will later prove a key link in our discussion on integrating law learning into the civic education project, which far exceeds the school but implicates federal policy. As she writes:

> rather than seeing the success of an education system based on the measurable achievements of students, such as scores in examinations or assessments, educational success through a capabilities perspective can be seen through the capabilities that such an education enables.[119]

Nussbaum's take is concerned with the knowledge, skills, values, and understanding that education enables a young person—more than morally, but also practically and intellectually—"to think in new ways, to 'be,' to develop agency in society and make decisions."[120]

With this said, we see similarities with Dewey and Kohlberg as well. One notes that the approach is essentially "resolutely pluralist about value," and maintains as well that central capabilities, when achieved, are "different in quality, not just in quantity."[121] In this way, the capabilities approach can be categorized as follows:

> [It is not a] theory of what human nature is, and it does not read norms off from innate human nature. Instead, it is evaluative and ethical from the start: it asks, among the many things that human beings might develop the capacity to do, which ones are the valuable ones, what are the ones that a minimally just society will endeavor to nurture and support? An account of human nature tells us what resources and possibilities we have. It does not, however, tell us what to value.[122]

Having now outlined the theory and its multi-faceted components, the question remains: what does Nussbaum's capabilities-oriented classroom look like? How do we educate citizens about capabilities rather than functions?

Unsurprisingly, Nussbaum maintains that whatever we are doing, we are failing. It's not a surprise to see why—one need only think back to our first chapter in this work. Pushes toward standardization and rote memorization have diluted the curriculum in such a way as to produce very little for the student in the way of citizenship education. Indeed, such an education—as Nussbaum conceives—effectively produces *bad* citizens! There are two reasons for this. For one, "people behave badly when they are not held personally accountable."[123] A standardized curriculum shelters the student in anonymity, encouraging them to stew in unchallenged ideas, preconceived notions, unchecked biases, and incorrect perceptions of law, institutions, and theories. This encourages a disconnect between the institutions they learn about and their responsibility to engage with the issues that persist within them. And, secondly, *bad* citizens are the result of an education that fails to expose people to counterarguments, arguments, dialog.[124] The current iteration of education—removing the debate—effectively dehumanizes and de-individualizes the curriculum favoring apathetic and discordant responses.[125]

Nussbaum identifies the following characteristics of a stronger civic education:

- Develop the students' capacity to see the world from the viewpoint of other people, particularly those whom their society tends to portray as lesser, as "mere objects."
- Teach attitudes toward human weakness and helplessness that suggest that weakness is not shameful and the need for others not unmanly; teach children not to be ashamed of need and incompleteness but to see these as occasions for cooperation and reciprocity.
- Develop the capacity for genuine concern for others, both near and distant.
- Undermine the tendency to shrink from minorities of various kinds in disgust, thinking of them as lower or contaminating.
- Teach real and true things about other groups … [to] counter stereotypes and the disgust that often goes with them.
- Promote accountability by treating each child as a responsible agent.
- Vigorously promote critical thinking, the skill, and courage it requires to raise a dissenting voice.[126]

This is an education for a more inclusive type of citizenship, "infused with the spirit of humanities: by searching critical thought, daring imagination, empathetic understanding of human experiences of many different kinds, and understanding the complexity of the world we live in."[127] Her methods promote especially the art of Socratic self-examination,[128] arguing that "the examined life" is the best preparation for citizenship.[129] Channeling value-relativism, Nussbaum postures that "[s]ocratic examination does not guarantee a good set of goals, but it at least guarantees that the goals pursue will be seen clearly in relation to one another."[130] She rightly indicates that people who fail to examine themselves are often too easily influenced; "irresolution is frequently compounded by deference to authority and peer pressure, a problem endemic to all human societies."[131] "When arguments is not the focus, people are easily swayed by the fame or cultural prestige of the speaker, or by the fact that peer culture is going along. Socratic crucial inquiry, by contrast is utterly authoritarian."[132] The critical attitude uncovers the structure of each person's position on a given political subject. Indeed, it allows for the uncovering and the sharing of assumptions, opening up opportunities to cultivate "points of intersection that can help fellow citizens progress to a shared conclusion."[133] Socratic values, to Nussbaum, "produce a certain type of citizen: active, critical, curious, capable of resisting authority and peer pressure."[134] In her words:

> This means a life that accepts no belief as authoritative simply because it has been handed down by tradition or become familiar through habit, a life that questions all beliefs and accepts only those that survive reason's demand for consistency and for justification. Training this capacity requires developing the capacity to reason logically, to test what one reads or says for consistency of reasoning, correctness of fact, and accuracy of judgment.[135]

For Nussbaum, critical thinking is intimately connected to a democratic and political life. If democracy would not be reduced to "a marketplace of competing interest groups," education must "foster a democracy that is reflective and deliberative."[136] That young people develop their ability to reason critically over their own prejudices is ultimately good for a democratic society. Indeed, Nussbaum's philosophy allows us to foster a "deliberative vision of a democratic society." Politics is but a tool for mobilizing the most convincing arguments from a variety of positions and views. Servicing this end is unquestionably an important role for all education systems, as they have the greatest "potential to help spread mutual understanding and remove, or at least reduce, the cultural and religious barriers arising from differences in for instance historical, social, cultural, and political development."[137]

2.5 Connecting the Dots and Moving On

The project of this piece—re-invigorating civic education to cultivate *better* citizens—is nuanced; the notion of law learning is likewise carefully poised at the nexus of moral learning and practical education. Even more theoretically, one could view the efforts of the above philosophers—and many other thinkers unnamed—as more than simply work toward better citizenship, but toward the cultivation of a "learning society, underpinned by a learning agenda"—this being a principle objective of moral education *writ large*.[138] I assume in this piece that education and learning ought to be recognized for their central connection to "society's well-being and social harmony,"[139] and thus, curricular changes promote the achievement of a stronger nation. However, this notion is far from agreed-upon. We saw this in the earlier discussion of civic education—where standardization yielded a bland curriculum that did little to empower or strengthen children and their relationship with government institutions or to law. In fact, it did just the opposite: promoting complacency, apathy, blind obedience, and false contentedness or else perceptions of the inaccessibility of institutions. Indeed, broadly speaking:

> in most western societies schooling has [in fact] been projected as an ideologically neutral activity in which promoting democratic participation and active citizenship is equated with promoting conformity and transmitting the dominant values and outlook of ruling elites on the 'majority' communities.[140]

Where, in fact, there is an injection of moral debate, of critique, of discourse beyond the routine, we fight over substance, lenses, and perspectives on values—the family, the teacher, the district all at odds.

But what do we sacrifice when we foster only the neutral classroom? Nussbaum, Kohlberg, and Dewey argue neither for politicizing or polarizing the classroom, nor for neutrality, but rather for a values-plural discussion and an embrace of difference. Without these, we stifle *individual growth*; the challenging and transformation of attitudes, values, and beliefs; the reconciliation of their own personal stories with the problems of the day; respect for one another on fundamental human dignity levels; a sense of involvement in change-making, a feeling of responsibility for the flourishing of other human beings. Max Weber, like Nussbaum, points out how modernity and modernization have indelibly contributed to the erosion of human development by prioritizing an ineffable "ambiguity": "modernization brings with it the erosion of meaning, the endless conflict of polytheistic values and the threat of the iron cage of bureaucracy. Rationalization makes the world orderly and reliable, but it cannot make the world meaningful."[141] One central concern, therefore, for us here is: can we go back—at least in the classroom—to an earlier sort of educational paradigm? What does that look like? Were we ever there—as a community, as an educational project, in the United States? To an extent, covering these questions is the subject of the next chapter: to set out to demonstrate that, indeed, such a practical and moral education as I proscribe in law learning, such an education for *civic ends, community engagement while staying true to individual-centered empowerment*, was very much a part of our educational history and national education philosophy thinking back to the colonial enterprise. It was since then corrupted and unmoored.

Yet, we still see the remnants—re-couched in terms of progress and educational advancement—even in the age of standardization. In 1997, the New York State Council on Curriculum and Assessment proffered the following statement, though it was hardly ever realized:

> The schools we envision are exciting places: thoughtful, reflective, engaging and engaged. They are places where meaning is made… Their teachers function more like mentors, wise advisors than information transmitters or gatekeepers. They create a bridge between challenging learning goals and students' unique needs. They are continually learning because these are schools where everyone would be glad to be a student, or a teacher—where everyone would want to be—and could be—both.[142]

One need not puzzle to see the influences of Dewey in the highly reflective nature of such a "utopian" educational vision, the perpetuity of the learning project, or Kohlberg in this notion of cultivating a community of symbiotic learners working toward some important end. We ought to bear this vision in mind, now having laid out the philosophical influences for law-learning as a curricular innovation. Together with Nussbaum, our thinkers offer a cohesive educational philosophy for producing self-reliant citizens grounded in civic discourse, arching toward justice, and predisposed toward critical thinking, respect for traditions, and argument; they paint a picture of classrooms that prioritize the cultivation of a community of debate based in respect and plurality of opinion; and place upon the *government as well as the student* the obligation for an education that ensures that their tools are fostered and received well.

We are again focused on the individual's ability to *critique*, on every pupil's power of perception, and believe that "empowerment" means something different to everyone. Education ought to be nuanced and discursive rather than didactic—there is no right or wrong way or singular explanation. Keeping this in mind, it might surprise us that a survey of the historical educational landscape before and into the common school favored, to some extent, an approach like this. Uncovering this reality is important, lest I proffer a solution with no mooring in precedent. Showing "law-learning" as a moral and practical education to be merely an outgrowth of a tried-and-true past will only help legitimate the notion for policymakers.[143]

Notes

1 Robert Coalson, "'There Is No Values-Free Form of Education,' Says U.S. Philosopher," available at: www.rferl.org/a/nussbaum_interview/2315794.html

2 Jürgen Habermas, *The Theory of Communicative Action, Vol. 1, Reason and the Rationalization of Society* (Boston, MA: Beacon Press, 1984); *Between Facts and Norms: Contributions to a Discourse Theory of Law and Democracy* (Cambridge: MIT

Press, 1996). His larger chronological argument is that though common and civil law in democratic nations had emancipatory origins, through the gradual legalization of culture, law became a "micro-manager" of people's everyday lives, and this "formalization or textualization of everyday life replaces the social solidarity of the lifeworld that formerly was forged tacitly through uncodified norms of communicative acts and reason." *See also* James Chriss, "Review essay view essay of Jurgen Habermas' Between Facts and Norms," Sociology & Criminology Faculty Publications (1998).

3 Jürgen Habermas, *Between Facts and Norms: Contributions to a Discourse Theory of Law and Democracy* (Cambridge: MIT Press), 306.

> Every association that institutionalizes such a procedure for the purposes of democratically regulating the conditions of its common life thereby constitutes itself as a body of citizens. It forms a particular legal community … with specific forms of life and traditions.

He borrows some of this idea from Max Weber's social theory and sociology of law, believing that a "postmetaphysical justification [of law] is required because of the increasing rationalization of Western culture has disenchanted the world." Mark C. Modack-Truran, "Habermas's Discourse Theory of Law and the Relationship between Law and Religion," 26 *Cap. U L. Rev.* 461, 462 (1997).

4 *See e.g.*, Mark Kelman, *A Guide to Critical Legal Studies* (Harvard University Press, Cambridge, Massachusetts 1987).

5 *See e.g.*, John Rawls, *Political Liberalism* (Columbia University Press, New York, New York, 1996).

6 *See e.g.*, HLA Hart, *The Concept of Law* (Oxford University Press, Oxford, England 1989).

7 Mark C. Modack-Truran, "Habermas's Discourse Theory of Law and the Relationship Between Law and Religion," 26 *Cap. U L. Rev.* 461, 462 (1997).

8 James Chriss, "Review essay view essay of Jurgen Habermas' Between Facts and Norms," Sociology & Criminology Faculty Publications (1998).

9 Jürgen Habermas, *Between Facts and Norms: Contributions to a Discourse Theory of Law and Democracy* (Cambridge: MIT Press), 109.

10 James Chriss, "Review essay view essay of Jurgen Habermas' Between Facts and Norms," Sociology & Criminology Faculty Publications (1998).

11 This is a fascinating step for Habermas to take because his larger school of critical theory holds, in the words of James Chriss:

> that values are created primarily by elites who, wielding enormous social and political power through ideological hegemony, control the substance of public deliberation and, hence, are able to pass into legislation laws that reflect and defend their own interests at the expense of the relatively powerless masses.

"Review Essay of Jurgen Habermas' Between Facts and Norms," Review (1998); Hugh Baxter, "Habermas' Sociological Theory of Law and Democracy: A Reply to Wirts, Flynn and Zurn," 40 *Phil. Soc. Crit.* 225–234 (2014).

12 Mark C. Modack-Truran, "Habermas's Discourse Theory of Law and the Relationship between Law and Religion," 26 *Cap. U L. Rev.* 461, 462 (1997).

13 Jürgen Habermas, "Knowledge and Interest," 9 *Inquiry*, 285–300, 297 (1966). To Habermas, as a normative basis for his theory, humanity is autonomous by its nature.

> The concern with emancipation from quasi-natural authority is not just a vague idea that hovers before one's eyes: it can be *a priori* comprehended. What raises us above nature is indeed the only fact of which, due to its very nature, we *can* have knowledge: namely, language. The idea of autonomy is given to us with the structure of language. With the very first sentence the intention of a common and uncompelled consensus is unequivocally stated.

14 James Chriss, "Review essay view essay of Jurgen Habermas' Between Facts and Norms," Sociology & Criminology Faculty Publications (1998).

15 Mark C. Modack-Truran, "Habermas's Discourse Theory of Law and the Relationship between Law and Religion," 26 *Cap. U L. Rev*. 461, 462 (1997).

16 James Chriss, "Review essay view essay of Jurgen Habermas' Between Facts and Norms," Sociology & Criminology Faculty Publications (1998).

17 Jürgen Habermas, *The Theory of Communicative Action, Vol. 1: Reason and Rationalization of Society* (Boston, MA: Beacon Press 1985; German original: 1981), 28. In terms of the larger order, "decision makers at the political center cannot ignore such power" (as they would otherwise be unlikely to be re-elected). Habermas's concept of legitimate law thus crucially rests on the communicative practices of civil society, which will channel their impulses into the political system and in this way prevent it from becoming self-reliant and detached from citizens.

18 Abdollah Shabani, BU Law Symposium, "Habermas' Between Facts and Norms: Legitimating Power?" Based on his earlier works, the process is thus: "Informal public opinion-formation generates 'influence'; influence is transformed into 'communicative power' through the channels of political elections; and communicative power is again transformed into 'administrative power' through legislation." Jürgen Habermas, "Three Normative Models of Democracy," I *Constellation*. No. 1, 8 (1994). Also, "legitimate lawmaking is understood as a result of institutionalized procedures that convert citizens' practice of self-determination in the form of communicative and participatory rights into the binding decision of political power."

19 Notably, many of the philosophies here—whether on law or education—have been considered naïve. Even Martha Nussbaum in *Political Emotions: Why Love Matters for Justice* (Cambridge, MA: Harvard University Press, 2013) refers to his complimentary vision of "constitutional patriotism" as "so moralized and so abstract that one can't have any confidence that it would work in real life" (222). However, she recognizes credit owed to him for recognizing the role emotions do play in his deliberate and discursive democracy with the "autonomous" citizens.

20 Alisha Haridasani Gupta, "Why Ruth Bader Ginsburg Wasn't All That Fond of Roe v. Wade," The New York Times (2020), www.nytimes.com/2020/09/21/us/ruth-bader-ginsburg-roe-v-wade.html. Note: this is consonant with my argument back in the Introduction, *see* James Chriss, "Review essay view essay of Jurgen Habermas' Between Facts and Norms," Sociology & Criminology Faculty Publications (1998), where I articulate the dissonance between law and culture and show how *Dobbs* revealed, using constitutional rhetoric, how the law needed to change (an Amendment, constitutional change, some enshrinement of privacy) for there to be actual change. *Roe*,

in other words was technical (and, indeed, it was, pretty much relegated to a medical decision) and not law changing. This comment shows further that *Roe* at its time was also dissonant with culture and pushed to quickly and without proper comprehensive legal framing. Not realizing this has only fueled the first.

21 Meredith Heagney, "Justice Ruth Bader Ginsburg Offers Critique of Roe v. Wade During Law School Visit," The University of Chicago Law School (2013), www.law.uchicago.edu/news/justice-ruth-bader-ginsburg-offers-critique-roe-v-wade-during-law-school-visit

22 Deepa Shivaram, "The movement against abortion rights is nearing its apex. But it began way before Roe," NPR (May 2022), www.npr.org/2022/05/04/1096154028/the-movement-against-abortion-rights-is-nearing-its-apex-but-it-began-way-before

23 Grace Hauck, "People with Nazi flags, signs supporting Florida Gov. DeSantis gathered outside Disney World," USA Today (June 2023), www.usatoday.com/story/news/nation/2023/06/11/videos-show-nazi-flags-desantis-sign-disney-world/70310731007 (showing the protesting of neo-Nazis outside of Disney World in support of DeSantis' presidential bid).

24 Jill Anderson, "The State of Critical Race Theory in Education," Harvard Graduate School of Education (February 2022), www.gse.harvard.edu/news/22/02/harvard-edcast-state-critical-race-theory-education

25 In this way, it is worth distinguishing this proposal from the 1970s "Street Law" movement. This I do in a later endnote.

26 *See e.g.*, Wolfgang Althof and Marvin W. Berkowitz, "Character and Civic Education as a Source of Moral Motivation," in Karin Heinrichs et al. (eds.), *Handbook of Moral Motivation* (Rotterdam: Sense Publishers, 2013), 567–584 https://link.springer.com/chapter/10.1007/978-94-6209-275-4_31

27 *See* Thomas Lickona, "Eleven Principles of Effective Character Education," 25 *J. Moral Educ.* 93–100 (1996).

28 *See* James Arthur, "Traditional Approaches to Character Education in Britain and America," in Larry P. Nucci and Darcia Narvaez (eds.), *Handbook of Moral and Character Education* (New York: Routledge, 2008), 80–98.

29 John Dewey's "hidden curriculum" Jackson, Philip, *Life in the Classroom* (New York: Holt, Rinehart and Winston, 1968).

30 John Dewey, *The Public and Its Problems* (Athens, OH: Swallow Press, 2016. Originally published in 1927 by Henry Holt and Co.). ("Indifference," he articulates:

> is the evidence of current apathy, and apathy is testimony to the fact that the public is so bewildered that it cannot find itself … What is the public? If there is a pubic, what are the obstacles in the way of its recognizing itself?).

31 John Dewey, *Democracy and Education* (New York: Macmillan, 1916), 34.

32 John Dewey, *Democracy and Education* (New York: Macmillan, 1916), 34

33 John Dewey, *Democracy and Education* (New York: Macmillan, 1916), 34.

34 John Dewey, *Democracy and Education* (New York: Macmillan, 1916), 34.

35 John Dewey, *Democracy and Education* (New York: Macmillan, 1916), 34.

36 John Dewey, "Individualism Old and New," in *The Later Works of John Dewey, Vol. 5*, 91 (Carbondale, IL: Southern Illinois University Press, 1984).

37 Naoko Saito, *The Gleam of Light: Moral Perfectionism and Education in Dewey and Emerson* (New York: Fordham University Press, 2006), 1.

38 Martha Nussbaum, *Not for Profit: Why Democracies Need the Humanities* (Princeton: Princeton University Press, 2016), 64.
39 John Dewey, *Moral Principles in Education* (Boston, MA: Houghton Mifflin, 1909), 37.
40 John Dewey, *Moral Principles in Education* (Boston, MA: Houghton Mifflin, 1909), 4.
41 "This in the sense that one cannot articulate one's feelings or even that, in the loss of one's own taste, one does not know 'what one really wants.'" Naoko Saito, *The Gleam of Light: Moral Perfectionism and Education in Dewey and Emerson* (New York: Fordham University Press, 2006), 2.
42 Naoko Saito, *The Gleam of Light: Moral Perfectionism and Education in Dewey and Emerson* (New York: Fordham University Press, 2006), 2.
43 Naoko Saito, *The Gleam of Light: Moral Perfectionism and Education in Dewey and Emerson* (New York: Fordham University Press, 2006), 2.
44 John Dewey, *Democracy and Education* (New York: Macmillan, 1916), 34.
45 Naoko Saito, *The Gleam of Light: Moral Perfectionism and Education in Dewey and Emerson* (New York: Fordham University Press, 2006), 5. This can also be quantified or characterized as "growth without fixed ends," which is, importantly, distinct (and evolved) from something like "self-realization" which has an end to it; "growth" to Dewey is an endlessly evolving natural process. It is borne out of Darwinian Naturalism.
46 John Dewey, *Democracy and Education* (New York: Macmillan 1916), 56. Importantly, again, this does not characterize childhood as merely precursory preparation for adulthood, but that it has its own intrinsic value.
47 John Dewey, *Moral Principles in Education* (Boston, MA: Houghton Mifflin, 1909), 24.
48 John Dewey, *Democracy and Education* (New York: Macmillan 1916), 34.
49 John Dewey, *Democracy and Education* (New York: Macmillan 1916), 34.
50 John Dewey, *Moral Principles in Education* (Boston, MA: Houghton Mifflin, 1909), 24.
51 For this, he was criticized by others as hopelessly naïve in its optimism and scarcely realizable. *See* Naoko Saito, *The Gleam of Light: Moral Perfectionism and Education in Dewey and Emerson* (New York: Fordham University Press, 2006), 6.
52 John Dewey, *Moral Principles in Education* (Boston, MA: Houghton Mifflin, 1909), 12.
53 John Dewey, *Moral Principles in Education* (Boston, MA: Houghton Mifflin, 1909), 8;

> In his book, *Theory of Valuation,* Dewey wrote that norms are in no way confined to activities to which the name "moral" is applied. In other words, there is not a specific set of activities that can be considered as moral activity. For Dewey, there is no particular "moral realm": moral study is the same as intelligent inquiry.

Xiandang Liu, "The Problem of Character Education and Kohlberg's Moral Education: Critique from Dewey's Moral Deliberation," 45 *Philos. Stud. Educ.* 136 (2014).
54 The ability to teach without indoctrination is predicated on a mastery of the distinction between "valuing" and "evaluating," which Dewey entertains in his *Theory of*

Moral Life. To value is personal in nature; it is one's developed attitude toward a thing or idea. By contrast, to "evaluate" is a process of critically appraising a value with a specific situation. People could value many things, but people ought to evaluate those valued ideas consistently in a changing process over time. According to Dewey, core ethical values need to be judged always in a pragmatic sense. Therefore, character education should provide students opportunities to "deliberate about core ethical values and apply the virtue of critical evaluation to a specific situation." It is important, however, to note the following:

> Dewey did not object to teaching certain virtues overtly. Dewey believed that humans could accomplish more "impossible" things if they developed certain virtues. But, valuation, the process of estimating each value within a specific situation with a critical perspective, was more important because we cannot solve problems with the same familiar patterns of thought.

Xiandang Liu, "The Problem of Character Education and Kohlberg's Moral Education: Critique from Dewey's Moral Deliberation," 45 *Philos. Stud. Educ.* 136 (2014); John Dewey, *Theory of the Moral Life* (New York: Irvington Publishers, 1996), 113.

55 John Dewey, *Moral Principles in Education* (Boston, MA: Houghton Mifflin, 1909), 8.

56 John Dewey, *Moral Principles in Education* (Boston, MA: Houghton Mifflin, 1909), 4. Dewey holds that moral education requires "the development of character through all the agencies, instrumentalities, and materials of school life."

57 John Dewey, *The School and Society and the Child and the Curriculum* (Chicago, IL: University of Chicago Press, 1991), 112–121.

58 John Dewey, *The School and Society and the Child and the Curriculum* (Chicago, IL: University of Chicago Press, 1991), 112–121.

59 John Dewey, *Theory of the Moral Life* (New York: Irvington Publishers, 1996), 135;

> Caspary summarizes three characteristics of moral deliberation from this definition: First, moral deliberation focuses on possible lines of action. This means that, in each problematic situation, we should clarify the relationship and imagine the possible lines of action. Second, with each possible line of action, we should also predict the possible responses and consequences. Third, we should know that moral deliberation is inter-personal and sensitive; it considers emotional feeling and intuition. Moral deliberation could help students evaluate each value within a specific situation critically.

Xiandang Liu, "The Problem of Character Education and Kohlberg's Moral Education: Critique from Dewey's Moral Deliberation," 45 *Philos. Stud. Educ.* 136 (2014).

60 John Dewey, *Theory of the Moral Life* (New York: Irvington Publishers, 1996), 135.

61 Xiandang Liu, "The Problem of Character Education and Kohlberg's Moral Education: Critique from Dewey's Moral Deliberation," 45 *Philos. Stud. Educ.* 136 (2014), 4.

62 Other skills include "initiative, insistence, persistence and industry, as well as 'force of character,' sensitivity to conditions, personal responsiveness." John Dewey, *Moral Principles in Education* (Boston, MA: Houghton Mifflin, 1909), 34.

63 John Dewey, *Theory of the Moral Life* (New York: Irvington Publishers, 1996), 135.

64 John Dewey, *Moral Principles in Education* (Boston, MA: Houghton Mifflin, 1909), 34.

65 John Dewey, *Moral Principles in Education* (Boston, MA: Houghton Mifflin, 1909), 34.

66 John Dewey, *Moral Principles in Education* (Boston, MA: Houghton Mifflin, 1909), 49.

67 Kohlberg's typology contains three different levels of thinking, with each level comprising two related stages. The first level, the "pre-conventional," typifies thinking that is concerned with rewards, bartering, and fear of punishment (typically aged 9 years old or younger). There, morals are shaped by parents and other authorities. The second, or "conventional level," has to do with conforming to the rules of the person's family, group or nation (typically adolescents, children believe there can be more than one viewpoint on an issue and rules are created by social acceptance). The last level is called the "postconventional level," and is identified with universal moral principles of justice and freedom. Only 10% of people reach the third level, they can create their own set of moral values and lives by them.

68 Emile Durkheim, *Moral Education: A Study in the Theory and Application of the Sociology of Education* (Minola, NY: Dover Publications, 1925). Durkheim's moral socialization perspective on moral education argued for moral education by way of "instruction and explanation, role models, and group reinforcement." *See* John Snarey and Thomas Pavkov, "Beyond Socialization versus Development: Kohlberg's Approach to Moral Education." 24 *Sociol. Focus.* 105 (1991). Whereas Dewey's conceptions were more about individualistic ascension, a moral socialization perspective is primarily about social solidarity, group conformity, and mutual support in service of moral development. Kohlberg would go on to democratize Durkheim, and lean more toward Piaget, so we need not spend more time on him. Indeed, his critique of Durkheim as propounding a "bag of virtues" was plain:

> Although it may be true that the notion of teaching virtues, such as honesty or integrity, arouses little controversy, it is also true that a vague consensus on the goodness of these virtues conceals a great deal of actual disagreement over their definitions. What is one person's "integrity" is another person's "stubbornness," what is one person's honesty in "expressing your true feelings" is another person's insensitivity to the feelings of others.

In other words, if there is no individual conception of morality, we lead to the false impression that there are "moral absolutes" that are culture bound, i.e., they are vulnerable to the likes and dislikes of special interest groups.

69 Jean Piaget, *The Moral Judgment of the Child* (London: Kegan, Paul, Trench, Trubner, 1932).

> Piaget came up with two levels of moral thinking. The first stated that rules are to be obeyed because an authority figure said to do so. The second and more mature level of thinking thought of rules as ideas to help people get along and can be altered as needed.

John Snarey and Thomas Pavkov, "Beyond Socialization versus Development: Kohlberg's Approach to Moral Education." 24 *Sociol. Focus.* 105 (1991).

70 *See* John Snarey and Thomas Pavkov, "Beyond Socialization versus Development: Kohlberg's Approach to Moral Education." 24 *Sociol. Focus.* 105 (1991).

71 Xiandang Liu, "The Problem of Character Education and Kohlberg's Moral Education: Critique from Dewey's Moral Deliberation," 45 *Philos. Stud. Educ.* 4 (2014).

> Morality is as much for Kohlberg as Dewey a morality of the practical, an ethics of action. For both men, to be just is to do. But, from here, Kohlberg and Dewey divide themselves on fundamental ethical principles. For Dewey, conscience, as

derived from obligation, is the ideal form of the practical good. Working towards this is, therefore, for the common good. Kohlberg argues that if the process of moral development is social action, the form it takes is justice. "Justice, in turn, is a matter of equal and universal human rights." Justice is not a rule but an ethical principle universal, applicable to all nations and men. Kohlberg is proposing here that concepts of the good are culturally universal. So while Kohlberg proposes a process-based "drawing out" of non-specific forms of virtue, the ultimate destination of this process has a very definite form and content: justice and equality.

72 Mark J. Connerty, "Three Theories of Development: A Comparison of Dewey, Kohlberg, and Noddings' Models of Moral Growth," Critical and Creative Thinking Capstones Collection. 67 (1998).

73 George Lind, "Moral Dilemma Discussion Revisited." The most famed, of course, is the *Heinz Dilemma*:

> Heinz's wife was dying from a particular type of cancer. Doctors said a new drug might save her. The drug had been discovered by a local chemist, and the Heinz tried desperately to buy some, but the chemist was charging ten times the money it cost to make the drug, and this was much more than the Heinz could afford. Heinz could only raise half the money, even after help from family and friends. He explained to the chemist that his wife was dying and asked if he could have the drug cheaper or pay the rest of the money later. The chemist refused, saying that he had discovered the drug and was going to make money from it. The husband was desperate to save his wife, so later that night he broke into the chemist's and stole the drug. Should Heinz have broken into the laboratory to steal the drug for his wife? Why or why not?

This "dilemma discussion" was developed in partnership with Moishe Blatt.

74 Here, I want to take a moment and discuss Kohlberg's position on the family and their role in moral education. Josu Ahedo Ruiz, et al., "Updating the Proposal of 'Just Communities' for Democratic Civil Education," 13 *Ramon Llull J. Appl. Ethics.* 53–75 (2022). Kohlberg at one point thought to strip the family of its role in moral education, arguing that "orientation of behavior" (*not* indoctrination)—which takes place in schools—is essentially most important in creating just-thinkers. He argued that "moral education should directly concern action and not just reasoning." Eventually, however, he came to see that the family could be involved (though he never advocated for a leading role for the family but prioritized the school) in affective emotional education. He postured:

> schools traditionally focus on a more technical education, more attentive to the development of intellect-based knowledge and skills. In contrast, socio-affective education based on developing self-assuredness, respect for others, following the rules, and acquiring skills that can be applied efficiently to work has been considered a task best left to parents.

75 Josu Ahedo Ruiz, et. al., "Updating the Proposal of 'Just Communities' for Democratic Civil Education," 13 *Ramon Llull J. Appl. Ethics*. 53–75 (2022)

76 Josu Ahedo Ruiz, et. al., "Updating the Proposal of 'Just Communities' for Democratic Civil Education," 13 *Ramon Llull J. Appl. Ethics*. 53–75 (2022).

77 Josu Ahedo Ruiz, et. al., "Updating the Proposal of 'Just Communities' for Democratic Civil Education," 13 *Ramon Llull J. Appl. Ethics*. 53–75 (2022).

78 Clark Power, "Moral Education through the Development of the Moral Atmosphere of the School," 15 *J. Educ. Thought* 4–19 (1981).

79 John Snarey and Thomas Pavkov, "Beyond Socialization versus Development: Kohlberg's Approach to Moral Education." 24 *Sociol. Focus*. 105 (1991).

> They do not learn that not all morally important matters are problems; they do not learn that reasonable people of goodwill have much in common and can disagree; and they do not learn that moral sophistication and the capacity to understand and discuss complex moral issues are not achieved instantly.

80 Kohlberg says as much in a passage from *of From Is To Ought*: "I simply point to the fact that no principle other than justice has been shown to meet the formal conception of a universal prescriptive principle" (Lawrence Kohlberg, *From Is to Ought: How to Commit the Naturalistic Fallacy and Get Away with It in the Study of Moral Development* (New York: Academic Press, 1971), 176).

81 Clark Power, "Moral Education through the Development of The Moral Atmosphere of The School," *J. Educ. Thought.* (1981).

82 *See* John Snarey and Thomas Pavkov, "Beyond Socialization versus Development: Kohlberg's Approach to Moral Education."

> Drawing unexpectedly from the ideas of Emile Durkheim, Kohlberg came to believe that the unit of education was the group, not simply the individual, and that moral education should change the school's moral culture, not just develop the person's moral reasoning.

83 He built schools to this effect. *See* Dina Sukma, et al., "Just Community Approach to Character Education: School Change or Student Change?" 4 *Int. J. Couns. Educ.* 15–22 (2019). Kohlberg founded the first "School of Community" in the spring of 1974 in the town of Cambridge US. In 1992, the Just Community model was piloted by Lind and Wolfang in German schools.

84 Josu Ahedo Ruiz, et al., "Updating the Proposal of 'Just Communities' for Democratic Civil Education," 13 *Ramon Llull J. Appl. Ethics*. 53–75 (2022).

85 Josu Ahedo Ruiz et al., "Updating the Proposal of 'Just Communities' for Democratic Civil Education," 13 *Ramon Llull J. Appl. Ethics*. 53–75 (2022).

86 Josu Ahedo Ruiz et al., "Updating the Proposal of 'Just Communities' for Democratic Civil Education," 13 *Ramon Llull J. Appl. Ethics*. 53–75 (2022); Lawrence Kohlberg, *From Is to Ought: How to Commit the Naturalistic Fallacy and Get Away with It in the Study of Moral Development* (New York: Academic Press, 1971), 185.

> The school would be governed by direct democracy. Every major issue would be discussed and decided at a weekly community meeting where every member (students and teachers) would have a vote. There would also be standing committees made up of students, teachers, and parents. A social contract would be drawn up among the members that would set out each person's responsibilities and rights. Students and teachers would have the same basic rights, including freedom of expression, respect of others, and freedom from physical or verbal harm.

87 Josu Ahedo Ruiz et al., "Updating the Proposal of 'Just Communities' for Democratic Civil Education," 13 *Ramon Llull J. Appl. Ethics*. 53–75 (2022).

88 Josu Ahedo Ruiz et al., "Updating the Proposal of 'Just Communities' for Democratic Civil Education," 13 *Ramon Llull J. Appl. Ethics*. 53–75 (2022).

89 Martha Nussbaum, *Not for Profit: Why Democracy Needs the Humanities* (Princeton, NJ: Princeton University Press, 2016), 18.
90 Martha Nussbaum and Jonathan Glover (Eds.), *Women, Culture, and Development: A Study of Human Capabilities* (Oxford: Clarendon Press), 61–104.
91 Martha C. Nussbaum, *Creating Capabilities: The Human Development Approach* (Harvard: Belknap, 2011).
92 Martha C. Nussbaum, *Creating Capabilities: The Human Development Approach* (Harvard: Belknap, 2011), 18.
93 Martha C. Nussbaum, *Creating Capabilities: The Human Development Approach* (Harvard: Belknap, 2011), 18.
94 Martha C. Nussbaum, "Capabilities and Human Rights," 66 *Fordham L. Rev.* 273, 290 (1997).
95 Martha C. Nussbaum, *Creating Capabilities: The Human Development Approach* (Harvard: Belknap, 2011), 18. In this way, they are "combined capabilities." Whereas variances from person to person are "internal capabilities"—innate equipment, trained traits, or abilities, "combined capabilities" reflect the "job of society that wants to promote the most important human capabilities so as to support the development of internal capabilities—through education, resources to enhance physical and emotional health, support for family, a system of education, etc."
96

> Nussbaum holds that human development relies upon ten fundamental functional abilities and opportunities: **life-supporting capabilities** (people live for as long as normally expected, not dying early, or having a life so reduced it is no longer worth living); **physical health** (capable of being healthy, including having good reproductive health), **physical integrity** (capable of exercising free movement, protected from harassment, including sexual abuse and domestic violence), **being able to use the senses, imagination and thought** (capable of using these in a truly human way, formed and shaped through an adequate education, not just limited to basic knowledge), **emotions** (capable of forming relationships with things and people outside themselves, love etc.), **common sense or practical reason** (see above), **connections** (capable of living with others and, in relation to them, manifest an interest in others, which requires a social basis for self-respect and avoidance of abuse, which also means being treated as a respectful person of the same value as others. This includes protection from discrimination). It is also about the **person's relationship to other species** (capable of having an interest in animals, plants and nature), **play** (capable of play, laughter, pursuing leisure activities) and **having control of one's political and material environment** (see above). A life that is deprived of any of the above capabilities is not a good human life.

Vasil Gluchman, 28 "Nussbaum's Philosophy of Education as The Foundation For Human Development," *Hum. Aff.* 328–338 (2018); Martha C. Nussbaum, "Human Capabilities, Female Human Beings," in M. C. Nussbaum and J. Glover (Eds.), *Women, Culture, and Development: A Study of Human Capabilities* (Oxford: Clarendon Press, 1995), 61–104; Martha C. Nussbaum, *Creating Capabilities: The Human Development Approach* (Harvard: Belknap, 2011).
97 Martha C. Nussbaum, *Creating Capabilities: The Human Development Approach* (Harvard: Belknap, 2011), 25

98 Martha C. Nussbaum, *Creating Capabilities: The Human Development Approach* (Harvard: Belknap, 2011), 152.
99 Martha C. Nussbaum, *Creating Capabilities: The Human Development Approach* (Harvard: Belknap, 2011), 152.
100 Martha C. Nussbaum, *Creating Capabilities: The Human Development Approach* (Harvard: Belknap, 2011), 152.
101 Martha C. Nussbaum, *Creating Capabilities: The Human Development Approach* (Harvard: Belknap, 2011), 290 (This distinction is related to Rawls's distinction between "social and natural primary goods." John Rawls, *A Theory of Justice* (Cambridge: Harvard University Press, 1971), at 62.

> Whereas he holds that only the social primary goods should be on the list, and not the natural (such as health and imagination), we say that the social basis of the natural primary goods should most emphatically be on the list.)

Allow me to take a pause here. This is our first encounter with John Rawls' *Political Liberalism*, albeit through Nussbaum. As I invoke his name and his ideas, I find it necessary to explain exactly *how* I can square his *Political Liberalism* (which is necessarily a theory of democracy and of democratic society)—and by extension the Capabilities Approach which draws inspiration from him—when I have already invoked Habermas' social and political theory earlier as a means of understanding the role of law-learning as part and parcel to empowering the citizen, specifically emphasizing how it strengthens autonomous and rational thought in discursive actors. In short, my answer has to do with the fact that this is a civics education innovation discussion, foremost, and a commentary on a view of democratic society second. This makes their differences less important and their common interests more so. *See* Amy Gutmann, "Civic Education and Social Diversity," 105 *Ethics* 557 (1995); *see also* (to some extent *contra*) Elizabeth Edenberg, "Civic Education: Political or Comprehensive?" in *Justice, Education, and Politics of Childhood: Challenges and Perspectives* (Johannes Drerup, et al.) (Cham: Springer, 2016), 187–206. In terms of civics outlooks predicated on their theories, the two have surprisingly common roots. My exploration (not written here but believe me it took a good amount of time!) into the intersection and divergence—and there are certainly both—between Rawls and Habermas has been fascinating, but it is worth only discussing in a footnote for fear of distraction. *See, e.g.*, Raymond Morrow, "Habermas and Civic Education," in Richard Desjardins and Susan Wiksten (eds.), *Handbook of Civic Engagement and Education* (Northampton, MA: Cheltenham, 2022), 28–41; John Rawls, "Political Liberalism: Reply to Habermas," 92 *J. of Philos.* 132–180 (1995).

Rawls and Habermas are often compared "as proponents of democratic education sharing a theory of deliberative democracy," though there are differences. Raymond Morrow, "Habermas and Civic Education," in Richard Desjardins and Susan Wiksten (eds.), *Handbook of Civic Engagement and Education* (Northampton, MA: Cheltenham, 2022), 28–41. Rawls' notions are based in social contract rather than communicative discourse; it pre-supposes a "well-ordered society" rather than taking a critical view of it, which, in turn marginalizes civic education to a certain extent. For Rawls, *Political Liberalism* requires less than those—like Habermas, who draws inspiration from Kant—who espouse a more comprehensive liberalism. *See* Elizabeth Edenberg, "Civic Education: Political or Comprehensive?"

in *Justice, Education, and Politics of Childhood: Challenges and Perspectives* (Johannes Drerup, et. al.) (Cham: Springer, 2016), 187–206, "The politically liberal state would only require the kind of education needed so that children as future citizens can understand the political conception of justice and cultivate important political virtues" John Rawls, *Political Liberalism* (New York: Columbia University Press, 2005). So, we are talking reasonableness in children, understanding "justice" and a virtues-education (Rawls, *Political Liberalism*). Now, Habermas has himself written on citizenship education, though not directly, in the forms of "constitutional patriotism" and "post-conventual identities." The "concept of constitutional patriotism provides an alternative to traditional, chauvinistic nationalism based on essentializing categories such as race, ethnicity, and religion, as well as the mythologizing of national histories." Raymond Morrow, "Habermas and Civic Education," in Richard Desjardins and Susan Wiksten (eds.), *Handbook of Civic Engagement and Education* (Northampton, MA: Cheltenham, 2022), 28–41. This new form of cosmopolitan solidary promises integration of "intercultural dialogue and mutual learning" (Morrow, "Habermas and Civic Education"). Indeed, Habermas draws support for this argument through a reconstruction of Kohlberg's theory of moral development; "whereas traditional societies are characterized by the dominance of conventional identities and moral reasoning that are centered and ethnocentric, post-conventional identities can decenter their own standpoint as part of considering the needs and perspectives of others" (Morrow, "Habermas and Civic Education"). The cultivation of such capacities become an obvious priority for civic education. *This is, in other words, an emancipatory education for a deliberative democracy that asks of citizens to participate in deliberative communication involving both "consensus and contestation.*" Tomas Englund, "Educational Implications of the Idea of Deliberative Democracy," in *Habermas, Critical Theory, and Education* (Mark Murphy, Ted Fleming, eds.) (London: Routledge 2009), 19–32.
At first blush, these are vastly different expectations which ought to yield vastly different proposal in terms of civic education. I do also acknowledge that Nussbaum herself has some words for Habermas in terms of criticizing his "constitutional patriotism" as "so moralized and so abstract that one can't have any confidence that it would work in real life." Martha C. Nussbaum, *Political Emotions: Why Love Matters for Justice* (Cambridge, MA: Harvard University Press, 2013), 222. However, she does say that "it is to his great credit that Habermas sees the need for some type of emotional support for good political principles and proposes to address the question" (Nussbaum, *Political Emotions*, 222). One would be surprised (as was I), that a civic education vision satisfactory to both political liberalism and more comprehensive liberalism is actually quite tenable. Namely, that it be a *demanding* form of civics, and that the student must develop the 'reasonableness' of citizens.' Amy Gutmann, "Civic Education and Social Diversity," 105 *Ethics* 557 (1995) ("[there is] a remarkable degree of convergence between those political and comprehensive liberals who embrace a demanding view of the political requirements of civic education."); Callan, Eamonn. "Political liberalism and Political Education." 58 *Rev Politics*. No. 1, 5–33 (1996). Reasonableness, to Rawls, is a moral requirement in terms of one's ability to respect other citizens. Also, the reasonable citizen recognizes the "burdens of judgment," which leads one to use public reason when "directing the legitimate exercise of political power" on matters of basic justice. John Rawls, *Political Liberalism*

(New York: Columbia University Press, 2005), 54; Amy Gutmann, "Civic Education and Social Diversity," 105 *Ethics* 557 (1995) (she also points out other values that must be imparted, such as toleration and fairness, etc.). Meanwhile, to Habermas—again, inspired by comprehensive liberalism in Kant—this same education is for the power of *deliberation and communication in democratic life* (Englund points out that there is a *lot* to do with Dewey here). Tomas Englund, "Educational Implications of the Idea of Deliberative Democracy," in *Habermas, Critical Theory, and Education* (Mark Murphy, Ted Fleming, eds.) (London: Routledge, 2009), 19–32. The difference appears, therefore, to be on the questioned role of autonomy and the individual. But, as Gutmann states, while political liberalism rejects "the political relevance of the common (comprehensive) liberal ideals of individuality and autonomy," it nevertheless stresses "teaching mutual respect as well as toleration" (Gutmann, "Civic Education and Social Diversity," 557). Therefore, "if we can reasonably agree on teaching not only toleration but also mutual respect as a substantive aim of civic education, then our metatheoretical conceptions of liberalism may turn out to be largely (even if not entirely) beside the point" in this specific sphere of inquiry (Gutmann, "Civic Education and Social Diversity," 557).

To be sure, I have placed the Capabilities Approach to Education, and, more specifically *law learning*, within a vision of Habermas' discursive and deliberative democracy that stresses autonomy and individual empowerment in the cultivation of norms. This, I don't think, is typically done. But I see no reason why not; Habermas' theory lends itself well to this idea in the context of civic education overhaul. Beyond a doubt, my conception of civic education is demanding—an education in law learning stresses virtues, as we shall see in Chapter 4, that are complimentary to both Rawls' and Habermas' notions, and will feature, as we shall see in Chapter 5, outcomes that contemplate a more "reasonable" if not "deliberative citizen."

102 Martha C. Nussbaum, *Women and Human Development: The Capabilities Approach* (Cambridge: Cambridge University Press, 2001), 290.

103 Martha C. Nussbaum, *Creating Capabilities: The Human Development Approach* (Harvard: Belknap, 2011), 39. Also "affiliation." "If people are well-nourished but not empowered to exercise practical reason and planning … [no] situation is fully commensurate with human dignity."

104 Martha C. Nussbaum, *Creating Capabilities: The Human Development Approach* (Harvard: Belknap, 2011), 39.

105 Martha C. Nussbaum, *Creating Capabilities: The Human Development Approach* (Harvard: Belknap, 2011), 39.

106 Martha C. Nussbaum, *Creating Capabilities: The Human Development Approach* (Harvard: Belknap, 2011), 18. This also includes control of one's material life. Where one is "able to own property and immovables and exercise ownership rights in the same way other people do."

107 Martha C. Nussbaum, *Creating Capabilities: The Human Development Approach* (Harvard: Belknap, 2011), 290.

108 Martha C. Nussbaum, *Creating Capabilities: The Human Development Approach* (Harvard: Belknap, 2011), 77.

109 Martha C. Nussbaum, *Creating Capabilities: The Human Development Approach* (Harvard: Belknap, 2011), 77. Like John Rawls, Nussbaum uses the notion of "reflective equilibrium" as the goal of the process of scrutiny. She views the

process as a Socratic attempt to attain clarity about the structure of one's own moral judgments in social justice; justification is achieved not by individuals acting alone but by debate among Socratically deliberating individuals.

110 Martha C. Nussbaum, *Creating Capabilities: The Human Development Approach* (Harvard: Belknap, 2011), 77. She also notes that it also endorses other aspects of Rawls' political liberalism.

> Given that all societies contain a plurality of religious and secular views of the meaning and purpose of human life, it seems strategically unwise to adopt a political view that opts for one of these against the others: such a political regime is likely to prove unstable, at least under conditions of freedom. But that is not the only, or even the primary objection to that sort of political doctrine.
>
> (89)

111 Martha C. Nussbaum, *Creating Capabilities: The Human Development Approach* (Harvard: Belknap, 2011), 114.

112 Martha C. Nussbaum, *Creating Capabilities: The Human Development Approach* (Harvard: Belknap, 2011), 18.

113

> Capability, not functioning, is the political goal. Capability must be the goal because of the great importance the capabilities approach attaches to practical reason, as a good that both suffuses all the other functions, making them human rather than animals and figures itself as a central function on the list. It is perfectly true that functionings, not simply capabilities, are what render a life fully human: If there were no functioning of any kind in a life, we could hardly applaud it, no matter what opportunities it contained. Nonetheless, for political purposes it is appropriate for us to strive for capabilities, and those alone. Citizens must be left free to determine their course after they have the capabilities.

Martha C. Nussbaum, "Capabilities and Human Rights," *66 Fordham L. Rev.* (1997), at 289. Most of the time. In the context of education, however, the functioning is a means to an end and thus must be prioritized.

> Children are different since we are trying to promote the development of adult capabilities. We may in some cases be justified in requiring functioning of an immature child, as with compulsory primary and secondary education, but we must always justify coercive treatment of children with reference to the adult-capability goal.
>
> (Nussbaum, "Capabilities and Human Rights," at 291)

114 Martha C. Nussbaum, *Creating Capabilities: The Human Development Approach* (Harvard: Belknap, 2011), 26. One *can* learn to reason and be deliberative, but they must also *choose it to act in that system*! We can, after all, "imagine a society that does well in creating contexts for choice in many areas but does not educate its citizens or nourish the development of their powers of mind."

115 Martha C. Nussbaum, *Creating Capabilities: The Human Development Approach* (Harvard: Belknap, 2011), 18 ("The approach takes each person as an end, asking not just about the total average well-being but about the opportunities available to each person.").

116 Martha C. Nussbaum, *Creating Capabilities: The Human Development Approach* (Harvard: Belknap, 2011), 18.
117 Martha C. Nussbaum, *Creating Capabilities: The Human Development Approach* (Harvard: Belknap, 2011), 18.
118 Martha C. Nussbaum, *Creating Capabilities: The Human Development Approach* (Harvard: Belknap, 2011), 18.
119 Vasil Gluchman, "Nussbaum's Philosophy of Education As the Foundation for Human Development," 28 *Hum. Aff.* 328 (2018).
120 Vasil Gluchman, "Nussbaum's Philosophy of Education As the Foundation for Human Development," 28 *Hum. Aff.* 328 (2018).
121 Martha C. Nussbaum, *Creating Capabilities: The Human Development Approach* (Harvard: Belknap, 2011), 18.
122 Martha C. Nussbaum, *Creating Capabilities: The Human Development Approach* (Harvard: Belknap, 2011), 31. We use the list of ten central capabilities as a basis for the idea of fundamental political entitlements and constitutional law (70). In Nussbaum's words, "I articulate political principles [through the list of central capabilities] that can be used as the basis for framing a set of fundamental constitutional entitlements, and the approach I support thus has a close link to law and nation-building" (71). In general, then, the Capabilities Approach focuses on the protection of areas of freedom so central that their removal makes a life not worthy of human dignity. When a freedom is not that central, it will be left to the ordinary workings of the political process … . Given a widely shared understanding of the task of government (namely that government has the job of making people able to pursue a dignified and minimally flourishing life), it follows that a decent political order must secure to all citizens the ten Central Capabilities (28); Nussbaum, *Creating Capabilities*, at 26; *See* John Rawls, *Political Liberalism*. One notes that this preference for capabilities (and thus for choice) is connected to a respect for a plurality of different views of life, harkening, in many ways to Rawls' "Political Liberalism." "The political aim is that all humans in a nation should get above a certain threshold level of combined capability, in the sense not of coerced functioning but of substantial freedom to choose and to act."
123 Martha Nussbaum, *Not for Profit: Why Democracy Needs the Humanities* (Princeton, NJ: Princeton University Press, 2016), 43.
124 Martha Nussbaum, *Not for Profit: Why Democracy Needs the Humanities* (Princeton, NJ: Princeton University Press, 2016), 43.
125 Martha Nussbaum, *Not for Profit: Why Democracy Needs the Humanities* (Princeton, NJ: Princeton University Press, 2016), 44.
126 Martha Nussbaum, *Not for Profit: Why Democracy Needs the Humanities* (Princeton, NJ: Princeton University Press, 2016), 45–46.
127 Martha Nussbaum, *Not for Profit: Why Democracy Needs the Humanities* (Princeton, NJ: Princeton University Press, 2016), 4–6.
128 For Nussbaum, three capacities are essential for the cultivation of humanity—first, self-examination of oneself and one's traditions. Second, "an ability to see themselves as not simply citizens of some local region or group but also, and above all, as human beings bound to all other human beings by ties of recognition and concern." And third, to be considered a world citizen. Additionally, she also calls for the narrative imagination. *Citizens cannot think well based on factual knowledge*

alone. The third ability of the citizen, closely related to the first two, can be called the narrative imagination.

The narrative imagination is not uncritical: for we always bring ourselves and our own judgments to the encounter with another, and when we identify with a character in a novel, or a distant person whose life story we imagine, we inevitably will not merely identify, we will also judge that story in the light of our own goals and aspirations.

See Martha Nussbaum, *Cultivating Humanity: A Classical Defense of Reform in Liberal Education* (Cambridge: Harvard University Press, 1998); Martha Nussbaum, "Education for Citizenship in an Era of Global Connection," 21 *Stud. Philos. Educ.* 290 (2002).

129 Martha Nussbaum, "Education for Citizenship in an Era of Global Connection," *Stud. Philos. Educ.* 290 (2002).

130 Martha Nussbaum, *Not for Profit: Why Democracy Needs the Humanities* (Princeton, NJ: Princeton University Press, 2016), 50.

131 Martha Nussbaum, *Not for Profit: Why Democracy Needs the Humanities* (Princeton, NJ: Princeton University Press, 2016), 50

132 Martha Nussbaum, *Not for Profit: Why Democracy Needs the Humanities* (Princeton, NJ: Princeton University Press, 2016), 50.

133 Martha Nussbaum, *Not for Profit: Why Democracy Needs the Humanities* (Princeton, NJ: Princeton University Press, 2016), 50. She also proposes, like Dewey, that Socratic argument and critical thinking be imposed in every class, the small classes are favored over larger classes, and more. She argues the following:

as a starting point, critical thinking should be infused into the pedagogy of classes of many types, as students learn to prove, to evaluate evidence, to write papers with well-structured arguments, and to analyze the arguments presented to them in other contexts.

I agree, in theory and in an ideal situation. Though I focus here on civics classes already in existence. (55).

134 Martha Nussbaum, *Not for Profit: Why Democracy Needs the Humanities* (Princeton, NJ: Princeton University Press, 2016), 72.

135 Martha Nussbaum, *Not for Profit: Why Democracy Needs the Humanities* (Princeton, NJ: Princeton University Press, 2016), 72.

136 Martha Nussbaum, *Cultivating Humanity: A Classical Defense of Reform in Liberal Education* (Cambridge: Harvard University Press, 1998), 19; *see also* Anders Berman, "Martha Nussbaum and Liberal Education," in *Martha Nussbaum: Ancient Philosophy, Civic Education and Liberal Humanism* (Anders Burman & Synne Myrebøe, eds.) (Huddinge: Södertörns Högskola, 2019), 78.

137 Vasil Gluckman, "Nussbaum's Philosophy of Education as the Foundation For Human Development," 28 *Hum. Aff.* 328–338 (2018).

138 To use a phrase by Roy Gardner, *Education for Values: Morals, Ethics and Citizenship in Contemporary Teaching* (Roy Gardner et al., eds.) (London: Routledge, 2000), 12.

139 Roy Gardner, *Education for Values: Morals, Ethics and Citizenship in Contemporary Teaching* (Roy Gardner et al., eds.) (London: Routledge, 2000) 13.
140 Roy Gardner, *Education for Values: Morals, Ethics and Citizenship in Contemporary Teaching* (Roy Gardner et al., eds.) (London: Routledge, 2000), 13.
141 Jo Cairns, "Introduction," in *Education for Values: Morals, Ethics and Citizenship in Contemporary Teaching* (Roy Gardner et al., eds.) (London: Routledge, 2000).
142 Jo Cairns, "Introduction," in *Education for Values: Morals, Ethics and Citizenship in Contemporary Teaching* (Roy Gardner et al., eds.) (London: Routledge, 2000), 21.
143 Paul Yates, "Legitimating the Moral Curriculum," in *Education for Values: Morals, Ethics and Citizenship in Contemporary Teaching* (Roy Gardner et al., eds.) (London: Routledge, 2000), 85 (likewise mobilizing a historical survey to moor curricular proposals in an ongoing national project aged centuries).

3 Contextualizing a New Critical Education within the Roots of the Historic Civic Education Project

This chapter sets out to situate our larger issue with civic education as part of a larger "educational devolution" from the once clear, historical goals and standards of the public education project both within and without the classroom a discussion of the history of education. I would contend that without a discussion of the history, we cannot fully apprehend the scope of the issue to which this work offers an answer; there is more to say about modern education than "standardization is ruining it"—in fact, we have completely lost sight of the point of public education, to which this proposal in many ways endeavors to bring us back.

The need to integrate a historical conversation is best accentuated by a metaphor to which I already referred earlier: "the field and rules of the game." In 2013, *Parks and Recreation*, an exceptionally lauded television program aired an episode entitled "The Cones of Dunshire."[1] There, Ben (a favorite character) contrived a new fantasy board game to channel his obsessive energy during a period of unemployment. He instructed colleagues and friends in two things: the fantasy world itself, which is the "common ground" of the game, "and" the ground rules: "four cones win, but in order to get a cone you have to build a civilization… which is where the Spirit Cards come in." His guiding advice for new players: "it's all about the cones."

Ben's words accomplished the two-fold educational goal: teaching the "common ground" *and* the rules. Both were necessary. Rules legitimate; rules distinguish "Cones of Dunshire" from, say "Settlers of Catan" or "Monopoly Deal." Furthermore, to be an effective game player, all must start with the same basic idea of landscape, a set of institutions, principles, and an *ethos.* As players get better based on that understanding, they might develop unique strategies to win; they might master the game; they might make new rules or point out larger issues. But importantly, any development occurs all within the confines of an existing landscape: nobody would think to throw a rule out that is integral to the identity of the game (maybe toss the cones out and play with triangles).

DOI: 10.4324/9781003596523-5

The previous chapter offered a philosophy on how best to educate players to apprehend, master, and even develop the "rules of the game" for our American democracy—commenting on how education ought to develop students' temperament, offering guiding moral learning that promotes senses of justice or the common good, and denoting a capabilities focus as essential to political participation. This chapter is instead about the "common playing field," or, for us, *the grander purpose of public education in America and its relationship to our governing ideals.* In other words, asking *to what end* do we educate and instill moral and practical wisdom in the manner discussed above? Today, we fail to agree on the objective of public civic education. We saw this clearly through our failure to even agree on a proper definition of its goals.[2] Is the game we are playing "how to best achieve a republican vision of government?" or is it "how to change and shake institutions"; is it "how to participate within our existing systems," or is it "how to be heard as a citizen." A review of the history does shed some light on the larger purposes of public civic education that might be helpful in mooring our proposal in at least an abstract notion of a "common playing field."

I hope to show how our education has devolved from helping support engagement with that "game" to something altogether different. We can recast our current civic educational predicaments as an unmooring from the purpose which we see clearest in our earliest schooling systems in the New England colonies. Although these schools are the most unfamiliar and unrelated to us in terms of our current iteration of public schools, they are the original game-makers[3] and carry essential lessons in the principles and preoccupations of schooling. In this way, we will see how standardization policies from beyond the classroom, together with the villainization of values and prioritization of neutrality *within* the classroom, all as we modernized to create the "public school," hurt the intersection of education and democracy more than helped. *They represent bad game teaching* and a complete misunderstanding of the *common field* of the game. Indeed, I perceive a values education—at odds with the current criticisms regarding its capacity to indoctrinate—as empowering per the original purpose of the education game, when focused on human development and the bettering of the person. It was this way in the 1600s, though with some caveats of course. Rather than attacking values education as an enterprise, we ought to reconsider what values students learn, the capacities they gain, and, more broadly, the goal of the whole educational project. In this, teaching children law as a theory—when construed as a value education necessary for the American citizen—can be instructive.

Below, I fixate on two through-lines that support and contextualize this proposal as a strong solution consistent with historical trends and storied public education principles. The first through-line I trace begs the reader to study how our ever-existent proclivity toward standardizing, nationalizing, mass-producing, and commodifying education has impacted the originally intended goal of delivering learning in ways that *empower and cater to the individual student*. This is taken in the broadest possible sense—for even early education was always about more than just one pupil's individual growth[4]—and speaks more to the notion of our system's gradual severing, more and more, from familial and community influence (for better and for worse) in terms of the substance of instruction and administrative assembly. Appreciating this will serve to support a curricular proposal that seeks to offset that loss of criticality, directedness, and versatility with self-examination that was once so sacrosanct in early education. In what I perceive to be a system that will *not* re-invent itself in a systemic way anytime soon, I think it is important to introduce a more unabashedly critical element to education—law learning—as a part of a larger, storied educational narrative rather than something out of left field.

The second through-line concerns change in the parameters of classroom education; how has *what* we learn changed? Though the civic enterprise of education, in my view, has remained consistent in theory,[5] the sources of learning from which we have drawn change, the reasoning behind our civic learning has changed, and our conception of civics has changed. This is important, as we shall see, as our current ongoing "culture wars" are symptoms of this change, and, lest values-learning be lost forever in the push for neutrality, the palatable presentation of such an education must be rethought. The argument proposed in this work concords with the belief that an education in ethical and moral values is necessary for an optimal society. From the Colonial Era into the 17th and 18th centuries, this was construed as something grounded in religious belief. Our derision from religion ought not obfuscate by the fact that it is still an important approach to education. As Locke had proposed: education is a societal progressor; that children were "blank slates to be written on—society could be changed through the education of children"[6]; specifically, a moral education led to an optimal society. For today's day and age, I argue that this same idea holds, though the education for creating the best citizens ought to be in law (rather than substantive religion) and its moral, ethical, and value underpinnings. And the idea is not farfetched—especially when you consider the history.

To prove this, I want to focus on two periods in our educational story[7]: the colonial schooling project and the common schooling project. These moments are emblematic of larger trends in *how, what, and why we teach*; they showcase key developments in our perception of "civics" learning and innovation in how we administrated the system to meet progressively changing educational objectives. This survey, albeit curtailed, prepares us once again to envision the current proposal within the framework of pre-existing principles and ideas and "game field" that can be described thusly: *educating for the empowered citizen.*

In the colonial period, our public schools bred a discursive community. The original education game was religiously imbued, but they were also preoccupied with civics in terms of the production of leaders, critics, and idealists to continue the intellectual tradition and progress. This was then unmoored in the common school era with its assimilative purpose, accompanied in turn by standardization and uniformity. It was an industrial education that lost the sense of the individual child and from which we never recovered.

Perhaps this was an inevitable "devolution"—we did, after all, open the game up to many players of diverse religious, social, cultural, and ethnic backgrounds—we did also have new industrial and commercial needs. However, we have reached a point now where, as a nation, we are entrenched enough to think critically about our current version of the game of "public education and democracy," our "common playing field," colored not by religion but in value-pluralism. This will only augment the work we did to understand how to best educate for "the rules of the game," or create leaders in this milieu of values-pluralism, with a facility in all the tools for leadership in this diverse democratic eco-system (debate, counterargument, rights, ethics, inclusive rhetoric, values) gained through learning law. Surprisingly: this is an education that the Puritans prized, one emphasizing individual growth and the community's role in that growth. We are no longer breeding people for the factory or holding onto a mistaken notion of shallow patriotism and singular ideology. Instead, we need to create a community of high-reasoning learners, a "priesthood of all believers," a united front, but in the secular sense.

3.1 Conscience, Community, and Colonial Classrooms: Civic Unity through an Education in "Reading and Writing" in Massachusetts Bay

Pointing to the Massachusetts Bay colonial school experience—albeit the first iteration of systemically public, accessible schooling[8]—might raise some eyebrows given my intention to measure changes in education (particularly, in terms of treatment of the individual student, and systemically, in terms of content) as impacting what I see as a consistent *civic* objective to the public schooling project. While the West has generally "accepted that the spread of formal schooling is the product of advancing progress, democracy, and enlightenment,"[9] there are those that challenge this notion of civic centeredness at the heart of American schooling history, especially targeting the colonial era. The colonial school, one may perceive, was a rank-and-file religious school where students learned to read the Bible and understand Calvinist principles.[10] Nothing democratic or civic about it! When, in 1647, the Massachusetts Bay Colony General Court declared that every town over 50 was required to "appoint a teacher for reading and writing," and every town over 100 families ought to have a Latin Grammar School to prepare students for Harvard College,[11] the generation of civic leaders was an at-best small motivator in comparison to larger religious zealousness. And, of course, other criticisms can come from those who would (rightly) say that Massachusetts Bay Colony's educational prioritization is hardly representative of other colonial approaches to education, and, furthermore, that colonial education—with its overtly religious leaning—could not be further from contemporary public education.

But I must disagree with these critics to a large extent.[12] While to be sure, Massachusetts Bay Colony's early grammar schools are no modern public schools, they taught civic substance in their own way, and they served a unifying role amongst people in their own way.[13] Suffice it to say, they undeniably offer a foundational point from which the Founders, later Horace Mann, and later even still John Dewey—all whose educational philosophy was unquestionably civic-oriented—sought inspiration for the schooling evolutions that yielded our current paradigm. *As we will see, one might argue that the largest difference between the view of a progressive education we have interrogated so far and that of the colonials was a focus on specific, articulated religious principles at the core of their study*, a "common playing field" that may be different from ours today. However, "the rules of the game" they proffered were important civic, instructive, and ought to inspire us today more than our more immediate relatives in the common school. In other words, the educational environments were functionally operating within the skills-focused civics sphere, and they were about critical thinking and strengthening of character. For the day, colonial education offered a versatile curriculum that endowed students with both capabilities to practically reason, ascend, and participate in their political sphere.[14]

3.1.1 The Conception of the Puritan "Commonwealth" and Its Impact on Schooling Policy

Individual civic empowerment through learning was at the center of the Puritan educational project, from both a systemic perspective and a pedagogical perspective. To see this, we begin first with a larger context. John Winthrop's chief concern for the Massachusetts Bay Colony was straightforward: they were ever at risk of devolving into a struggling conclave of "beasts" who would forget that they were members of a covenanted community who's social and political freedoms were limited by the grander vision of a "city upon a hill." In other words, we are contending with a society whose perception teetered delicately on the proverbial brink of savagery. What stops its bestial collapse? Winthrop proposed that civil liberty and just society exist "in the moral law, and the political covenants and constitutions amongst men themselves"[15]—a statement that, at first blush, conveys notions of *obedience*, *common values*, *accepted social mores*, *strong central institutions*, *uniformity*, *aversion to dissidence*. Indeed, it sounds rather cold and one-dimensional—no room existing for polite dissent or alternative belief, no room for new ideas. To a certain extent this was true,[16] but allow me to suggest that this is a narrow reading.

Winthrop states "amongst men themselves," inviting a notion that all men must come to agreement, and that all citizens ought to be leaders in their enterprise. This is a rather non-hierarchical and plural notion; indeed, so long as you are playing according to the rules of *one* game (upholding a moral law as found in scripture, singular religious identity, and common social mores), criticism, debate, and development through dialogue would be invited and encouraged. In this, we will find the education project necessary and key.

In fact, Ralph Clover develops this idea further, looking into the fascinatingly "contradictory" notion of Winthrop's commonwealth.[17] The commonwealth was an "organic body—timeless, self-sufficient, and subject by the consent of its members to a government *divinely empowered to pronounce laws for the common good*."[18] But, it was marked, indeed, by two symbiotic forces "intertwined in a network of mutuality:"[19] the government and social covenant on the one hand, the individual on the other.[20] As to the government-side, the notion of the "commonwealth" seems to be superficially intolerant ("divinely empowered" and unilateral in authority). Indeed, a social covenant[21] connoted values, ideas, and purposes—perpetually renewed and reaffirmed to all by devoted leadership. It worked alongside set laws and to divinely articulated values that are universal, "good, just, and honest."[22] To be sure, the development of capable leadership and strong, central institutions were paramount; the purpose of later school laws in 1647 were, in part to ensure a steady stream of pupils to Harvard College so as to rear the next generation of clergymen who would concern themselves with intergenerational intellectual and religious maintenance.[23] This undoubtedly influenced the expediency with which Harvard College[24] was founded, and, as a direct consequence, the development of elementary and secondary education.[25] And, to be sure, in high-level leadership, Massachusetts was not wanting[26]; in terms vision, the colony was well-placed.[27] Yet, the Puritans did *not* content themselves to leave matters in the hands of a ruling elite leading blind sheep; no, the charge instead was to emphasize and develop the individual's sense of "mutuality" with other colonists and instill a respect for the unwritten and written laws and orders and values of the colony. It was, in fact, empowerment.

Taking a closer look at the "individual" in Clover's construction, we see how Winthrop and his contemporaries envisioned a "citizen"—indeed, *expected* a "citizen"—to *not* blindly adhere to divinely wrought, clitist notions of right and wrong, or of socially determined behavior and duty. Winthrop was of a generation of "men [seeking] to express new ideas in traditional terms."[28] His citizens therefore had self-awareness, criticality, and a facility enough to dialogue with persisting values. The vision of the community—indeed as espoused in the later constitutional and representative government—was of a "divinely ordained diversity of moral equals"[29]—non-hierarchical in one sense, prideful in the ability of all citizens, properly equipped, to contribute something unique, to maintain a difference of opinion, and for the community to grow by way of that dialogue.[30]

To see this at work, one need not look further than the publication of New England's initial law codex, *Laws and Liberties* in 1648. Inhabitants had called out for the codification of laws so as "to study and understand the laws presented in the document to encourage greater self-government."[31] This self-starting initiative alone is the ultimate sign of a citizenry well-equipped and active in their politics.[32] But, even further, publication of the laws "enabled the citizens to read and internalize them—law in this sense was instructive, not merely prohibitory, and citizens consented to the laws through their practice of obedience."[33] In this way, we get a vision of "true citizenship [is a] more robust, ongoing understanding of consent through active obedience and even enforcement."[34] Indeed, the founding generation's commitments to equality on the basis of morality, industry, and communion,[35] presented a "unique mixture of liberty and authority that held the active role of individual citizens as members of society."[36] And it was this that the schooling story helped to fortify; education "shaped the souls of citizens by helping them to develop the right sorts of habits and opinions about the political community and their own role in it,"[37] reinforced identity and purpose. In other words, such an eduation:

> [balanced an] appreciation for the value of the individual in their emphasis on both the cultivation of individual gifts and their robust conception of citizens as the industrious keepers of their own liberties, [as well as] an aspirational principle of civic communion.[38]

The next question, then, is *how*.

3.1.2 Administrating and Legislating the Schooling System as a Civic Enterprise

Conceiving of the schooling story as a civic enterprise relies on this appreciation for the balance between government and individual in a religious landscape, yes, though *not* as part of a religious project. Schooling, I argue, was *not only* religious or political or social indoctrination. We see this manifest *ab initio* in how the first public "grammar" school, Boston Latin School (1635), was founded not by any church, but by a Boston town meeting. Truly embodying the conception of a "priesthood of all believers," the rapid agreement reached by the community to install the school demonstrates the compactness of the Puritan community, the vigor of their local governments, and the principled nature of the schooling initiative focused on elevating all voices. This was not a new notion; English colonists had transplanted from England a universal appreciation for educational objectives and a methodology for realizing those goals. Specifically, their ready-made educational configuration of household, church, and school, cooperating with each other to engender in children the virtue of piety, civility, and learning.[39] Indeed, both father and mother[40] saw it as a mission to avail themselves of every opportunity to educate his own children, instill piety, and keep abreast of their children's spiritual demeanor, and their aptitude for political and town participation.

At first, schools merely provided the "tools for acquiring religious knowledge," of which basic literacy was chief, while the family supplied "knowledge itself."[41] But so central was the importance of schooling to the maintenance of competent citizens and regenerative leadership—importance both religious and pragmatic in nature—that laws quickly developed to push town responsibility[42] in education.[43] While certainly Massachusetts—and especially Bostonian—youth may have been the beneficiaries of the great teaching from their parents, especially in basic literacy,[44] nothing rose to the level needed to join the ranks of Puritan political leadership (which also, of course, meant religious leadership). The "town" school, in the eyes of religious leadership, would become a "vestibule to learning," help cast a wider net for leadership induction, and more effectively "[bring] up of young scholars, and [fit] them for academic learning, that still as they are judged ripe, they may be received unto the College."[45]

The pragmatic, secular nature of the leaders' dilemma cannot be understated: the replenishment of the clergy, assurance of the next generation's direction, and the development of intelligent, law-abiding, and righteous citizens. This mentality is systemically reflective, once again, of a founding commitment to the moral equality of persons; "the Word of God, *not only preached but read,* was the inheritance of all men and women regardless of station."[46] As Sarah August Morgan Smith writes:

> the development of the colony unquestionably benefited from the promotion of the sort of basic education that would facilitate citizens' understanding of and adherence to the laws, while also helping them to cultivate the personal habits and virtue that would make their individual callings safe and purposeful within the community.[47]

Pushes toward systematizing schooling for political and religious purposes began with chiding. The General Court would berate those parents who failed to engender in children an ability to read, and in 1642, empowered the "chosen men appointed for managing the prudential affairs" of each town as follows:

> [to] take account from time to time of all parents and masters, and of their children, considering their calling and employment of their children, *especially of their ability to read and understand the principles of religion and the capital laws of this country.*[48]

The wording of the law is significant, as suggests Smith:

> [Such a declaration by The General Court illuminates] several aspects of the public nature of education as understood by the Puritans. First, the delegation of the subject to the care of those charged with administering the "prudential affairs" of the several towns underscores the civic purposes of education: if education of the young is one of the "prudential affairs" of public life, and if prudence, or practical wisdom, is the preeminent political virtue,

> then education must contribute something to the welfare of the community. The essentially civil character of education at this most basic level is further underscored by the fact that such institutions were controlled by the towns directly, and not officially under the oversight (although clearly subject to the influence of) the churches.[49]

The later schooling laws in 1647 might have equally used religious rhetoric but only as a thin veil to highly secular, civic purposes. *The Old Deluder Satan Law of 1647*, specifically, mandated that every Massachusetts township "shall then forthwith appoint one within their town to teach all such children as shall resort to him to write and read," and that "where any town shall increase to the number of one hundred Families or Housholders, they shall set up a Grammar-School."[50] The rational was to protect against the "chief project of that old deluder, Satan, to keep men from the knowledge of the Scriptures."[51] *For the sake of our religion, way of life, and our very souls*, education served as the bulwark of unity and strength.[52] The law stressed urgency and universality, for evil does not discriminate based on wealth. Thus, the protection of the community as a *whole* is predicated on the empowerment of *all*.[53] For the zealous Puritans, the law makes the bold statement that "salvation is as universally available as the educational end of reading, due to the infinite divine bounty that transforms the believer and gives both education and society their common purpose."[54] At once frightening, empowering, collectivizing, and unifying,[55] the colonial leadership mobilized theology to create a common enemy, one shrouded in mystery and threatening to all, around which they could begin an unencumbered restructuring of the educational model around formal schooling *without* running afoul of a traditional family–church–state balance. Indeed, formal schooling was now seen as a separate project, one specifically relating to community and one's versatility with the moral of the day, and the most effective way to achieve this pragmatic, secular, inter-generational objective.

The Old Deluder Satan Law incited residents to think about the status of their community's spiritual welfare as predicated on each child's intellectual elevation. The satanic threat, clergy maintained, was too overwhelming to leave the important educational project un-systematized, and, more than the church or the family, the town—ever-growing, ever-touching the lives of all its residents—*was* the be the best mechanism for innovating protections and against that threat.[56] Suddenly, conversations around formal schooling blossomed out from the homes of the elite to town-halls and church gatherings.[57] With every new revision of the law over time, one notes that three aspects remained consistent: (1) the conferral of power (and expectations) to the town, (2) the consideration of *all* classes of people, and (3) the *gravity* of the importance of schooling to the survival of the community reiterated to each family and child.[58] In this way, *everyone* was a defender against the adversary. *The Old Deluder Satan Law*, in its religious appeal, catalyzed the idea of compulsory and accessible education as a populist preoccupation and informed the people that a shared commitment to a unified purpose—upon which the Puritan community was already committed—meant the support of formal learning.

Over time, the foundational invocation of the devil as a common enemy meant to appeal to the masses and inspire the gradual prioritization of formal schooling in the colonial project, might have even served to increasingly secularize formal schooling content in Massachusetts Bay Colony—especially toward the end of the century. Indeed, alongside the frequent revising of the schooling law came increasing interest in more diverse types of learning. This makes sense; if more people attended school, the focus *had* to shift from the project of building the next class at Harvard to vocational or commercial skills.[59] And, indeed, this became manifest in the transiting emphasis in newly minted town schools from classical studies to, first, advances in English-learning education, and, eventually, and the advent and success of town-operated "writing schools."[60] With notion of a common, deeply venomous enemy urging Puritans toward new educational commitments, died the elitism of formal schooling and gave rise to the engrained town-school as a skills-factory.

3.1.3 Into the Classroom: Conceiving Literacy Education and Individual Focus as Civics

But, so far, all that has been proven was that (1) a responsibility is thrust upon each citizen, (2) that the system prioritized religious learning over basic literacy, and (3) this was unifying in purpose for the Puritans. How, then, does this make for an especially empowering civic education? To see this, let us look closer at the classroom itself. In terms of intellectual outcomes, students we required to be able to "*read and understand the principles of religion and the capital laws*"[61] of the country. This is something more than "capable of reading the hymns," which was important but not *the* central purpose. Rather than just rote learning, this policy sought a robust capacity to truly understand *the content of* religion and law. As Smith articulates:

> understanding in this sense seems to imply something more than mere comprehension, for the true value of leaning the principles of religion, for example, was not simply to know that an action was forbidden, but to be able to reflect on and apply one's knowledge to one's own life.[62]

By way of deciding to formally offer an elementary education system, New Englanders were not just indicating but proclaiming their commitment to widespread reading literacy as a basic and fundamental skill for all commonwealth citizens.[63] This was a leap in the movement toward cultivating a sense of the public value of more advanced levels of education for at least some portion of the population. In this way, the Puritan view on education was more than merely superficial: the true purpose of learning at all levels "was to free the mind to engage with matters beyond the merely utilitarian."[64] If one town or another failed in their charge to adequately provide for the education of children, they were highly stigmatized; it was held as a sign of "serious moral degeneracy," for without the opportunity to engage their minds and their spirits in the process of reflection and study, children were either drudges or open to their bestial proclivities.

Puritan leadership channeled a very distinct perception of self-identity, one which an elementary education needed to instill in children. "With Reformed Protestants, they insisted that *all* of human nature is corrupted, including human reason and will."[65] *But*, the Puritans continued to insist that "if human beings are created in God's image then they image God's rationality … reason remains definitive of what it means to be human."[66] For Thomas Hooker, for instance, "a man is a living creature imbued with a reasonable soul: and every living creature indued with a reasonable soul, is a man."[67] The schooling system—in terms of administration and the classroom experience—placed a premium on reason for the religious and intellectual welfare of their children and their community.[68] Yes, the climax of a Puritan education was the reading of the Bible, but more specifically it was providing the "conditions under which it was likely that the greatest number of people could be brought to their *own* religious awareness."[69] And, *still*, the Puritans were concerned with cultivating a universal social morality, a "right thinking," and ensuring equal access to this knowledge for all community members regardless of class.[70] The Puritans uniquely mobilized theological dogma to outline and develop a system of education that met their needs and contexts: the Puritan story was not only about reform and advancement, but unification and collectivization. To the Puritans, education served to preserve the faith and protect the believer. This is civics.

Committed to the Reformation ideal of *sola scriptura*,[71] the Puritans believed strongly in the power of education as a tool for personal and social reform.[72] Even before the advent of any accessible school, Smith notes:

> community favored a habit of [discussing and reflecting] on such teachings by ordinary believers in the form of conventicles—a "little assembly, a meeting of a private character," particularly one "for the exercise of religion otherwise than as sanctioned by the law."[73]

All such forms of engagement with the wider world of learning—whether town-meetings, administrations, schools, sermons, catechisms, religious conversation with family, personal practices—requiring individuals to "engage with texts, as readers, auditors, speakers, authors."[74] To be sure, the success of each of these modes depended upon the widespread ability to read. If anything, the story of Massachusetts Bay Colony's educational transformation is a case-study in the reconfiguration of the role that unified purpose plays in the survival—both spiritual and physical—of a new community. Learning served them the role of efficient, principled way to consistently rally toward the achievement of important social objectives like the strengthening of the town and empowerment of citizens. Through religious rhetoric, Massachusetts Bay Colony began working as a unit, ever-diligently, toward attaining their proverbial true "brotherhood of all believers" bonded with accessible education and universally accessible (at least in theory) tools for empowered participation in government and religious life.

If we are talking about a religious people, with religious community laws, and an education stressing this, then their education was a civic education. For the Puritans, instruction in reading was paramount, even more than writing.[75] This is how, after all, one would study the word of God or understand the laws of the colony. What we see is a colonial commitment to the purposeful encouragement of individual industry, not only to keep the community functioning, but also to keep children from the sort of "wanton, dishonest, or immodest behavior" that might tempt them were their hands idle.[76] The division of governance amongst the schools echoes the founding commitment to communion as well, the special care toward one's fellow citizens that recognizes in their good—and their virtue—the good of the community. We read and write to keep government accountable; we learn with that aim; we learn for the good of bettering our community and perpetuating our intellectual progress through generations.

3.2 Discourse Declines; the Game Gets Confused: The Unmooring of Education from the Common School to the Present

Having uncovered how our oldest schooling roots were civic *specifically* in terms of their vested interest in cultivating citizens who were involved, versatile with the tools of governance (in the Puritan case, facility with laws and religious principles and mores), let us jump forward in time to the progenitor and closest ancestor of the modern public school: the common school. Unfortunately, this point saw the schooling project lose sight of our main point in the game of *educating for the empowered citizen* by building savvy strategists and enthusiastic participants in our institutions. I join others[77] in contending that Horace Mann's Common School became something of a patriotically propagandist protestant school in an era of new multiculturalism, prizing uniformity of ethics, values, and learning. Of course, there is the reasoning for this: the common school was up against a distinctive milieu from the colonial enterprise in terms of industrialization and immigration; "the school was to prepare the children of all religions, ethnic backgrounds (particularly the foreign-born) for the intelligent responsible exercise of citizenship,"[78] to preserve—as they perceived them—republican institutions and cultivate political community. However, it is noted that history obviates a transition from developing leaders, critical thinkers, and dialogs in all ranks of the citizenry to an era of indoctrination. To retain a leadership quality in education might have been unsustainable as we grew as a nation, but this turn was a poison that we still cannot shake from our impression of public education.

To Mann and other great common school reform voices, mass learning was "a primary vehicle for defining ourselves as a nation."[79] For Mann, specifically, a uniform school experience needed to be offered to all regardless of class, standing, ethnicity so that, collectively, they might ensure that they met emerging needs—in their time and in all times—and sustainably realize the expectations of democracy.[80] Now, the common school was theoretically rooted in the frameworks of the colonial period. Inclusive of ideas of "individual choice," of "social contract, which sought to engender an agreeable and necessarily inclusive form of societal planning."[81] The notion of "common and equal opportunity" promised a "community within society, reinforcing the impact that a mutual value system could deliver."[82] However, a great divergence also took place—for Mann, *inculcating values were more important than developing intellect.* True, "education would serve individual interests founded in liberal philosophy as well as communitarian goals founded in both democratic and republican theory."[83] But, to Mann's mind, the impartation of values on children was the way to do this; specifically, *the protestant values, their values, ought to be the values of a nation*. Among these values: "tolerance," "individual choice," as well as the more overtly religiously influenced collection made famous in Mann's *Twelfth Annual Report* in 1848, "principles of piety, justice, regard to truth, love to their country, humanity and universal sobriety, industry, frugality, chastity, moderation, and temperance, other virtues which are the ornament of human society, and which a republican constitution is founded."[84]

In the classroom, this was clearer than ever as the common school famously would avoid controversial topics that would prove emotionally and intellectually divisive.[85] The common school endeavored to educate all children "without divisions along religious, cultural or economic lines" by precisely realigning toward a single religious value-set.[86] The national ethic was developed "along with Bible readings without comment"[87] provided the necessary moral grounding. "Immigrant children would receive moral and religious teaching, powerful enough, if possible, to keep them in the right path amid the moral darkness which is their daily and domestic walk."[88] One notes that this might have been par for the course, as well, in colonial schooling. However, there is a difference when such an effort is being made in an era of multiculturalism *with assimilationist intent* rather than to cultivate critical leaders in a preexistent religiously zealous community within which to operate. Indeed, Mann proposed a school that developed *his* perception of a national ethic in an epoch where "multiculturalism, especially in the form of religious diversity, posed a problem for public education." As Mann himself expressed:

> [a]ll those who are worthily laboring to promote the cause of education are laboring to elevate mankind into the upper and purer regions of civilization,

> Christianity, and the worship of the true God; all those who are obstructing the progress of this cause are impelling the race backwards into barbarism and idolatry.[89]

And to be sure, this yielded no shortage of protests as to the practical "revolutionary" consequences of this new reformed educational philosophy—ulterior (especially Catholic) voices argued that it "stamped out differences among students, [secured] conformity to rules and regulations teachers ... disconnect[ed] students from networks of personal communication. communities built on emotional bonds, shared loyalties, religious affiliations, expressive idiosyncrasies."[90] In its own time, it surely served as a counter-course to prevailing sentiments that described Mann's education as "sectarianism in disguise,"[91] and an "inefficient and improper monopoly"[92] on the education of children from parents or the Church.

Of course, Mann would disagree with this conception—though in his disagreement he further proves the propagandistic point.[93] He would seek solace in arguing that the public school belonged to the state: to "encourage inquiry, not to impose interpretations." The school must indeed avoid promoting any religious view but was required to instruct only in "commonly held" values. To be sure, there was a threat of homogeneity, would argue Mann, but, as a bulwark against dominating ideology, he would point to local control over education. This political structure, to his mind, would be the best way in which to transmit social and economic knowledge to the community.[94] But, even this, when the whole "common field" of education game was envisioned as "assimilating students to an American culture with singular values-identity," any diverse approach was quashed.[95]

And it is (incorrect) mentality—that there is an "American culture" to assimilate into—that colors our educational landscape even today.

Consider, for example, the mid-1900s when the common school gave way to the public school under Dewey's own paradigm for more secular and child-centered than ever before. There, "the religious function of the school shaded into the patriotic and the achievement of a broad objective of moral goodness into the nurturing of good citizens."[96] Dewey endeavored a vision of the school whose object was less about the "teaching of morals in an *authoritarian sense*, but more about serving a 'cultural revision' function."[97] However, the legacy of Mann permeated through, and Dewey's vision for a "common experience of the school [developing] a common faith that would transcend individual and group differences without negating the latter" was seldom realized. His ideas faced cyclical disfavor over time. Indeed, as time rolled on and the purpose of education became concerned with developing "excellence" or patriotism (say, during the Cold War),[98] any perceived ills in education were Dewey's doing. His public school was guilty of "permissiveness, valuelessness, and lack of academic standards in the public schools."[99] Until, finally, in the 1970s, 1980s, and into the present, calls for the propagandistic values that Mann had set forth manifested again in textbooks and curricula across the country. Today, schools at all levels toe the line in values-instruction or favoring outright values-neutrality. And even in this schools cannot *really* shake the protestant values identity. Echoing Charles Glenn and others, at no other time in our history do we witness such direct challenges to the very premise underlying the "myth of the common school," that is, that the values promoted through public education are in fact "neutral, nonsectarian, and indeed obvious to any to any reasonable person."[100]

3.3 The Game Revisited

The schooling project is almost entirely obstructed by an effort to remain "value-neutral" and thus avoid the controversies that come with diversity. "Educators across the nation work through the political and pedagogical minefields" in any conversation having to do with character, in issues as far-ranging as critical race theory to banned books.[101] We have rejected, in many ways *because* of our reliance on the common school philosophy, any movements for involving values pluralistically and relatively in the classroom, associating *all* values education with teaching of common "core" values rooted in the thinking of Mann's era. To challenge this again inculcates questions of indoctrination, the "hidden curriculum," the transmission of an "American" culture, and the proper mode for forming student beliefs and world views.[102]

The debate, indeed, rages beyond these pages: "where do we fall on the fundamental question of how to preserve basic freedoms in a pluralist society governed by majority consent and founded on democratic principles?"[103] How do we allocate power in the education project—to the benefit of the individual (parental), local (community), and national (societal) interests?[104] But, as Michael McConnel points out, we need not hang so tightly on the ideas of the common school reformers. Indeed:

> American society has not remained static since the days of the common school reformers. Sociological and psychological developments in teaching and learning theory have left us with an understanding of pedagogy unforeseen in the mid-1800s. Concepts of individual rights and liberties, the rise of the administrative state and government regulation of schooling, even mass compulsory state-controlled education itself, were far from the consciousness of the common school reformers, much less the constitutional framers of the previous century. High literacy rates generated largely through mass schooling, together with the rapid development of mass media and the technological explosion of recent decades, have left parents far more knowledgeable and capable to advocate on behalf of their children's educational interests.[105]

In an era in which calling into question the treatment of values education in school implicates "a tangled web of thorny concepts such as curriculum fragmentation, religious centrality, critical inquiry, rational deliberation, tolerance, and religious viewpoint,"[106] we are overlooking a key notion: the benefits of existing in this time of social media, psychological advances, and mass literacy, all of which provide a foundation for progressing our model of teaching, reorienting ourselves in the educational landscape, and moving past misapprehended educational limitations. This is sorely needed as our rootedness in standardization, uniformity, and neutral teaching are damaging the very soul of this democracy.

My proposal: let us look back to our oldest view of the "common field of the educational game": to engender an "education for the empowered citizen," as was the case, I have argued, in the colonial schooling enterprise. With this, the "rules and tools for this game" lay in the values-relativist teaching approaches of Dewey and Kohlberg and the Capabilities Approach of Martha Nussbaum. We need not abandon values but reconceive them in unique ways: mainly, to let them organically emerge (in their diversity!) in discursive schooling settings that emphasize only equality, critical inquiry, and rational deliberation as frameworks—all cross-cultural and uniform.[107]

We *must* move away from associating education with indoctrination or specific values-inculcation. Indeed, in creating a game, you want diverse and willing co-players. Our educational game began with a singularly important vision for a "common ground": education for an empowered citizenry and for the next generation of leaders; the rules and tools of the game being mass literacy, civic involvement, and social mores. It was not "the best New Englander" or the quietest churchgoer or the humblest man, but a "priesthood of all believers."

Having set this out—our "common ground" and the "rules of the game" firmly in mind—we must now discuss the way they ought to be introduced. How, indeed, do we foster practically a contemporary community of learners, idealists, revolutionaries, and innovators—so long as they are *invested* citizens—preoccupied with advancement and intellectual maintenance? It is a matter of reframing our civics education in all schools, providing a platform—already part of curricula everywhere (though ineffective)—for discourse through *law learning*; law being our national tongue, our discourse, our means of change-making and inter-connection. This next chapter will show *how* law learning can be the robust education we need to answer the challenges posed by the generation of apathy. I will approach this by, first, examining how law learning is already doing the critical work demanded by Dewey, Kohlberg, and Nussbaum for law students in the law school context. Then, in arguing for the expansion of law learning from just the siloed law students, I will show three ways in which such an education empowers *all* citizens: combatting complacency, redefining the citizen's relationship with authority, and developing one's values.

We *must* move students to rethink values by engaging with our most intrinsic systems and national legal scaffolding—doing so not through neutrality or the avoidance of controversy, but through engagement with it. The discussions that take place, the place and appreciation of counterarguments, the skills, and critical thinking perspectives are all the means of playing the game—and something enjoyed already by the privileged law student. But the need for debate and facility with issues through the lens of order, law, and national needs is necessary as a general education. Learning law is a tool for the empowered development of a "priesthood of all believers;" the best means of values-learning, as it is the common language of citizenship, touches all cultures, bridge pluralities without inculcating or pushing values, and promises discourse over blind-belief.

Notes

1 Season 6, Episode 9 (November 21, 2013).

2 *See*, Chapter 1.

3 One might argue that the colonial school could not possibly serve as a good reference for the founding of the "public school" system as current conceived—indeed, the "game" as it were—either in terms of its purpose or identity, pointing to the sheer number of interruptions (seismic shifts in national philosophy, identity, etc.) that have taken place between then and new. Consider, for instance, the American Revolution which reset our constitution and national identity with new ideals and visions, or else the industrial revolution and the US's turn toward commerce and industry. To argue against this would be distracting from our major theme here, but I would like to do so in the future. For now, suffice to say, scholars have tackled the question of the connection between the colonial era and modern schooling, politics, values, etc. For a deeper bibliography, consider: Elizabeth Payne, *Meet the Pilgrim Fathers* (New York: Random House, 1966); Jim Cullen, *The American Dream: A Short History of an Idea That Shaped a Nation* (New York: Oxford University Press, 2016).

4 One need not look any further than some of the public schools of the early 1800s, some of which were established to turn out factory laborers, like the New York Public School Society which employed a monitorial model of education, "where a single master taught hundreds of students, employing older students to pass lessons down to younger pupils with an emphasis on rote skill building, discipline, and hierarchical obedience." David Hemphill and Erin Blakely, "Narratives of Progress and the Colonial Origins of Schooling," 456 *Counterpoints*. No. 1, 7 (2015).

5 Indeed, going back to the founders. *See, e.g.*, James Carpenter, "Thomas Jefferson and the Ideology of Democratic Schooling," 21 *Democr. & Educ.* 1–11 (2013).

6 *See* John Locke, *An Essay Concerning Human Understanding* (New York: Penguin Classics, 1999), Book I, Chapter 1, Section 2.

7 For a more comprehensive history of education, *see* Wayne Urban, et al., *American Education: A History* (Routledge: London 2019) (6th Edition).

8 Hanor Webb, "The Birth of Our Nation's Public Schools," 36 *Peabody J. Educ.* No. 84, 86 (1958).

9 David Hemphill and Erin Blakely, "Narratives of Progress and the Colonial Origins of Schooling," 456 *Counterpoints*. No. 1, 7 (2015).

10 David Hemphill and Erin Blakely, "Narratives of Progress and the Colonial Origins of Schooling," 456 *Counterpoints*. No. 1, 7 (2015).

11 Hanor Webb, "The Birth of Our Nation's Public Schools," 36 *Peabody J. Educ. No*. 84, 86 (1958).

12 For a greater bibliography on others who construe religious education in a civics light, *see, e.g.*, Mark Chapman, "Newman and the Anglican Ideal of a University," 18 *Journal of the History of Modern Theology* 212–227 (2011).

13 *See* Sarah Augusta Morgan Smith, " 'With A Publick Spirit': Community and Commitment in New England, 1630–1689," dissertation for the faculty at Rutgers University.

14 For this reason, the schooling developments in Massachusetts Bay Colony are relevant to our inquiry here; knowing what they taught, the values they preached, and the means of delivering those values to students must be queried. Those critics who argue for the un-civic education and the irrelevance of the colonial model of publicly accessible schooling—on account of their religiosity, no less—to answering pressing contemporary schooling questions, would throw away a valuable learning tool. It would be, likewise, as if to throw away the common school history because it was "not set up exclusively to promote democracy or other enlightenment goals, but rather to meet the increased knowledge requirements of industrialized labor, assimilate new immigrants, and meet the growing need to build consumer markets." David Hemphill and Erin Blakely, "Narratives of Progress and the Colonial Origins of Schooling," 456 *Counterpoints*. No. 1, 7 (2015). That's correct, for sure, but those aims were not mutually exclusive. This proclivity for polarity against using any overtly religious project as a model for something secular has harmed more than it has helped current schooling conversations, and I trudge forward to seek what this specific history tells. Indeed, it even bolsters the argument that, in harkening for a reform to our civic education on a moral and practical front that is moored in tried-and-true principles, we need look no further than our own story.

15 Sarah Augusta Morgan Smith, " 'With A Publick Spirit': Community and Commitment in New England, 1630–1689" (citing John Winthrop, "Journal") (James Savage, Richard S. Dunn, and Laetitia Yeandle, eds.) (Cambridge: Harvard University Press, 1996), 586.

16 And, to a certain extent, this is true. Think on Rhode Island, for instance, founded by Roger Williams who felt the Puritan Massachusetts Bay Colony too stringent on religious living and frustratingly closed-minded in many ways.

17 Ralph H. Clover, "The Rule of Law in Colonial Massachusetts," 108(7) *U. Pa. L. Rev.* 1001–1036 (May 1960).

18 Ralph H. Clover, "The Rule of Law in Colonial Massachusetts," 108(7) *U. Pa. L. Rev.* 1001–1036 (May 1960).

19 Sarah Augusta Morgan Smith, " 'With A Publick Spirit': Community and Commitment in New England, 1630–1689" (citing John Winthrop, "Journal") (James Savage, Richard S. Dunn, and Laetitia Yeandle, eds.) (Cambridge: Harvard University Press, 1996), 586.

20 Ralph H. Clover, "The Rule of Law in Colonial Massachusetts," 108(7) *U. Pa. L. Rev.* 1001–1036 (May 1960).

21 Ralph H. Clover, "The Rule of Law in Colonial Massachusetts," 108(7) *U. Pa. L. Rev.* 1001–1036 (May 1960). (Mitchell, Stewart, Allyn Bailey Forbes, and Malcolm

Freiberg, eds., *Winthrop Papers* (5 Vols; Boston: The Massachusetts Historical Society, 1929–1947), 3:198).

22 Sarah Augusta Morgan Smith, " 'With A Publick Spirit': Community and Commitment in New England, 1630–1689" (citing John Winthrop, "Journal") (James Savage, Richard S. Dunn, and Laetitia Yeandle, eds.) (Cambridge: Harvard University Press, 1996), 586.

23 Marcus W. Jernegan, "The Beginnings of Public Education in New England," 23 *The School Rev.* 320, 326 (1915); *see generally Laws and Liberties* (1648); *see also New England's First Fruits* (1643).

> After God had carried us safe to New-England, and we had builded our houses, provided necessaries for our livelihood, rear'd convenient places for God's worship, and settled the Civil Government: One of the next things we longed for, and looked after was to advance *Learning* and perpetuate it to Posterity; dreading to leave an illiterate ministry to the church, when our present ministers shall lie in the Dust.

24 Harvard College was modeled after nonconformist colleges like Emmanuel at Cambridge. *See* Daniel R. Coquillette, "Radical Lawmakers in Colonial Massachusetts," 67 *N. Engl. Q.* 179–206 (1994).

25 *New England's First Fruits* (1643).

> After God had carried us safe to New England, and wee had builded our houses, provided necessaries for our livelihood, rear'd convenient places for God's worship, and setled the Civil Government; One of the next things we longed for, and looked after, was to advance Learning, and to perpetuate it to Posterity; dreading to leave an illiterate Ministry to the Churches, when our present Ministers shall lie in the Dust.

26 As historian Marcus Jernigan aptly describes of the Puritans, the "progress of a civilization depends on the ability and energy of its leaders, and in this respect, Massachusetts was most fortunate." Marcus Jernegan, "The Beginnings of Public Education in new England," 23 *The School Rev.* 326 (1915); *see generally Laws and Liberties* (1648).

27 The proportion of educated leaders was higher than any other colony, with nearly one hundred graduates of Oxford and Cambridge settled before 1650, nearly three-fourths of whom were clergymen. For further information, *see* Marcus Jernegan, "The Beginnings of Public Education in new England," 23 *The School Rev.* 326 (1915) ("The migration to New England to 1643 is commonly reckoned at about 20,000, or 4,000 families. Thus, there would be one person in 40 families, or one for every 200 emigrating, who had received university training.")

28 Ralph H. Clover, "The Rule of Law in Colonial Massachusetts," 108(7) *U. Pa. L. Rev.* 1001–1036 (May 1960).

29 Sarah Augusta Morgan Smith, " 'With A Publick Spirit': Community and Commitment in New England, 1630–1689".

30 Clover, ("The Rule of Law in Colonial Massachusetts," 108(7) *U. Pa. L. Rev.* 1001–1036 (May 1960).), pointing to this this expectation, and his greater contradiction, ever apparent in the prelude to the 1648 *Laws and Liberties*:

> If any of you meet with some law that seems not to tend to your particular benefit, you must consider that [laws] are made with respect to the whole people, and not to each particular person: and obedience to them must be yielded with respect to the common welfare, not to thy private advantage, and as thou yieldest obedience to the law for the common good, but to thy disadvantage: so another must observe some other law for thy good, though to his own damage; thus must we be content to bear one [another's] burden and so fulfill the Law of Christ.

Notice how, from the outset, our author addresses the notion of difference of opinion, of balancing personal interest with public good. This connotes an expectation of freethought, even in a society ostensibly risen to the ranks of holiness. I am struck by this; reflective, indeed, on its resonances with Kohlberg's "just community" predicated on finding justice in the balance between our own values and the collective good: *we are in this colonial experiment together; we rise and fall on the backs of our brothers and sisters.*

31 Ralph H. Clover, "The Rule of Law in Colonial Massachusetts," 108(7) *U. Pa. L. Rev.* 1024 (May 1960).

32 Ralph H. Clover, "The Rule of Law in Colonial Massachusetts," 108(7) *U. Pa. L. Rev.* 1024 (May 1960).

33 Sarah Augusta Morgan Smith, " 'With A Publick Spirit': Community and Commitment in New England, 1630–1689".

34 Sarah Augusta Morgan Smith, " 'With A Publick Spirit': Community and Commitment in New England, 1630–1689".

35 Ralph H. Clover, "The Rule of Law in Colonial Massachusetts," 108(7) *U. Pa. L. Rev.* 1001–1036 (May 1960). (Their ultimate commitment to the rule of law was itself a reflection of New Englanders' commitment to the moral equality of persons: the magistrates were presumed to be equally subject to the laws they enacted and enforced, and were prohibited from exercising unlimited discretionary power over the people whom they governed).

36 Sarah Augusta Morgan Smith, " 'With A Publick Spirit': Community and Commitment in New England, 1630–1689".

37 Sarah Augusta Morgan Smith, " 'With A Publick Spirit': Community and Commitment in New England, 1630–1689".

38 Sarah Augusta Morgan Smith, " 'With A Publick Spirit': Community and Commitment in New England, 1630–1689".

39 Joseph Watras, "Education and Evangelism in the English Colonies," 14 *American Ed. Hist. J.* 205 (2008). And, as it happens, the school was the weakest of the triumvirate. The families—for whom children would mostly apprentice and where whom most would spend their time—were clearly the strongest educational presence, followed by the churches—ever-empowered with the role of providing full religious literacy to those who gathered for services.

40 Sarah Augusta Morgan Smith, " 'With A Publick Spirit': Community and Commitment in New England, 1630–1689". *See e.g.*, Richard Mather's *Farewell Exhortation* (Cambridge, MA: Printed by Samuel Green at Cambridge in New-England) (1657) (arguing that everyone—including women, who were often "more with [their] children" than men—set themselves to the task of "teaching them [their children] as soon as ever they are capable of learning.")

41 John D. Burton, "Philanthropy and the Origins of Educational Cooperation: Harvard College, the Hopkins Trust, and the Cambridge Grammar School," 37 *Hist. Educ. Quart.* 141 (1997).

42 With this said, the colonist and newly forming "town" governments, or the representatives of a group of people who had associated themselves for political or religious purposes in order to satisfy their needs, oft had a tumultuous relationship. Through taxation—at first via voluntary levies and later through formal taxation—and activity, towns became formidable and prevalent entities in their own right, at once a vehicle of community action and organizational apparatus for community care. To the townsmen, "town government—the political establishment of town meeting and selectmen—was an arbiter regularizing his relations with his fellows in the community." And, by 1642, by the time of the first educational ordinance, 21 towns had been founded in Massachusetts. For a full bibliography on the town development and taxation, *see* Carl Bridenbaugh, "The New England Town: A Way of Life," 56 *Journal of the American Antiquarian Society* 19–48 (1946); Darrett R. Rutman, "The Well Ordering of the Town," in *Winthrop's Boston*: *A Portrait of a Puritan Town, 1630–1649* (Chapel Hill: UNC Press, 1965); Robert Francis Seybolt, *The Public Schools of Colonial Boston*, 1635–1775 (Cambridge: Harvard University Press, 1935); *see also*, Marcus W. Jernegan, "The Beginnings of Public Education in New England," 23 *The School Rev.* 326 (1915) ("In 1638, [the State] ordered that every inhabitant ought to be liable to contribute to all charges both in church and commonwealth, 'whereof he doth or may receive a benefit'").

43 Marcus W. Jernegan, "The Beginnings of Public Education in New England," 23 *The School Rev.* 326 (1915). *See* Walter Small, "The New England Grammar School," 10 *Sch. Rev.* 319–330 (1902) (Boston Latin School (1635), and schools in Charlestown (1636), Cambridge (1640), Salem (1637), Dorchester (1639), Roxbury (1645), Braintree (1646)). The 1630s saw only a few formal schools develop that could feed into the newly established Harvard College. In other words, there existed a narrow field of opportunity for students to develop the skills they needed to become clergymen and replace an ever-aging leadership. Simultaneously, Harvard College's admission requirements were rigorous:

> when any scholar is able to read Tully or such classical author, *extempore*, and speak true Latin in verse and prose, and decline perfectly the paradigms of nouns and verbs in the Greek tongue, then they may be admitted into college, nor shall any claim admission before such qualification.

44 At least when it came to prospects for the ministry, by the age of seven or eight, a child—through a combination of family, church, and perhaps some school learning—was expected to have mastered English sufficiently to read a passage from the Bible containing three-syllable words, learnt his catechism, and absorbed some of the self-discipline and awareness of sin that characterized a good Puritan. *See* Lawrence Cremin*, American Education: The Colonial Experience 1607–1783* (New York, Evanston, and London: Harper & Row, 1970), 169. Furthermore, by 1642, the Puritan leaders had begun enforcing the *Massachusetts Bay School Law of 1642* which *required* parents to teach their children how to read and write. This, however, still met with little effectiveness.

45 *New England's First Fruits* (1643)
46 Sarah Augusta Morgan Smith, " 'With A Publick Spirit': Community and Commitment in New England, 1630–1689".
47 Sarah Augusta Morgan Smith, " 'With A Publick Spirit': Community and Commitment in New England, 1630–1689".
48 Sarah Augusta Morgan Smith, " 'With A Publick Spirit': Community and Commitment in New England, 1630–1689".
49 Sarah Augusta Morgan Smith, " 'With A Publick Spirit': Community and Commitment in New England, 1630–1689".
50 *The Old Deluder Satan Law of 1647*, The Laws and Liberties of Massachusetts, Reprinted from the Copy of the 1648 Edition, Harvard University Press, 1929.
51 *The Old Deluder Satan Law of 1647*, The Laws and Liberties of Massachusetts, Reprinted from the Copy of the 1648 Edition, Harvard University Press, 1929.
52 *The Old Deluder Satan Law of 1647*, The Laws and Liberties of Massachusetts, Reprinted from the Copy of the 1648 Edition, Harvard University Press, 1929. (the penalty was 5 pounds).
53 Robert Middlekauf, "Education in Colonial America," 41 *Curr. Hist.* 5–8 (1961).
54 James Stillwaggonn, "The Old Deluder, Educational Salvation, and the Limits of Distributive Justice,"10 *Policy Futures Educ.* 352 (2012).
55 The conflation of social thriving and threat—in this case religious—would become a model for educational laws concerning public schools moving forward. Both Horace Mann and Thomas Jefferson evoked threats in speaking about the priority of education. James Stillwaggonn, "The Old Deluder, Educational Salvation, and the Limits of Distributive Justice,"10 *Policy Futures Educ.* 352 (2012).
56 James Stillwaggonn, "The Old Deluder, Educational Salvation, and the Limits of Distributive Justice,"10 *Policy Futures Educ.* 352 (2012). Now, while the initial reception of the law was one of ambivalence, and the development of schools did *not* exponentially uptick because of its passage, there is nothing to suggest the Puritan's disagreed with this burgeoning mentality. Indeed, so many other immediate threats, including incursions of native tribes, harsh winters, and little in the community chest, might have played a role in the slow-start to public education.
57 *See* Darrett R. Rutman, "The Well Ordering of the Town," in *Winthrop's Boston: A Portrait of a Puritan Town, 1630–1649* (1965).
58 For a more extensive history, *see* Marcus W. Jernegan, "The Beginnings of Public Education in New England," 23 *The School Rev.* 327 (1915).
59 Jon Teaford, "The Transformation of Massachusetts Education," 10 *Hist. Educ. Quart.* No. 287, 290 (1970).
60 Jon Teaford, "The Transformation of Massachusetts Education," 10 *Hist. Educ. Quart.* No. 287, 290 (1970)
61 Sarah Augusta Morgan Smith, "'With A Publick Spirit': Community and Commitment in New England, 1630–1689". Showing this also in the context of catechesis in New England.
62 Sarah Augusta Morgan Smith, "'With A Publick Spirit': Community and Commitment in New England, 1630–1689".
63 Sarah Augusta Morgan Smith, "'With A Publick Spirit': Community and Commitment in New England, 1630–1689".

64 Sarah Augusta Morgan Smith, "'With A Publick Spirit': Community and Commitment in New England, 1630–1689".
65 Andrew Forsyth, "Puritan Natural Law," in *Natural Law and Common Law in America* (Cambridge: Cambridge University Press, 2019), at 7.
66 Andrew Forsyth, "Puritan Natural Law," in *Natural Law and Common Law in America* (Cambridge: Cambridge University Press, 2019), 8.
67 *A Survey of the Summe of Church-Discipline, Part I: Ecclesiastical Policie Defined* (London: Printed by A. M. for John Bellamy, 1648), 44.
68 Andrew Forsyth, "Puritan Natural Law," in *Natural Law and Common Law in America* (Cambridge: Cambridge University Press, 2019), 7.
69 John D. Burton, "Philanthropy and the Origins of Educational Cooperation: Harvard College, the Hopkins Trust, and the Cambridge Grammar School," 37 *Hist. Educ. Quart.* 141 (1997).
70 John D. Burton, "Philanthropy and the Origins of Educational Cooperation: Harvard College, the Hopkins Trust, and the Cambridge Grammar School," 37 *Hist. Educ. Quart.* 141 (1997).
71 For theological reasons—their belief in the 5 *solas*, *sola scriptura* specifically predicated on an ability access the message of the Bible to fortify one's deeds, combined with Martin Luther's two kingdoms framework—couched in secular social justice objectives—chief among them an interest in offering accessible education to all classes—reformers advocated for social change on systemic and individual levels. Focusing on the systemic rather than the individual level, schooling reform in the 1520s was grounded in Luther's theological doctrine of the two kingdoms. Education, ever essential to the maintenance and ordering in both the heavenly *and* earthly realms, assured the preservation of the Gospel, the spiritual flourishing of *each* of the Christian faithful, the development of the next generation of religious thinkers, and community cohesiveness. In Luther's words, the "best and greatest welfare, safety and strength lies not in the wealth of arms and allies," but "rather in its having many able, learned, wise, honorable and well-educated citizens." Newly empowered with knowledge, *the common people* on this earth can then "reliably gather, protect, and properly use treasure and all manner of property." To this end, Luther and his contemporaries called for a moral and intellectual rebuilding of the populace, stressing devotion and discipline to *both* spiritual and material goals, an education that prized and empowered the day-laborer as much as the priest. At once, Luther arguments mobilize ideas of equality, individualism, and self-reliance—and crafts a system that prizes these values—in a way never before seen but remains relevant today.
72 John Morgan, *Godly Learning: Puritan Attitudes towards Reason, Learning and Education, 1560–1640* (New York: Cambridge University Press, 1986).
73 Sarah Augusta Morgan Smith, "'With A Publick Spirit': Community and Commitment in New England, 1630–1689". Showing this also in the context of catechesis in New England. In these settings, attended by both men and women, women served as lay leaders and teachers; as such, female literacy and learning were not only personal but social, or community, goods. David R. Como, "Women, Prophecy, and Authority in Early Stuart Puritanism," 61 *Huntington Libr. Quart.* No. 2, 203–222 (1998). See also Kenneth Charlton, Chapter 6, "Women as Agents," in *Women, Religion and Education in Early Modern England* (Routledge, 1999), 154–187.
74 Sarah Augusta Morgan Smith, "'With A Publick Spirit': Community and Commitment in New England, 1630 1689".

75 See E. Jennifer Monaghan, "Literacy Instruction and Gender in Colonial New England," 40 *Am. Quart.* 18–41 (1988).

76 E. Jennifer Monaghan, "Literacy Instruction and Gender in Colonial New England," 40 *Am. Quart.* 18–41 (1988).

77 For a full bibliography on this, *see* Charles L. Glenn, *The Myth of the Common School* (Amherst: University of Massachusetts Press, 1988); Carl F. Kaestle, *Pillars of the Republic: Common Schools and American Society, 1780–1860* (New York: Hill and Wang 1983).

78 *See* Rosemary Salomone, "Common Schools, Uncommon Values: Listening to the Voices of Dissent," 14 *Yale L. Policy Rev.* 169 (1996).

79 Rosemary Salomone, "Common Schools, Uncommon Values: Listening to the Voices of Dissent," 14 *Yale L. Policy Rev.* 169 (1996).

80 Rosemary Salomone, "Common Schools, Uncommon Values: Listening to the Voices of Dissent," 14 *Yale L. Policy Rev.* 169 (1996).

81 Rosemary Salomone, "Common Schools, Uncommon Values: Listening to the Voices of Dissent," 14 *Yale L. Policy Rev.* 169 (1996). As Mary Mann wrote, "Common and equal opportunities of education for all was the primitive idea of those men who had been so signally made to feel how unequally human rights were shared."

82 Rosemary Salomone, "Common Schools, Uncommon Values: Listening to the Voices of Dissent," 14 *Yale L. Policy Rev.* 169 (1996).

83 Rosemary Salomone, "Common Schools, Uncommon Values: Listening to the Voices of Dissent," 14 *Yale L. Policy Rev.* 169 (1996).

84 Mann, Twelfth Annual Report (1848).

> The reformers understood well the political limits of transposing any form of standardization or state-imposed ideology onto the individualistic American culture. And so they attempted to strike a tolerable balance between individual and collective goals while meeting their own nationalistic objectives. State government would maintain final authority over education by providing minimum standards and assuring equal educational opportunity.

Rosemary Salomone, "Common Schools, Uncommon Values: Listening to the Voices of Dissent," 14 *Yale L. Policy Rev.* 169 (1996).

85 Mann, Twelfth Annual Report (1848). Rosemary Salomone, "Common Schools, Uncommon Values: Listening to the Voices of Dissent," 14 *Yale L. Policy Rev.* 169 (1996).

86 Michael McConnel, "Multiculturalism, Majoritarianism, and Educational Choice: What Does Our Constitutional Tradition Have to Say?" *University of Chicago Legal Forum* 134 (1991).

87 These readings, as opposed to the Catholic practice of looking to the church to understand moral views, relied on individual interpretation. It is also important to note that, given Mann's emphasis on "cultural assimilation and a state-controlled centralized authority," Mann's common school system "made no room for the input or involvement of parents." His vision of a universal system of education, implicitly religious though it was, made the state the primary agent in "shaping the character of the American people." *See* Sacha M. Coupet, "Valuing All Identities beyond the Schoolhouse Gate," *Loyola University of Chicago* 17 (2020).

88 Michael McConnel, "Multiculturalism, Majoritarianism, and Educational Choice: What Does Our Constitutional Tradition Have to Say?," 123 *U. Chi. Legal F.* 134 (1991). "Education was inseparable from religion, and where there was diversity in religion it was difficult to achieve consensus regarding education." This manifested in problem on administrative, financial and pedagogical levels.

89 Michael McConnel, "Multiculturalism, Majoritarianism, and Educational Choice: What Does Our Constitutional Tradition Have to Say?," 123 *U. Chi. Legal F.* 134 (1991).

90 Barbara Finkelstein, "Exploring Community in Urban Educational History Cities: Consensus and Conflict in American Educational History," 309 (Donald & Diane Ravitch eds., 1983).

91 *See* Rosemary Salomone, "Common Schools, Uncommon Values: Listening to the Voices of Dissent," 14 *Yale L. Policy Rev.* 169 (1996); Michael McConnel, "Multiculturalism, Majoritarianism, and Educational Choice: What Does Our Constitutional Tradition Have to Say?," 123 *U. Chi. Legal F.* 134 (1991) ("But while the common school reformers imbued their systems with religious exercises, they were equally insistent that these exercises be "nonsectarian."

> In practice, this meant that the common schools would teach those tenets of Protestant Christianity that were most widely shared and exclude those doctrines about which there was serious disagreement. The result was a watered-down piety closely resembling liberal Protestantism..

92 *See* Rosemary Salomone, "Common Schools, Uncommon Values: Listening to the Voices of Dissent," 14 *Yale L. Policy Rev.* 169 (1996).

93 Michael McConnel, "Multiculturalism, Majoritarianism, and Educational Choice: What Does Our Constitutional Tradition Have to Say?," 123 *U. Chi. Legal F.* 134 (1991).

94 Michael McConnel, "Multiculturalism, Majoritarianism, and Educational Choice: What Does Our Constitutional Tradition Have to Say?," 123 *U. Chi. Legal F.* 134 (1991).

95 His underlying assumption was problematic even in this: he believed there *was* a single "American" culture, and this culture was religiously valued, into which all citizens should be assimilated. Michael McConnel, "Multiculturalism, Majoritarianism, and Educational Choice: What Does Our Constitutional Tradition Have to Say?," 123 *U. Chi. Legal F.* 134 (1991). ("The common school movement was explicitly anti-multicultural, with respect to both culture in general and religion. One opponent of funding of parochial schools testified that "the task of absorbing and Americanizing these foreign masses... can only be successfully overcome by a uniform system of American schools, teaching the same political creed" and assured the Congress that this uniform system would "continue us" as "a united, homogeneous people.")

96 Robert Michaelson, *Piety in the Public School* (New York: Macmillan, 1970), page 87.

97 Toni Marie Massaro, *Constitutional Literacy: A Core Cirriculum for a Multicultural Nation* (Durham: Duke University Press, 1993), 25–26.

98 Diane Ravitch, *The Schools We Deserve: Reflections on the Educational Crises of Our Times* (New York: Basic Books, 1985), 82–83.

99 Diane Ravitch, *The Schools We Deserve: Reflections on the Educational Crises of Our Times* (New York: Basic Books, 1985), 82–83.

100 Rosemary Salomone, "Common Schools, Uncommon Values: Listening to the Voices of Dissent," 14 *Yale L. Policy Rev.* 169 (1996).

101 Rosemary Salomone, "Common Schools, Uncommon Values: Listening to the Voices of Dissent," 14 *Yale L. Policy Rev.* 169 (1996).

102 To this, of course, many offer answers and many arguments take place. Some argue, as Nussbaum, that we offer more a "mutli-cultural approach" to values-learning. Others are against any values taught in school at all. This gives rise, as well to debates about parental choice and control. As McConnel writes,

> when we formed a nation out of a continent of diverse cultures and peoples, when we guaranteed diversity and freedom of belief, we committed ourselves to a multi-cultural polity. The competing civic republican ideal is not practicable in a nation of this sort. It will either impose a single moral-cultural vision at the expense of the minorities, or no moral-cultural vision at all (if such a thing is possible), at the expense of coherence and value.
>
> (Michael McConnel, "Multiculturalism, Majoritarianism, and Educational Choice: What Does Our Constitutional Tradition Have to Say?," 123 *U. Chi. Legal F.* 151 (1991))

103 Michael McConnel, "Multiculturalism, Majoritarianism, and Educational Choice: What Does Our Constitutional Tradition Have to Say?," 123 *U. Chi. Legal F.* 134 (1991).

104 Michael McConnel, "Multiculturalism, Majoritarianism, and Educational Choice: What Does Our Constitutional Tradition Have to Say?," 123 *U. Chi. Legal F.* 134 (1991).

105 Michael McConnel, "Multiculturalism, Majoritarianism, and Educational Choice: What Does Our Constitutional Tradition Have to Say?," 123 *U. Chi. Legal F.* 134 1991).

106 Michael McConnel, "Multiculturalism, Majoritarianism, and Educational Choice: What Does Our Constitutional Tradition Have to Say?," 123 *U. Chi. Legal F.* 134 (1991).

107 Rosemary Salomone, "Common Schools, Uncommon Values: Listening to the Voices of Dissent," 14 *Yale L. Policy Rev.* 169 (1996).

> As a result, there is an anti-discrimination principle within equality that transcends culture. Nevertheless, despite the consensus that individuals should treat other individuals with equal dignity and respect, there is less agreement as to the degree to which equal treatment should be required and enforced as a matter of law, and whether the government should take affirmative steps to achieve substantive, and not just formal, equality for certain groups in society.

Part II

A New Proposal

In a recent piece that drew attention to the issues arising concerning civics in the United States, Richard Haass, President of the Council on Foreign Relations, proposed that "no people should assume their history, their heritage, and what is central to it."[1] Indeed, "collective identity, along with an appreciation and understanding of what lies behind it, is a matter of teaching, not biology."[2] My proposal, in many ways, is about the task of acculturating "collective identity," what we as citizens, and as a nation, value and expect of ourselves."[3] There are many such values and expectations, as I will discuss below. We expect, for example, all our citizens to be able to appreciate and mobilize resources in the form of institutions, opportunities, and ideas. We expect familiarity with the "central elements of [our] tradition."[4] And we expect obedience to the law as much as criticism and outspokenness. Schools and States, however, do not agree amongst themselves on how to teach these things or even that they ought to be taught; again, only a handful of states and the District of Columbia require a full year of civic education; 31 states require but half a year; 10 states have no requirement.[5] Haass notes that this unhinges our collective identity; "one third [of citizens] believe violent action against the government is justified," and many simply know nothing of their own political systems.[6]

But I have spoken about this already, concluding (as Haass concludes) that even were civics to be taught more widely, we would not know what to teach "under the banner of civics."[7] Haass proposes that a solid education be provided in government, structure, its operation, different forms of democracies.[8] It ought to expose students to canonical "American" texts, and include basics about American economy, society, and its evolution. And, furthermore, civic education ought to emphasize "the need for civility, the importance of compromise, the centrality of facts and where to find them"—the *behaviors* required in democracy.[9] In terms of history, a successful civics course might promise the following:

DOI: 10.4324/9781003596523-6

> major debates, events, and development be studied, that any single framing be avoided, and where there is disagreement, that the various perspectives be presented. One possibility is for students to be assigned a range of readings and then asked to debate competing interpretations in the past.[10]

While, in the short term, "any single national curriculum would surely fail,"[11] it is a need of the most urgent and critical vein.

While certainly the contemporary civics landscape is one of impotent standardization with unclear objectives unmoored from a unifying purpose, I disagree that a national solution is unrealizable or that we are unable to conceive of a uniform substance to such an education. To teach law to elementary and secondary school students as a form of a civics, not as a matter of professional education, but as a theoretical education, enriches the minds and builds toward collective identity. As we shall see, law touches every citizen, reflects key values, is built on facts and responses to real situations, and, when conceived as robustly as I do below, provides an essential education regardless of a citizen's background, beliefs, or political persuasions. Bearing in mind our goal for education—itself not quite new, but unearthed and harkening back to the colonial period's initial public education enterprise toward a "priesthood of all believers"—"school for the purpose of empowering the citizen"—such an education promises to be a uniquely potent means of achieving the re-envisioned schooling objective.

Notes

1 Richard Haass, *The Bill of Obligations: The Ten Habits of Good Citizens* (New York: Penguin Press, 2023), 135.

2 Richard Haass, *The Bill of Obligations: The Ten Habits of Good Citizens* (New York: Penguin Press, 2023), 135. He quotes, as well, Ronald Reagan in a speech about "new patriotism" saying

> this national feeling is good, but it won't count for much, and it won't last unless it's grounded in thoughtfulness and knowledge. An informed patriotism is what we want. And are we doing a good enough job teaching our children what America is and what she represents in the long history of the world?

3 Richard Haass, *The Bill of Obligations: The Ten Habits of Good Citizens* (New York: Penguin Press, 2023), 135.

4 Richard Haass, *The Bill of Obligations: The Ten Habits of Good Citizens* (New York: Penguin Press, 2023), 135.

5 Richard Haass, *The Bill of Obligations: The Ten Habits of Good Citizens* (New York: Penguin Press, 2023), 135.

6 Richard Haass, *The Bill of Obligations: The Ten Habits of Good Citizens* (New York: Penguin Press, 2023), 135.

7 Richard Haass, *The Bill of Obligations: The Ten Habits of Good Citizens* (New York: Penguin Press, 2023), 135.

8 Richard Haass, *The Bill of Obligations: The Ten Habits of Good Citizens* (New York: Penguin Press, 2023), 135.
9 Richard Haass, *The Bill of Obligations: The Ten Habits of Good Citizens* (New York: Penguin Press, 2023), 135.
10 Richard Haass, *The Bill of Obligations: The Ten Habits of Good Citizens* (New York: Penguin Press, 2023), 135.
11 Haas alludes as well to the Civics Secures Democracy Act of 2021, which explicitly states that "nothing in this act shall be construed to authorize the Secretary of Education to prescribe a civics and history curriculum," as a means of showing the futility of a national paradigm.

4 An Empowering Civic Education through Law Learning

At first blush, the notion of teaching something as complicated as law learning to primary and secondary school students may seem far-fetched. To be sure, I am not proposing to enroll 12-year-olds in intensive substantive criminal procedure and trial techniques classes. The vision I maintain for the citizen—congruent with Nussbaum—is not outcome-oriented, i.e., to create a nation of lawyers (heaven-forbid!), but rather the manipulation of an augmented legal education to build *capacity and capability* to think and hold a sophisticated conversation, understand systems and involve themselves in the national community and national challenges. And, congruent with Dewey and Kohlberg, learning law is an ethical education, instilling values we would identify with American citizenship (enshrined in the legal codes and common law) *while also* being values-plural in posture and approach, an education complementary to values learned through the family or faith community. The objective of the sections below is to defend each of these positions and build out a case for law as an empowering civics education.

This proposal is unique from other law learning models that teach citizens technical laws, means of exercising rights, or the ability to discern when a law is applicable in this or that case.[1] Law learning is born out of the conception that law offers students a set of skills (mental and practical) or *tools in one's toolbox* (namely, legal reasoning or *law-think* and facility with political institutions) that can elevate the way one goes about their role as citizen. The theory of law learning proposes that students should be exposed to the "idea of law and the American system" early on, and teachers should provide the means to engage with the law's problems, challenges, values, and premises. In this way, students might then go on to be social revolutionaries, idealogues, lawyers, activists ... or none of those things; law learning is *empowering* not for the roles it necessarily opens for students, but for the common rhetoric it facilitates in all citizens, the common understanding, the common *capabilities*, the common appreciations of our institutions that provide a baseline for citizens to flourish or act—if they want to do so—in America's political milieu.[2] What I am concerned with here, indeed, is cultivating higher reasoning skills and substantive systems-awareness necessary for *all* citizens.

DOI: 10.4324/9781003596523-7

It should come as no surprise that teaching law—a subject that features a plethora of desirable learning outcomes and is itself a dynamic force—in childhood education is no novel concept. But, of course, it is not always done in a constructive way.[3] Hong Kong is one example where, in 2001, they announced a change to their national civics education which incorporated the act of learning their Constitution, the Basic law, national security education. This was then complimented with a moral and ethical education. Born out of a familiar concern that the younger generation's "passive attitudes" might "undermine society's development in the long term," their "Values and Education Curriculum Framework" was designed to "cultivate national pride and empower citizens to participate in civic functions diligently and effectively."[4] It is a similar objective to the one I propose here, yet Hong Kong's approach has one fundamental distinction: the government de-emphasized the cultivation of critical thinking skills,[5] mobilizing law learning to set "standards behind which people judge right and wrong, their decisions, behavior, and attitudes."[6] Students ideally would then take greater care to weigh their opposition to this or that policy against the "country's welfare and the values held by society."[7]

This is *not* our project of learning law for the purposes of this manuscript. To learn law in this context, and what the above example serves to distinguish, is *not* to confer standards, and values or to indoctrinate. Rather, the act of learning law must teach students the opposite: *how* to ask questions, *how* to think about values and rights, and *how* to form informed opinions. My position is that this new curriculum will help deconstruct large and daunting institutions and institutional ideals for students—ideals now explored only descriptively—so that the American system can become more accessible to younger students, and the propensity for creative innovation more familiar.

Having put forth this foundation, the rest of this chapter sets out to establish how exactly the process of introducing students to law problems and questions yields such an empowering education. I divide the matter into three sections. The first (Section 4.1) explores the transformative aspect of education in law by way of discussing the acquisition of *law-think* and legal reasoning skills in the law school classroom. On a practical level, this proposal expects two things of students and civics classrooms. First, methodologically, civics instruction must encourage (and develop the skills for) students to practice *law-think*—to "[nurture] reflexes that support [one] when faced with questions and issues, regardless of the subject matter … [empowering one to impose] order and structure on [one's] thoughts and ideas."[8] Second, substantively, civic instruction encourages students to study (albeit on a simplified level) law—in the form of federal and state constitutional provisions; statutes; administrative rules; and common law judicial precedent—in areas relevant to the citizen, including but not limited to laws of contract, juvenile court, property, family welfare, business, taxation, evidence, equity, judicial procedure, law reform and criminal law,[9]—and, by extension, the sort of ideas that law is predicated upon: among them, weighing values, competing interests, working with constituencies, and defending policies. The value of this type of education is best seen, indeed *only* seen, in action in the law school classroom. Looking at the law school classroom is therefore helpful in showing how learning law earlier develops skills and perspectives essential to the budding American citizen, not just to the budding lawyer. We will see *why* law students have hailed *law-think* as a transformative tool for all professional and even personal challenges they might go on to face.

After this, I will endeavor to explore the notion of *law-think* or legal reasoning more generally and conceive of the skills and ideas a younger citizen non-lawyer would gain from an education in law. This will be done in two parts (Sections 4.2 and 4.3). First, I want to examine how this empowering education strengthens students' abilities to conduct themselves in external interactions (*combatting complacency; intrinsic motivation; the conception of themselves in relation to authority*). Implicit in this, as well, is a conversation about capabilities and practical tools that ought to be at the disposal of American citizens for them to lead meaningful political and social lives. And secondly, I want to reflect on how an education in law, in terms of its delivery and its substance, might push the student to reflect on internal self-identity, the cultivation of universal values that are deemed part and parcel of our national system, and, even more importantly, the discipline's prioritization of a plural posture to values which allows for the *reinforcement of privately held values*,[10] as well as the maintenance of classrooms that prize diversity, dialogue, and difference.[11]

4.1 The Empowering Training of Law-Think: Learning from the Law School Student Experience

When the wide-eyed prospective 1L joins her classmates for her first day of law school, she likely comes to the bustling community of aspiring change-makers knowing no law. She knows no substantive contract law, property law, or criminal law. Any factual knowledge she would have acquired up to that point—be it elementary math, middle school science, high school calculus, or college-level American history—would be of relatively little use to her as she wades into the judicial opinions and legal ideas of the first-year law school curriculum.[12] What *may* be of use to her are the methodological skills she has acquired because of her substantive learning up until that point—the critical reading skills she honed as a literature major in college, the analytical skills required to ace calculus. These skills are transferrable *tools in her toolbox*, and they have little to do with the substantive facts or figures or topics that originally prompted their acquisition. As Graham Ferris points out, even at this early point, the law is especially suitable indeed from a Capabilities Approach perspective as it

> starts from the qualities and needs and abilities of the learner. The aim is to enhance the situation of each learner by creating new capabilities or

> enhancing existing ones. What the learner does with these capabilities is not the business of the educator.[13]

Law—when conceived of as a liberal education as much as (if not more than) a professional education[14]—"serves the student, and aims at the welfare of the student, and [does so] by supporting student autonomy and the student's capacity for effective self-authorship."[15] Law is, as we shall see, can be a critical education that shifts and transforms perspectives.[16]

As our student progresses through her years in law school, her learning focuses on this, cultivating tools in her toolbox, skill sets over substance. As 1L turns to 3L, the student will learn more than *what* the law is, but also *law as a methodology*, law-think, or, as the proverbial adage goes, *how to think like a lawyer*.[17] As Bethany Henderson puts it:

> [t]hinking like a lawyer means developing and honing analytical skills—a set of intellectual habits. It means nurturing reflexes that support you when faced with questions and issues, regardless of the subject matter. And it means imposing order and structure on your thoughts and ideas—figuring out how to convey them in the clearest, most precise, and most powerful way possible.[18]

The way in which this process of cultivating *law-think* takes place depends, to some extent, on the way in which educators go about teaching their legal subjects. A discussion on *law-think* education's transformative nature, therefore, is best achieved by way of diving into examples of the jurisprudential slants teachers confer onto their discussions of cases, precedent, and laws—*how they read discrete legal issues as representations of the larger system*—to examine why they are effective in cultivating for students a nuanced perception of our legal system *and* building *law-think* skills. I will offer two examples, a moral pedagogy of law and a critical pedagogy of law, of such approaches and the manner in which they uniquely develop *law-think* skills. In both, we will see dissent, criticism, and examination infuse themselves in all aspects of law classroom pedagogy so as to become, using Nussbaum's language, even law school experience's "entire ethos."[19] To learn law is to be invited to critically explore values in tension, complex policies, questions, and ideas—the very same things that underlay the causes that affect all citizens, that many seek to change today, and that civics education, purportedly, ought to teach students. By exploring the way in which an education in law-think is delivered, we can thus see the way in which the student's mind is transformed to conceive of issues differently and place awareness differently.

There is a reason that over half of our previous presidents had passed the bar before assuming office, and this same reason counsels in favor of inviting civics students to learn law! The way in which the law student is taught to deconstruct ideas through common texts and precedents, build impressions of systems, and intimately study the values being balance therein, is a universally marvelous education that ought to be more widely accessible.

4.1.1 Law-Think Developed through Moral Teaching

Let us consider, first, how one learns law-think from a teacher who espouses a moral-centered view of the law and law teaching.

Historically, legal education "rests on a fundamental belief in the separation of law and morality."[20] Christopher Columbus Langdell, a thought-leader behind modern legal education, stressed that legal reasoning was a "deductive process by which one derived right and wrong answers from principles inherent in the opinions of appellate judges."[21] The legal mind, commensurately, is rational, analytical, logical, and dispassionate. Grounded in the "pragmatism of problem solving," "legal education becomes a form of discrimination, of selection, of seeing and valuing facts that count toward a decision."[22] While there are many benefits gained from a razor-focused disposition and eagerness to take apart cases for technical solutions, there are also obvious drawbacks.[23] Indeed, it was Oliver Wendell Holmes, though a legal realist in his own right, who argued that the teacher—departing from Langdell's the scientific view—ought to instruct students in law "in the grand manner," which intimates that legal education has a dimension beyond the substantive, beyond technical answers.[24]

A pedagogy that stresses learning law in the context of fairness, justice, and morality asks students to consider more than "what the law says," but judge the law's *rightness* in terms of its institutional impact on vision and values.[25] In other words, to see the "rule of law" as separate from given positive laws. One considers "constantly the normative bases for individual, corporate, and governmental responsibilities"[26] as well as the power-dynamics inherent in the resolution of disputes. What are the moral obligations of the legal actors? The role of the lawyer in serving as a positive force within the system?[27] And how ought we weigh disparate case outcomes on the basis of fairness and consistency with notions of justice?[28] By adopting the disposition that "the law expresses values which require both affirmation and critical scrutiny,"[29] the instructor invites students to simultaneously learn law, learn a value-set, and also to "see how their experience affects their values, and how these values effect their assessment of the law."[30]

What sort of value-set is important for the budding lawyer? The benefit of a moral legal education is made manifest when a young lawyer goes out and *does right* by the client, "doing what is a proper, not only what is legal."[31] Thinkers who argue in favor of infusing morality in legal education argue that injustice "depends on people's inability to examine how their own values may reinforce dominance," or in misapprehending the weighty role that any one individual actor can play in the judicial and legal process.[32] These values are the strength of the lawyer. Through the study of opinions, legislation, statutes, and administrative orders, the lawyer builds more than any subjective opinion on a given constitutional issue, but an appreciation for how this or that case fits into "a normative morality of higher principles."[33] In other words, the teacher instructs the student in how the law is founded on notions of "human dignity, human aspiration, procedural fairness, due process, equal treatment, [and] fundamental human rights."[34] In turn, the law student works to perpetuate these values—to *do right*, to abide by the moral obligation and responsibility to act toward these systemic aims, the common good, and common goals.[35]

The teacher wishing to impart such wisdom—or, more aptly, to engage the student in reflecting on their own personal perspectives—will not only communicate expert knowledge and judgment, but rather identify "where the profession puts its defining values and exemplars on display, [such that] future practitioners can begin both to assume and critically examine their future identities."[36] "Professional identity cannot be imposed nor is it forced upon unwilling candidates."[37] Ultimately, the goal of such a formative education must enable students to become self- reflective about and self-directing in their own development [as professionals.][38]

Understanding one's moral obligations within the system also has a very tangible practical dimension in terms of the conferral of skills. If one is conscientious of their moral direction as a lawyer and views the system as also working toward complimentary normative goals, the lawyer gains an ability to tap into a sense of community morality—the bounds of *right* and *wrong* in the system, a clear view of institutional values. Having a pulse on this can help one predict tomorrow's positive law, anticipate injustice, and forge policy in a way consistent with these values.[39] *Law-think* education, in other words, when delivered through a moral lens, cultivates in students a compass such that "personal convictions have become the most reliable guide [to] institutional morality."[40]

In addition to acquiring a sense of community morality, there are two other very notable results produced by this approach to learning law.[41] The first is that students—future reformers—become conditioned *to believe in the integrity of the law*.[42] While one may dispute the inherent corruption of institutions, the inequity of policy, or disagree with this or that law, their urge to reform *starts at a place of hope* that the system is good rather than a place of disillusionment manifested in a desire to abolish institutions or systemically disengage entirely.[43] The lawyer—the beneficiary of a bastion of knowledge of institutional values and the constant tension of ideals manifesting as law—even when reforming hold steadfast to the hope that there are good actors, good institutions trying to do the right thing.[44]

The second result is—perhaps surprisingly—*law obedience*. In appreciating the system as a reflection of higher normative principles, and acknowledging the prevalent balance between the ideals present in the law, the lawyer is more likely to obey discrete positive rules even when they disagree with them for no other reason than an understanding that the law generally promotes order, fairness, and democracy.[45] To follow the law is to preserve order and confer necessary legitimacy upon the system.[46] As Thomas Aquinas remarked, the need to obey what one considers an "unjust" law "is not based on the good of being law-abiding, but only on the desirability of not rendering ineffective the just parts of the legal system."[47] A legal education endows a perpetual appreciation for the multi-layered nature of the system and the competing interests of laws and policy.

Importantly, however, this is not to say that the lawyer *must* acquiesce to *all* positive laws *always*. Lawyers, like all citizens, can evaluate the inherent injustice of a law and commensurately practice all manner of civil and private disobedience in contexts where a moral obligation seems to supersede any duty to obey the law. Indeed, a legal education endows them with an even greater capacity for doing so, as well as a commensurately higher standard by which to judge injustice.[48] John Rawls contended that, in all cases, civil disobedience should be limited to "instances of substantial and clear injustice," where "normal appeals to the political majority have already been made in good faith and [have] failed," and the dissenter has already considered it "wise and prudent" based on the circumstances.[49] However, the lawyer, trained on the distinction between the "rule of law" and the positive law at issue, has an ever greater "duty of caution in evaluating each of these steps."[50] A legal education empowers one to reflect deeply on the very basis for an injustice and its bearing on the larger system, and, in the event of a need to respond, do so by informed, efficient and legitimate means. In other words, an education in the "rule of law" translates to tempered responses; painstakingly considered circumstances, and informed judgments about policy. Are these not helpful to the non-lawyer civics students as well?

4.1.2 A Different Approach: Law-Think By Way of a Critical Legal Studies Lens

Moving away from a moral pedagogy of law, teachers mobilizing lenses from "new legal realism" and "critical legal studies" ("CLS") offer a more functional and grounded approach to learning law as it impacts real people. Whereas the "rule of law" conversations encountered above persist mostly in the study of doctrine made available through appellate opinion and formalist observations concerning precedents,[51] these approaches—favoring a practical, empirical, interdisciplinary, and socially contextualized approach to law learning[52]—typically find their manifestation in more clinical or experiential settings.

Importantly, however, these jurisprudential lenses can and are applied to the same questions and cases as the morality approach.[53] Indeed, law students will encounter all these jurisprudential approaches in their three years of school; all of these are instrumental in the art of *law-think*.

Pedagogically, the teacher here is concerned with capturing the "area of contact between judicial behavior and the behavior of laymen."[54] The learning experiences are based on a nose-to-ground philosophy that veers away from the "doctrinal education to interdisciplinary education … precisely because the normative expectations for behavior to which courts are quite plainly sensitive are not those captured by [theory alone]."[55] In other words, cases are brought "down to earth," distilled and analyzed according to the idea that law is decided by people with their own biases, prejudices and influences.[56]

"New legal realism," to begin, pushes students to consider law *not* as a siloed "grand discipline" distinct from others, but one highly influenced by other fields, its actors by social and political contexts, its practice by a lawyer's experiences and background. In this way, they become open to realizing the economic, philosophical, and social norms that can influence judicial decision-making, legal systems, and ideas.[57] The pedagogy emphasizes law's impact on those who lack power in society, reducing legal questions to consider their real human impact, and searching for real answers to real issues.[58] This is important, as "students believe what they are told, explicitly and implicitly, about the world they are entering, they behave in ways that fulfill the prophecies the system makes about them and about that world."[59] Thus, by teaching with a mind toward furthering justice, acknowledging privilege, meeting the needs of the vulnerable, and understanding "law, legal culture and legal meaning more broadly, they are effectively cultivating a better, more culturally literate class of lawyer."[60]

Unsurprisingly, therefore, the school of thought is driven by an adherence to evidence-based teaching practices and multiple perspectives, inviting interdisciplinary approaches to law in the interest of the following central objective: showing that the "law's key task is effective translation of the 'human world using legal categories'."[61]

CLS endeavors to go even further in conceiving of the law as an amalgamation of competing policies and real influences that impact decision-making.[62] CLS claims that the legal system has been "socially constructed to reflect prevailing interests of power and domination" and that "the mythology of legal discourse serves to mystify and pacify the oppressed."[63] Therefore, to view "rules as given [as] static, and almost immutable and does not prepare either the social reformer who wants to change the rules or even the traditional lawyer who must anticipate for clients possible changes in the direction of rules."[64] It is the occupation of the student-turned-lawyer to mobilize their empirical skills, as well as their knowledge of the law's influences, to "penetrate the surface of social reality" and expose the actual workings of society, and to deconstruct the status quo by utilizing institutions to re-appropriate power.[65] This is an incredibly empowering model of the lawyer, one in which their knowledge base endows them with the responsibility to effectuate change for all citizens.

Naturally, therefore, the practical learning outcomes conferred by these technical, deconstructive approaches to law learning, somewhat differently from the first value-based approach, are all about individual problem-solving and socialization. The first skill is an ability to *isolate a few different layers and influences for any given issue*. Consider, for instance, the reformer who seeks to advocate for welfare as a tool for helping the impoverished. An education steeped in these jurisprudential lenses obviate dozens of different questions that go into answering this one: does welfare—empirically—help those in poverty or merely perpetuate dependency? If it does, to what extent is that an issue for the State? Do welfare systems contravene countervailing interests of autonomy and liberty? To what extent does public opinion of "dependency" impact our conception of welfare? What political interests are at stake when it comes to the retention or dissolution of welfare programs? Would somebody outside my position think of different answers than I to any of these questions? An appreciation of the dialectic tension between countervailing interests ultimately allows for more comprehensive and creative responses.

More than just *asking* the questions, learning law through a critical lens instructs on *how to navigate* these problems and resolve tensions through analysis, critical thinking, and the coordination of multiple interests and values. As an example, consider Martha Fineman's vulnerability theory project and its applications in all areas of law.[66] Martha Fineman developed an alternative human rights paradigm criticizing the "dominant conception of the universal legal subject as an autonomous, independent adult." By challenging the "myth" of autonomy and acknowledging the universally constant vulnerability of all individuals, she makes an argument for recasting the "welfare" state as a necessarily "responsive" one, de-stigmatizing it as a product of collective responsibility to care for those less resilient than others.[67] She argues that "dependency is universal and inevitable in our individual lives and inherent in the human condition."[68] The fact that some "manifest the realities of dependency" and are stigmatized is abhorrent and indicative of the "self-delusion" of welfare debates. Indeed, "we all live subsidized lives."[69] To wit, Fineman, through legal instrumentation, redefines—and pushes students to reflect on—conceptions of the "legal subject," "the State," "equality," "injury," "responsiveness," "justice," and "civil society" that speak to the universal, constant vulnerability of the human condition.[70] She does this, indeed, in many different areas of law—family law, insurance law, child law, schooling law—in a way that colors the issues and discussions that take place in those fields. Agree or disagree, to argue for the entire re-conception of "welfare" through the mechanisms of our legal system exemplifies the power of the CLS-trained mind steeped in data adherence, creative consideration of conflicting values, knowledge of systemic inner-workings, and defiance of ingrained biases.

Both the CLS and new legal realism approaches are all-encompassing and multilateral; indeed, their reliance on on-the-ground facts helps us in the art of methodologically compromising ideas to resolve issues efficiently, effectively, and in a way mindful of our larger systemic goals and individual interests. It involves removing oneself from the hierarchical notion of "law" as having a true *right and wrong*, from tacitly endorsing the idea that law is somehow this distant, unchangeable, noble system, and from the idea of only considering the facts that one is *supposed* to consider (based on how things have been done before), and decide things in a larger, more dynamic way. As a natural consequence of empowering thinkers holistically, these functional approaches to law learning encourage pluralistic approaches to larger systemic problems. Approaches and considerations and perspectives, I argue, that should be learned earlier through civics education as a tool for the burgeoning citizen-activist.

4.1.3 Extrapolating Outwards: Law-Think Education, What It Looks Like and Why It's Empowering

One commonality between the above approaches to teaching law—one moralistically and the other critical, technical, and functional—is a vision of law as a subject poised to be diversely taught and a system of thought that is *larger* than any one problem, *dynamic* in its room for improvement, *comprehensive* in its reach, and *malleable* by active actors. Learning law from either lens or both begs students to affirmatively engage with persisting social questions, tap into societal moral values, engage with empirical realities undergirding hot-button issues, develop their own unique responses to deeply rooted questions of justice, and acquire both a fluency in and versatility with the mechanisms in which law operates. One can readily see how transformative the act of learning law becomes, in its varied styles of delivery, on one's perceptions of institutions, ideas, and values: "the activity of a legal education … including the reading of thousands of appellate opinions, yields a rich, if incompletely articulable intuition about legal questions."[71] For law education, especially, the above also highlights how pedagogy is both a moral practice and a political practice. A politically conscious pedagogy in law "illuminates the relationship between power, knowledge, and ideology, while self-consciously, if not self-critically, recognizing the role it plays in a deliberate attempt to influence how and what knowledge and identities are produced within particular sets of social relations."[72]

Now, I do not suggest that *all* law teachers are so meticulously preoccupied with reflecting a jurisprudential (or event critical) intention to color their substantive courses.[73] Reasons for this are myriad, speaking to tropes like the homogeneity and elitist nature of law faculty recruitment,[74] the ill-trained nature of the law professoriate in educational effectiveness or assessment principles,[75] the consequences of external accreditation standards and expected learning outcomes on syllabi,[76] and, most frustratingly to my mind, the claim that introducing "theory" is somehow in opposition to, or unrelated to, a practice-ready or professional education[77]—that focusing on one is detrimental to the other. In many ways, critics are correct to contend that "legal education trains its own allies … [legal education] is a conserving and conservative force."[78] This perspective parallels in many ways the industrial educational philosophy that we saw with Mann's common schooling ideal; the roots of legal education derive from a "spartan society of early nineteenth century America [where] the stern business of personal, social, and political survival left little possibility for thought and the cultivation of institutions of professional education."[79] This proposal, commensurately, pushes from this mentality, acknowledging that the consequences of this approach on legal education might be read as similar to the consequences wrought in the public school landscape.[80]

While many fascinating strides are being made to bring out the "liberal" education aspect of law school, examining them is beyond the scope of this piece.[81] Yet, where instructors *do* offer these incredibly erudite conceptual lenses to students by which to examine their fields, they transform the nature of the *law-think* learning experience. When they study law through a cultural-critical lens, just as one example,

> the professor will be in a position to navigate the inevitable dichotomy of the cultural context within which the law evolved and the cultural contexts of students' perception of the law …, such a focus [allows one] to capitalize on such gaps as teaching moments to demonstrate to the students how their cultural perceptions differ from embedded legal cultural assumptions and the historical assumptions that motivated lawmakers to adopt particular laws.[82]

Or, as another example, when they study law through the lens of race, the student develops powers of "inclusive, candid, and sustained inquiry" that will help them understand the merits of laws as much as laws themselves; an education that is both professional *and* facilitative of the common good as "law will advance good depending on [the education of] its architects."[83] One sees how this is incredibly valuable; indeed, in this way, a legal education become a more humanistic education. This critical approach to navigating legal systems, governmental institutions, and constitutional ideas is, I maintain, part and parcel to *law-think* and it should also be a central aim of civics education.

Martha Nussbaum's proposed educational reformulation in line with the Capabilities Approach anticipates similar interdisciplinarity and philosophical coloration. Indeed one's capabilities are best achieved through a liberal education producing conscientious citizens; "an education is truly fitted for freedom only if it is such as to produce free citizens" who can "call their minds their own" and maintain "the ability to separate mere habit and convention from what they can defend by argument."[84] Such an education, to Nussbaum, is best applied at the university-level, and rooted principally in philosophy. But I see steps toward her vision made with civics reform rooted in law-learning in primary and secondary schools. She maintains that liberal education ought to be "committed to the activation of each student's independent mind and to the production of a community that can genuinely reason together about a problem, not simply trade claims and counterclaims."[85] So too is this achieved in the high school civics classroom, where law is the principal subject of study through interdisciplinary, critical, and moral lenses![86] The law provides a catalyzing substance that channels moral debate, an ultimate values-plural education in many ways, one Dewey would laud (as we will see in a later section). And, as Kohlberg would cheer, the education is resounded practical, the law manifesting the most pressing societal issues faced by the nation and to which citizens' voices must be applied.

Let us explore this "practical" or reality-conscious aspect to law learning further. *Law-think* is a skill first and foremost, a sharp tool for both deconstructing complicated issues and appreciating the goals and ideals of the existing system, a gateway to Nussbaum-ian capabilities of practical reasoning and political participation, to be sure. With law as its subject, the education pushes one to think and reason about *real* data that supports *real* decisions on a technical legal issue *with impact*, the people that would be affected by a policy change, the systems that would be implicated by a legal decision. The critical thinking tool, in other words, cannot be applied without also learning about people, institutions, and influencers that contribute to disputes. This is highly complementary of Nussbaum's preoccupation with an education *for* democracy; one that pushes students to understand (and ultimately maintain) the relationship between nation and individual.[87] Talking about the confluence of all these facts—again, which students already (haphazardly) learn as a part of civics training—in the specific context of how judges decide cases and how legislators cooperate to create laws, provides a forum for students to learn how to prioritize social values and constraints, negotiate ideas, and build working systems necessary in a democracy *all based on real events, real people, real problems*. They get to know traditions and principles through the exploration of precedent; they get to judge for themselves "injustice," and they get hands-on training in cultivating opinions and resolving current issues.

We can see paralleled in this the Kohlberg's "dilemma discussion" for moral development both in terms of activity and atmosphere—a useful tool for showcasing law learning as a moral education as much as a grounding citizen education. The aims of both the "dilemma discussion" and the "case analyses" are complimentary; material for class can be used to enlighten students to broader political and social issues that exist.[88] In the former, students are confronted with social problem, an individual issue of great moral controversy, and asked to discuss.[89] The purpose of the "exploration of moral reasoning" that takes place is to "demonstrate (a) the diversity of opinion possible, (b) the potential consequences behind various alternatives, and (c) an awareness of the student's own position."[90] Practically, students learn "participatory skills such as listening, critically analyzing, formulating their own opinions, responding to others clearly and cogently expressing their position and attitudes" in real-life social scenarios.[91] They are forced to defend opinions logically, to evaluate the validity of their peers' thoughts, and to develop autonomous reasoning skills *essential* to navigate complex moral situations.[92] So, too, is this the case in the case-analysis, *law-learning* landscape. Even more so! Lawyers are held up to be "arbiters of justice," champions for ulterior voices, leaders on the back of their superior education[93]; at least theoretically, "to be entrusted the reins of law is a great responsibility," educated for the frontlines of actions toward justice and the common good.[94] The student is pushed to consider their own moral persuasions, those of their peers, and, indeed, content constantly with implicated questions of societal values and priorities that must be interrogated. The work of the teacher in both settings, indeed, is to "foster the moral development of his students by different methodologies: clarifying dialogues, discussing real moral dilemmas, role-playing, procedures for active neutrality, simulations, conflict resolution."[95] The teacher helps each student issue more judgments that approximate a universal principle of justice.[96] The process of teaching students how to reason, of helping individuals generate a sense of judgment, helps students develop a "deeper sense of sympathy for their classmates and their clients,"[97] all while preparing them to practice law. And this is, to be sure, an essential education in leadership that is useful for *all* people.

It is worth considered, furthermore, *how* the teacher goes about this work; indeed, complimentary to educators' choice in jurisprudential–conceptual approach, is the much lauded and storied law school pedagogical tool, the Socratic Method. Exceptionally democratic,[98] this method for which law education is exceptional predisposed, promises that "the student and the instructor are equals in their capacity to learn and their observations of the world."[99] It is, indeed, a "way for teachers and students to strive toward a consciousness that is grounded in a humane and liberating dialogue."[100] As we saw above, the educator's jurisprudential approach to the subject of law, when combined with the pedagogical tool of the Socratic Method, "deconstruct[s] the individual perspective of reality. It dismantles arbitrary perspectives and reliance upon external sources. Once deconstructed, such a pedagogy rebuilds a consciousness geared toward the critical intervention in [real social issues]."[101] Educators work with their students for synthesis and awareness that allows students to explore their common condition and work to transform political and social conditions. This style of teaching in the classroom—often question and answer, repeatedly probing students positions on concrete cases, questioning assumptions—pushes students to interrelate and debate, think on their feet, reason, and defend; in this way, the curriculum of legal education all reflect a view of the world.[102]

The fact that there is no single universal truth that governs the outcome of a legal case or interpretation of statutes (as there is none in Kohlberg's dilemma discussion) does not suggest that there are no answers to problems and questions. Instead, the value in a legal education is that students must struggle to find the reasoning behind answers and discern which solutions are best to the problem.[103] And, as Ryan Peterson writes, "this willingness to struggle with others, and the recognition that your 'truth' may not be the absolute, is nothing less than what democratic societies requires."[104] Martha Nussbaum herself reserves particular praises for the Socratic Method as a highly productive pedagogical tool.[105] As she describes:

> one of the reasons that people have insisted on giving all undergraduates a set of courses in philosophy … is that they believe such courses, through both content and pedagogy, will stimulate students to think and argue for themselves, rather than defer to tradition and authority.[106]

People who fail to "examine themselves," "often prove to easily influenced."[107] Indeed, "irresolution is frequently compounded by deference to authority and peer pressure, a problem endemic to all human societies."[108] I would take it one step farther, failure to examine themselves, and failure to be versatile in understanding the issue also speaks to Kim Lane Scheppele's point that demagogues are free to run and mobilize law toward nefarious aims. "The critical attitude uncovers the structure of each person's position, in the process uncovering shared assumptions, points of intersection that can help fellow citizens progress to shared conclusions."[109] In this way, "progress can be made through a reflection that seeks the common good."[110]

Law learning produces, indeed, exceptional capabilities for political participation and practical reasoning skills, at least as it comes to dealing with the issues of society. The type of citizen it produces is one who is active, critical, curious, capable of resisting authority and peer pressure.[111] Learning about law and morality is also about understanding of the values inherent in our democracy and society. It provides the opportunity for us think critically about how laws ought to be applied, about where they align themselves in an argument, in what ways—and to what degrees—should countervailing interests, conflicting duties, and mitigating situations be brought to bear to reconcile injustice with the "rule of law." Learning law, in this way, cultivates a student who thinks always on multiple levels, one who is "less inclined to fall for rhetorical arguments that spark an emotional response without offering a clear vision of what should be done and how it can be done effectively."[112] Indeed, the student walks away not only with a certain perception of "justice," but also a value-set that can be used to evaluate what is and is not just.

Both jurisprudential approaches to learning law are valuable for the skills they endow, and indeed, should both feature in any sort of law learning curriculum that could take place in a civics classroom. But, as a final point, on a universal level, the value in *law-think* for the non-lawyer—as distinct from the iteration presented in Hong Kong—is also in simply offering an education that *requires* students—without getting out of their seats—to engage with different ideas, multiple perspectives, and plural approaches to common, pressing problems. This, in my view, is a fundamentally American project. *Law-think* is not about standards, nor is it about obeying the law blindly—though the respect they gain for the law may indeed impugn them to do so—but rather it is about combatting complacency, working together, hearing each other out, and cultivating a younger, more eager, capable, and inquisitive generation able to tackle complex issues and put forward changes that reflect the spirit and progressiveness necessary for the sustaining the American experiment. Indeed, law learning is an education that informs one of both "the mechanisms of our democratic system, [and] its spirit … what it means to be an American and even what America means."[113]

In the above, I have considered the way in which students interact with *law-think* in the law school setting, the questions they are pushed to ask, perceptions challenged, and the role that the law school classroom plays in building thoughtful, consciences professionals. I then extrapolated more universally to discuss what *law-think* looks like as an education on the ground, and, in turn, framing it as a useful tool for the non-lawyer citizen, both from a Capabilities Approach and Moral Education perspective. I postured that the education is something transformative and necessary for today's environment. In these next sections, I want to explore specifically the *consequences* of such an education, developing the contention that *law learning* as a citizen education project promotes important external-facing skills and inward-facing skills that are timely and necessary. In terms of external citizen skills, I discuss the impact this new civic education might have on the individual's relationship with authority. In terms of internal skills, I explore how the values-plural posture of the education will impact one's self-awareness and self-identity.

4.2 Resulting External-Facing Skills: Relating to Authority and Tradition

In thinking more about our present national relationship with authority, one shudders. According to a 2022 Pew Research Study, just 20% of Americans "trust the government to do the right thing," while 8% describe the government as being "responsive to the needs of Americans," and just over half have only "some" confidence in the nation's future.[114] Overall 46% of young people do not trust the government and 49% have "little faith" in the justice system.[115] To make matters worse, per the 2022 COVID States Project, nearly a quarter of Americans are amendable to overthrowing the government, with one in ten Americans saying it is appropriate "right now."[116] These are dire statistics but they are also unsurprising. The directorial staff at the COVID States Project argues that "[beginning with the American Revolution, we] are taught in grade school that it is at some points in history justifiable to engage in violent protest," and, given the state of the nation, the desire has understandably "moved from the sphere of chest-thumping to the sphere of reality."[117] These statistics are especially concerning given that most civics educators would consider, among their many other duties, engendering a healthy-relationship with government as a principle task.

In a nation that prizes rule of law and perpetually legitimate government, America cannot be well-contented to have a significant portion of their population ready to overthrow the standing regime.[118] There *must* be an interest in changing the general disposition. This proposal, again, maintains that the point of upheaval we have reached is owed in some ways to an authority that is disengaged from mass-opinion, out-of-touch, ruling by fiat rather than consensus. An education in law offers a chance for long-awaited bridging, providing a voice and path to individuals interested in making their position known to government. On its own merits, law learning, while not stymieing any urge to dissent from authority,[119] primes effective criticism; it cultivates helpful dispositions, orientations and institutional awareness that students can rely upon to express their discontent.[120] In short, it has the potential for making the student at once tempered, more effective, and *better* advocates and political participants, content and empowered to work *within* the system rather than burn it to the ground. Aside from potential critics and protesters, though, this education will also produce more generally cognizant, rationalizing, aware citizens capable of apprehending national problems and participating in conversations about solutions balancing complex ideas about authority, policy, and institutions.

4.2.1 Law Learning Transforms One's Reaction to Authority and Helps One Navigate Institutions

To begin, law learning focuses on fostering more productive debate and conflict resolution skills.[121] Students, whether learning to argue both sides of a case, examining the balancing acts of court decisions, or studying the way federal agencies make rules on the back of public comment, become intimately familiar with different sorts of institutions by way of their work product—which is already a step beyond the descriptive lessons currently taking place in the civics classroom—and thereby appreciate the challenges, roles, aspirations, and shortcomings of each institution. Instead of just learning that the Supreme Court has nine justices, for instance, students learn the burdens of *stare decisis* in court opinions, the idea of standards of review balancing interests, and methods of interpreting statutes, all of which inform what the law (and the democratic system) is and how it is produced. This ultimately prepares students for democratic discourse; they, in turn, become more *aware and accountable* parties to the ongoing national conversation on policy and in relating to authority. They are *aware* because they are the beneficiaries of an education in (1) how the individual relates to institutions of authority, (2) how those institutions deal with problems and (3) how they change policies (and the consequences of doing so); *accountable* because this awareness may incite a feeling of obligation to lead, speak out, and participate in a more nuanced process.[122]

I offer two examples, having to do with recent phenomenon, to showcase how law learning can be transformative. First, consider how this education might serve as a bulwark against the general inclination toward "folk-politics,"[123] the phenomenon where protest—the very obvious way in which many citizens interact with authority, though not always to any avail—is reduced to fleeting displays of anger rather than attempts to amend the structural and systemic nature of problems.[124] Second, I want to discuss institutional ignorance and the relationship between *law-think* and successfully navigating institution to achieved desired outcomes. Let us begin, however, with protest and political participation.

Such "folk-politics" protests, grounded in "flimsy justifications," featuring empathizers with little knowledge of the issue (many joining only in solidarity), and greater preoccupation with numbers than messaging, are occurring with greater frequency.[125] In their emotiveness, protesters are gradually becoming more "separate [] from the opportunity to learn something true."[126] And, to be sure, even where causes are worthwhile, the act of protesting them haphazardly can be reductive or worse.[127] One such engagement that comes to mind is the act of "protest voting" where activists choose to cast their vote for a non-establishment party—or simply abstain altogether—as a means of rebellion.[128] Their contention, to some extent, is that "only protests and direct action can bring about change, and that voting and participation in electoral politics is a waste of time."[129] These actions, widespread as they are, are credited with, among other things, the democratic loss of the 2016 election and its consequences on left-leaning policy, low political engagement, and worse—are antithetical to the democratic process.[130] Barack Obama himself maintains that, though one may aspire to a perfect policy change, "aspirations have to be translated into specific laws and institutional practices—and in a democracy, that only happens when we elect government officials who are responsive to our demands."[131] In other words, the shortsighted, all-or-nothing pension of such protests is counter-productive.

Learning law, in this case things like process, studying statutes, appreciating the way we allocate resources, studying agency policy, helps the student appreciate the slow nature of change, as well as the reality that no policy—favorable or unfavorable—is the product of an all-or-nothing stance. Indeed, by studying those "specific laws and institutional practices" that they both like and dislike—their history, interpretation, and evolution in the courts, their problems, arguments in favor or against—students learn to accept, at once, that a state of conflict is natural and ever-present in the democratic process, that sustained law evolution is an involved process, and, indeed, that *they*—the citizen, the voter, the individual—are part of this growth and development from being able to comment on agency rules to writing congress to protesting *the merits* of the law rather than just how they make us feel.

Central to this thesis, therefore, is that upon dispensing with this all-or-nothing mentality, sitting in this appreciation of constant conflict (which the study of law is predicated upon), students can thus be free to make reasoned, rather than purely emotional, judgments about how to act in support of their ultimate cause, and, with nuance now given to the ideas behind policies they dislike, perhaps even respecting the reasoned opinions of others in doing so. Furthermore, and to this example of "protest voting," students will become more amenable to half-measures—casting a vote for a candidate *more* in-line, if not entirely in-line, with their beliefs rather than resorting to abstention—in the interest of small incremental change and favorable law evolution.[132] *This* is what we need to teach; to understand law process, to achieve higher reasoning skills, reorients the student to what "success" looks like—a resolution, with ground-work laid upon which to build, rather than an all-out revolution at every turn.

This speaks, furthermore, to the need to develop good reasoning skills for students. The law—and learning it—requires that special attention be paid to arguments about words or doctrine.[133] One's opinions and ideas, as well as the means of expressing those ideas with reason and temperance, *can be practiced and improved.*[134] Graham Ferris offers that law learning does this especially well through "modelling"; "timely and useful feedback of useful vocabulary and conceptual structures"; "breaking down the complex end operations into simpler sub-operations that students can master"; "use of narratives to illustrate the importance of success and failure in reasoning and expression"; and "through questions and answer" about issues, contentious debates, and huge social problems.[135] It is a deconstructive education that, when employed, at least in theory, ensures students know the many different parts of an issue before expressing a view. This is useful in elevating the logic behind protest and activism.

Moving to our second example, law learning also helps the citizen navigate different authoritative institutions to resolve disputes effectively, efficiently, and favorably. Whereas the above has to do with a tempered response to authority, this has to do with the capability and capacity for citizens—through law learning—to hold institutions accountable and indeed direct criticism appropriately through awareness of the system.

In the wake of the *Dobbs* decision, the approval rating of the Supreme Court had plummeted to a mere 40%.[136] Protesters in the street and citizens at home have challenged the legitimacy of the court,[137] argued for packing the court with new justices,[138] cutting back federal jurisdiction, and disobeying outright undesirable Supreme Court decisions.[139] To many, a "successful" protest and resulting policy shift might look like overthrowing the judicial process itself, or at least overhauling the Court as institution. But, again, this proposal maintains that, by way of law learning, citizens would benefit from a reoriented perspective on this subject. Were students exposed to the meat of the *Dobbs* decision on paper in a classroom, a dialogue opened to discuss openly the past and future of the right to privacy as well as the balancing implicit in substantive due process, perhaps students' immediate responses might shift from overhauling institutions to working within them. In other words, "success" *can* be, and *should* be, conducted through the existing system rather than from without.

To be clear, this is *not* about students blindly adhering or contenting themselves with *Dobbs*, its reasoning, outcome, or consequences (which to many will surely be life-altering). But it is about offering nuance and context to the controversial decision—with the mind that other similar decisions will undoubtedly come. Rather than demonizing the institution, its authority, and the individuals therein—leading to divisiveness and mistrust—I argue for endowing students a way to reflect on this case critically and answering, borrowing from the rhetoric of movement lawyering,[140] the important question: what's next. In learning law, specifically in this case by exploring the way substantive due process rights were made and guaranteed in court, students can begin to wrestle with the way in which "aggressive court decisions changing policy may push society too fast too soon," that perhaps "better routes to reform exist through social movement mobilization in politics and legislative policy change."[141] Or not! Perhaps, in balancing the weight of *stare decisis* and practical consequences for themselves, the student reaffirms their vitriol for the court. This is fine, but, importantly, the students see, objectively, a new path forward within other institutions separate and apart from the court.[142] There is no abandonment of the process, only a critical mind assessing institutional strengths and weakness, acceptance of their shortcomings, and urge to find the most effective way toward dispute resolution.

It produces, indeed, exceptional skills of political participation and practical reasoning skills, at least as it comes to dealing with the issues of society. Socratic values, that, to be sure, produce a certain type of citizen: "active, critical, curious, capable of resisting authority and peer pressure."[143] This ability—accustoming oneself to the act of balancing institutional authorities and situating your case best within them—is important for *all* citizens, not just lawyers or protesters or activists, for two reasons. First, it favors an analytical perspective and, with the knowledge of when and how we can be helpful in pushing a cause for which we are passionate, inspires us all to get involved institutions, rather than to feel ourselves demoralized, or give ourselves in to the impulse to villainize. Importantly, by way showing us new paths forward carved into the fluid system, law learning engenders a feeling that *the individual does matter to our authorities, that they are essential to the debate, that the system reflects their ideas and interests, and, commensurately, that they are empowered to make change.* Though one may not see this directly in the context of the Supreme Court in the case of *Dobbs*, surely, they will in the context of the legislature, state governments, private and public enterprise, and other siloes within the system to which they should be exposed in class. And second, the act of law learning conditions students—whether future reformers or non-political absentees—to act with a foundational *belief in the integrity of the law and the democratic system.*[144] This is essential for an ordered society. Law learning does not hinder one's ability to dispute the "inherent corruption of institutions, the inequity of policy, or disagree with this or that law," rather it trains the student to act *from a place of hope* that the system is good—even if working within one or another institution is not amenable to your cause—rather than a place of disillusionment manifested in a desire to abolish institutions or systemically disengage entirely.[145] In other words, one's relationship with authority becomes healthier.

4.2.2 A Point of Comparison: The Jewish Tradition, a Culture of Learning Law

There is a balance that needs to be struck between respecting law[146] and its institutions on the one hand and critically appraising it, developing it on the other hand. A law education for *all* citizens is the first step; and to show how successful such an educational innovation can, allow me a slight diversion into a parallel world where this has been commonplace for centuries—one, in fact, from which this whole manuscript draws inspiration: the Jewish Tradition.[147]

Owing to a history of external persecution in diasporic experience, Judaism is incredibly developed in terms of their reasoning—their *how*, *to what end*, and *why*—for teaching children (Jewish) law young as a means of cultural preservation. Judaism's educational tool is one focused on building a cultivate a *better* citizen of the Jewish community.[148] The Jewish duty to educate necessarily requires learning what Jewish Law is and how Jewish law works, both for oneself and one's children, given *halakha*'s "intentional blending of law, personal ethics, and sense of community connectedness."[149] More specifically, studying *halakha* is about equipping the students with an understanding of how law functions, what arguments are at play on a given question, how can and should people act properly within and "evolving Jewish law."[150] Indeed, Jewish law learning is a civics education—intentionally educating for the betterment of Jewish peoplehood and citizenship. And it is one that is *mandated* for adults *and* children. Exploring what *law learning* looks like in the Jewish Tradition, substantively and practically, is instructive as we try and envision a national civic education project.

Substantively, the study of "Jewish law" includes working with *all* different aspects of the tradition, including those law discussions that have no practical application to modern life. Anybody connected to traditional Jewish communities would see this is directly part of a standard seminary curriculum.[151] But why study law, and especially law that has no real impact on daily life? There are two main reasons I would like to focus on. The first is the wisdom gained in the very process of working with law, or, in other words, the benefits of learning to think deeply about principles through text. The second is about becoming "acculturated" to thinking about legal structures and ideas in higher ways and understanding how laws are developed by Jewish actors. The importance of learning law for its own sake, is, to the mind of Jewish people, *the mechanism by which their culture and tradition passes down through generations.*

This notion is highly applicable to the national conversation I have been engaged with thus far; think back especially to Haass' comments and his concern that, without civics education, we fail to transmit collective identity: "collective identity, along with an appreciation and understanding of what lies behind it, is a matter of teaching, not biology."[152] The Jewish Tradition understands this; it develops an education program to ensure the appreciation and continuation of the "central elements of [their] tradition."[153] Louis Wirth explains as follows:

> the education in the case of the Jews, specifically designed to bring about, survival [is] an education in a way of life, changing with the changing circumstances in which the Jews found themselves in different times and places, but rooted in the Torah and the Talmud (which literally means "teaching") and in the accumulated lore of centuries.[154]

Indeed, preoccupations with continuity and cohesion—much like the American Common Law Tradition—are bedrock to the composition of Jewish law. Consider the following story out of the Talmud, as framed by Elliot Dorff:

> When Moses visited the academy of Rabbi Akiba, who lived some 1400 years after him, he did not even understand what Rabbi Akiba was saying (let alone agree with it). Nevertheless, Moses was comforted when Rabbi Akiba cited one of the new laws in Moses' name because that indicated that there was a sense of continuity in the tradition, however much it had changed in form. This sense of continuity can be maintained only if those who have studied the tradition carry on its spirit and substance in new settings.[155]

The prospect of pouring over a common history, value-set, ideals, and principles every time one opens a page of Talmud, re-envisioning and reinterpreting the law's meaning through ages and varied places, ensures the Jewish community remains connected and that individuals are conscientious of their role in perpetuating this connection. Indeed, this *supposed* to be an exercise so deeply engrained in Jewish Life—taking place daily, at fixed times and in fixed places every day—to become routine and habit.[156] I take this rigorous commitment, as well as the embedded nature of law learning in Jewish Tradition, as part of a larger observation: for the Jewish people, law *is* a cultural tool, a value-set, a rule-book that ought to be well-accessible and well-studied by as many people as possible as the primary vehicle by which one learns to "play the game" of Judaism. As Rabbi Dovid Zauderer writes:

> even if one doesn't understand what's being studied, he should still show up to learn—for the act of sitting there to learn is itself considered a meritorious act and will be rewarded in kind. Furthermore, we have a tradition that any Torah that was studied in one's lifetime—even if he didn't understand it at all—he will merit to study it and understand it for all eternity.[157]

To this point, it is also worth making one other comment—embedded in Dorff's reference to Rabbi Akiba's "academy"—on a practical aspect learning law for the community-congealing project: learning law in groups. The *Mishnah Berurah* states the following:

> even though one fulfills his mitzvah of Talmud Torah if he studies alone on his own, the mitzvah is substantially enhanced by studying as much as he can together with a group, because G-d's Name is glorified even more when Jews come together to study His Torah.[158]

This practical invocation quite furthers the notion of learning law *for* collective identity. As we saw above, on one level, Jews learn law to perpetuate tradition by debating letter of the law as a matter of habit; on the second, one *best* does this work by *means of connecting with others*, a bonding activity, debating viewpoints. Indeed, one could conceive of the very act of going in learning law in seminary or in groups, therefore, as a way of manifesting their "patriotism" and "duty" and "service" to Judaism. The louder the debate and the argument in a *Beit Midrash* the better; debate and contention being foundational to Jewish Tradition as epitomized by the biblical notion of *makhloket l'shem shamayim* ("an argument for the sake of heaven"). The power of the law is not *only* reading from the law, therefore, but connecting with other human beings—of varied persuasions and opinions—on the subject. This amplifies the project of *chiddush* ("re-analysis"), as we will see latex, but most importantly strengthens the collective consciousness. This, indeed, instructs us well in how to conceive of civics in classrooms—spaces for values discussion, debates, controversy all through the lens of law.

The second reason for why Judaism stresses the study of law that needs reflection is precisely the same as what we have been talking about to this point: learning respect for the institutions, the need to develop them, and the importance of appreciating how to navigate them. Learning law is a community citizenship education, a professionalization process, and a developmental tool; to the Jewish community the skills one acquires through law learning, especially higher reasoning, ensures that the next generations grow to be filled with impactful, thoughtful citizens and capable actors. Law is just one other course subject in primary and secondary schools meant to provide children with the tools necessary to be productive adults in the real world. As Rabbi Zauderer articulates:

> each person is obligated to learn each day Tanach (Bible), Mishnah, Talmud, and *Halacha* (Jewish law). However, if he only has time to learn one thing, then it should be *Halachah*, which is most practical for him to know what to do in his daily life.[159]

With this, Zauderer captures an essential idea: one cannot operate (Jewishly) effectively—critically, rationally, community-mindedly—without understanding Jewish law and the skills obtained by learning it.

In the seminary, pouring over pages of Talmud, children learn not only how to apply a general rule to a situation, but also how to think about the ways in which laws are applied. For example, a student might be asked to consider whether a general rule, "no carrying on Shabbat" applies to one who, say, pushes a stroller, or operates a self-driving car, or hitches a ride with a friend who is driving. While many students could offer quick answers, seminary children will learn the reasoning, rhetoric, and explanations behind the prohibition arrive at conclusions, and, importantly, recognize the complexity and nuance needed to engage in public life within the Jewish community. Part of the instruction (and a very advantageous aspect of the education) is:

> [to] help children learn to reason by more than one method: more than just by logic, Jewish Law reasons by analogy and analysis, and it recognizes both the value of adhering to precedent and innovation, or how the needs of the time serve a role in developing Jewish Law.[160]

As to the first aspect, Jewish law understands that "while a system can have precedent, it must still be able to change."[161]

On this note, it is important to realize that the Jewish Tradition is ever active in a process of *chiddush*, reanalysis, and innovation of sources to find a novel solution to a problem. Students of Jewish law seek out "novel and innovative truth to ancient problems, and the community is often witness to (and involved in) the process by which a new idea becomes normative."[162] It begins, familiarly, with reasoning by analysis and by argument from deeply important, binding core texts as well as countless important medieval and post-medieval text that need to be understood and analyzed. The students learn to read and understand texts and codes, and from there apply them to novel considerations. These individuals, capable of harmonizing seemingly incompatible texts and understanding which tools to apply depending on the types of contradictions a text presents, is one accustomed to a model of thinking that is nuanced and complex. Indeed, reasoning by analogy empowers the student to understand that each situation one encounters may share similarities with others but is nevertheless unique.

Beyond this, to learn Jewish law develops one's capacity for agreement on matters of policy, and, in the event that there is disagreement, civil discussion. Consider, for instance, the following situation:

Two students who are faced with a question of whether and under what circumstances Jewish law would sanction divulging a secret with which you have been entrusted. The debates could be endless on the reasoning and citations for one answer or another, but, perhaps, students could arrive at a unified conclusion that the secrets of others are, per *halacha*, best kept absent extenuating circumstances in the interest of cultivating a policy of trust and loyalty.

Implicit in this example are the following lessons: reconciling policy matters, building arguments, finding common ground. These are matters that, for the rest of society, preoccupy only the specialized graduate student in law. But, as the Jewish community serves to exemplify, perhaps these skills are necessary universally.

Again, we can see how Jewish law learning helps children learn the "rules of the game" while playing. Even further, it shapes how they view authority with criticism *and* deference, curiosity, *and* rigorous devotion. The Jewish tradition prizes a very active, empowered community participant, and the analogical and higher reasoning skills are the key tool for this. They, indeed, help a person identify the rules of the game through comparing situations as he or she experiences them. Furthermore, by constantly exercising the ability to see others' perspectives, an added benefit is that children learn to appreciate that there may be more than just one side to a question.

Students of Jewish law, being required from an early age to embark on a moral and religious learning experience, cultivate a culture of community-orientation, and develop good citizen characteristics with common mindsets, as well as key analytical abilities, truly think differently. To be taught essential skills in formal classrooms, educated morally by parents practicing the faith, connected to the community, and pushed to succeed professionally—are all congruent with the aims of learning Jewish law young. And, indeed, we see the results made manifest in examining how Jewish adults approach education, continued and ongoing learning, and connecting with community.

Moving back to the wider national conversation, to follow the law is to preserve order and confer necessary legitimacy upon the system.[163] A legal reasoning education endows a perpetual appreciation for the multi-layered nature of the system and the competing interests of laws and policy, as well as provides for a mental shift toward criticality and curiosity, higher-reasoning, and motivation to interact theoretically with the system that governs you. At the same time, this is not equivalent to indoctrination[164]; students are able to evaluate the inherent injustice of a law and commensurately practice all manner of civil and private disobedience in contexts where a moral obligation seems to supersede any duty to obey. Indeed, such an education endows them with an even greater capacity for doing so, as well as a commensurately higher standard by which to judge injustice.[165] A legal education empowers one to reflect deeply on the very basis for injustice and its bearing on the larger system, and, in the event of a need to respond, do so by informed, efficient and legitimate means. In other words, an education in the "rule of law" translates to tempered responses; painstakingly considered circumstances, and informed judgments about policy.

Just as act of learning a little history in school is helpful for the student to understand their socio-cultural milieu in context, so too is learning a little "law learning" is helpful to balance legal obedience with institutional awareness and healthy criticism of authority. While certainly *law-think* is not about standards, nor is it about obeying the law blindly—though the respect they gain for the law may indeed impugn them to do so—it is about combatting complacency, working together, hearing each other out, and cultivating a more eager, capable, and inquisitive generation able to tackle complex issues from within and put forward changes that reflect the spirit and progressiveness necessary for the sustaining the American experiment. Indeed, law learning is an education that informs one of both "the mechanisms of our democratic system, [and] its spirit ... what it means to be an American and even what America means."[166]

At its core, learning law evolves the student from a place of throwing bombs toward another where one works stalwartly, cleverly, and critically from that place which isn't quite right,[167] to that place which is a little bit better. Effectively, it takes away the hierarchical notion of "law" as having a true *right and wrong*, and decide things in a larger, more dynamic way. As a natural consequence of empowering thinkers holistically, these functional approaches to law learning encourage pluralistic approaches to larger systemic problems. As Judge Sam Bratton once observed, "constitutional and statutory provisions contribute to our form of democracy, yet democracy itself does not find its perpetuating source in them. It is enshrined in the hearts of men who cherish liberty and human dignity."[168] To empower all citizens with law learning—legal reasoning; *law-think*—will only serve to augment their relations with authority in line with the needs of our democracy all while bolstering a sense of 'collective identity."

4.3 Resulting Internal-Facing Skills: Self-Examination, Reinforcing One's Values, and Self-Identity

To continue with my exploration of the transformative consequences of an education in law learning for the student, I next reflect more deeply on the values-aspect of the project. Specifically, this section endeavors to show how learning law impact students' self-awareness and self-identity such that they are more effective in their external interactions and even in realizing certain capabilities of political participation and external reasoning. But how does this project cultivate these internal skills, reoriented perspectives, and realizations? As a moral development education, law learning does so by embracing[169] a values-plural posture while also being grounded in foundational mores, universal values, that ground American society, law, and legal system. In true Deweyan fashion, this values-pluralism complements and bolsters a student's preconceived values acquired through other community affiliations (family, church, etc.), while also reflecting how they might be reconciled with more widespread, societally held values as they are manifested through law and cases studied in classrooms. This, ultimately, helps students become *better* citizens by virtue of being aware and appreciating the socio-cultural milieu, understanding the nuance of values-balancing taking place in the law institutions, and fostering more in-touch citizens free both in the mind to higher reasoning and motivated to reinvigorate democracy with their ideas.

4.3.1 Universal Values and Internal Skills

To begin, certainly, law and the legal system *do* reflect and inculcate certain discrete "universal values," nameable ideals that the system puts forward as essential for citizens.[170] To name just a few, consider: the "common good," "justice," "equality," "fairness," "temperance," "diligence," and "involvedness." These are universal and anchoring—law and its systems being an exceptional medium for their conveyance. *Kelo v. New London*,[171] for example, encapsulates discussions surrounding fairness and injustice in the property context, while maybe *A.C. v. Raimondo*[172] better broaches topics of citizen involvement, of diligent self-advocacy, individualism, and state responsibility. Even if you disagree with these specific lists of values, one cannot disagree as to the existence of universal values. Amy Gutmann, for instance offers up "conscious social reproduction" where all else fails as an American value undergirding education and our democracy.[173] This idea connotes a collective commitment to bettering the society we share; our laws, our education system, "these are practices and authorities to which we, acting collectively as a society, have consciously agreed."[174] And who could disagree with the universal notion of bettering the system? Answers to the question of *why* understanding universal "American" values over others—and to be sure the list can go on—are important have been offered in dozens of ways by many authors, but allow me to offer two reasons relevant to our discussion of the benefits inherent in all citizens studying law and the law system.

First, each of these values are important tools for constructing and understanding how one is *supposed* to go about interacting with others outside of themselves. As Lawrence Kohlberg proposes, "a moral principle is [one] for resolving competing claims, you versus me, you versus third person."[175] Justice and equality, especially, are principled bases for resolving competing claims; they connote impartiality, in that "disputes are resolved on the basis of an external judgement rather than in favor of one or the other because of their characteristics."[176] Simply, we are not supposed to have a sense that the system owes us better treatment; we are no better than others. Furthermore, they teach us that we are *autonomous*, able to navigate our lives in ways we see fit so long as we comprehend the consequences of our actions, and that the system will judge us accordingly (with no preferential treatment).[177] And, lastly, they teach us balance in that all arguments and confrontations are to be treated on their own merits, contending with the unique circumstances, weighing contexts, and checking ideals.[178]

Studying legal reasoning is an excellent way to learn these values especially and to see them in practice. When one reads a court opinion, the transcript of a sentencing hearing, or even an appellate brief, students are necessarily exposed to the application of these principles in favor of arguments and outcomes. Consider, for example, cases where the justice system forgives or mitigates punishments for individuals stealing food to save themselves from hunger. There, we see a weighing of the idea of justice and a balancing between principles of order and justice leading to the outcome that "one's right to life comes before another's right to property."[179] Or, in another context, consider how criminal sentencing decisions—and their appeals to higher courts—are all about wrestling with the issues of weighing standards like individual history and background, the context of crime, perceived severity of transgression, values of recidivism, deterrence, and rehabilitation, all in the interest of just outcomes. Furthermore, and just as importantly, when one studies these things over time, one is exposed to the way the law, and society, has evolved in their views of these principles; embedded in the history of our law systems is the collective values and principles of our society applied to everyday cases and contexts. In this way, the law instructs students in the benefits of slow and balanced change, consistent morality, and equitable interactions between people and systems.

Whereas the first reason why these values were important was inter-personal and relational, the second reason concerns their importance in the project of personal growth on the back of understanding one's situatedness within institutions and amongst people. As Jane Aiken argues, exposing students to content implicating values like justice and fairness, especially in a legal education, teaches "students the ability to deconstruct power, to identify [their] privilege, and to take responsibility for the ways in which the law confers dominance [oftentimes in their favor]."[180] With this understanding, one might "learn to use [their] power and privilege in socially productive ways."[181] Principally, studying law *can*, in its purest form,[182] beg lessons in self-consciousness, self-understanding, and self-reflection for the citizen.[183] Consider, for instance how, in studying judges and judging, one can be compelled to see the process as an "inherently situated activity," one where a judge "cannot escape the effects of his or her own particular situation."[184] The manner in which decisions are decided, the backgrounds of parties to a case, the inability to relate to others' experience, are factors in this process put on display in court opinions, interpretations of statutes, and even administrative ordinances. For the citizen, the act of exploring one's own instinct, biases, upbringing, and prejudice by way of interrogating reactions to the law and its institutions, as well as examining the predispositions of those institutions making the laws, is important for helping to shift how one perceives the world, its challenges, and their impact on different people in a diverse society. This self-reflection, in no short order, can be helpful in cultivating in students a sense of collectivity and interconnectedness with others who are all availing themselves of a shared system. The practice of learning law promotes connection and embeddedness and reflection.[185]

4.3.2 Self-Examination as Value (and Skill); Law Learning as Exceptional Subject for Supporting Self-Examination of Values

Indeed, a through-line through this conversation on the inculcation of universal values is this notion of "self-consciousness, self-understanding, and self-reflection." I would say, in fact, that, both as a byproduct of the process of *law learning* and a systemic value, these attributes, or more specifically the value of individual self-examination, need also be added to the list of universally held values in the American system. This merits some further reflection.

Recalling our earlier encounter with Habermas,[186] I predicated this proposal on a particular view of law as an institutionalization of practical discourse between citizens, communities, institutions on social norms.[187] Law is, indeed, mediated through "intentional social relations," implying that autonomous,[188] thoughtful "flesh-and-blood' individuals are in a regular dialogue with their laws and legal systems to best reflect their values."[189] From the laws, therefore, we can divine necessarily important societal principals; and, on the other side, we take solace in the fact that "all practical questions can be judged impartially and decided rationally"[190] and that *all* actors are empowered to take yes or no positions on "various claims pertaining to propositional truth, normative rightness, and subjective truthfulness" in a given matter.[191] This implies, therefore, that I extend this conception of law to include an autonomy-based conception of law and rights, one of positive liberties and laws that support principally *enabling of individuals to live autonomously and in control of their own lives.*[192] The story of laws, rights, liberties and duties are, by consequence, reflective of the "growth of the individual: the free individual [as] one that develops, determines, and changes her own desires and interests autonomously and from within. This is not liberty as the mere absence of obstacles, but liberty as autonomy or self-realization."[193] Criticism of this school of "positive liberty" abounds[194]—it is anti-paternalistic in terms of the role of government in ration to individual decision-making, to name but one complaint—but a chief factor, to my mind, undergirding the opposition is this notion that people are ill-equipped to make decisions for themselves that take into account others. As John Christman has put forward "positive liberty concerns the *ways* in which desires are formed—whether because of rational reflection on all the options available, or as a result of pressure, manipulation or ignorance."[195] And, in all likelihood, this is a correct assessment: we are ill-equipped to make choices that balance interests, or predisposed to pressure to act one way or another depending on our influencers, or to take into account values outside our own. Our systemic, universally held value to self-examination is, however, indelibly implicit in rhetoric about autonomy and independence. Though unrealized, my view is that this rhetoric begs us to do better. And I believe we can. To meet the standards of a system that is required by an idealized "positive liberty view," we need to educate in self-examination, and we need to raise the capabilities of our citizens to *truly* be autonomous and critically minded.

Martha Nussbaum emphasizes the importance of self-examination to the citizenship project and to the Capabilities Approach to Education; "the unexamined life threatens the health of democratic freedoms, and the examined life produces vigor in the nation and freedom in the mind."[196] She argues for the need to "to confront the passivity of the pupil, challenging the mind to take charge of its own thought."[197] The issue is, indeed, pressing as modern citizens "have never stopped to ask themselves what they really stand for, what they are willing to defend as themselves and their own."[198] To put it another way, while our legalistic American tradition might value autonomy, independence, self-determination, Nussbaum might identify that few of us know how to act on these notions so as to realize them; few of us effectively appreciate what *we* believe, let alone how these beliefs might be applied to society-wide questions enough to efficiently and fairly participate politically.

However, such reflection is an important part of any fully autonomous life.[199] Bernard Williams[200] has written that without an individual awareness of one's core values, man is without reason to live; where we are *all* without this awareness, "our system and social scene degrades into a value-less, neutral, and shaky cultural-relativist position; we become scared to *believe* in anything, and, more importantly, to check authority where they try to establish values, ideals, or principles by fiat."[201] As Graham Ferris furthers, a graduate legal education "validates the desire to talk about [this] question, and provides a model discourse and vocabulary to help a student to articulate and reason about" core values and how they figure into systemic conversations.[202] I agree, and add that this can be done earlier than in graduate school. After all, "to give people a conceptual vocabulary is to influence them; but to deprive them of it is to cripple them, not to empower them."[203]

An education in law and law learning, as a moral-development education, is optimal to *confront, to measure the firmness of our own beliefs*, and build key capabilities for flourishing within the civic structure. It does this in two ways. The first has to do with the universality of law to the American experience—law speaks to people where they are at; law connects deeply with us at innermost levels.[204] As Alexis de Tocqueville once declared, "[t]here is hardly a political question in the United States that does not sooner or later turn into a judicial one."[205] Citizens get involved in the law every day, whether to avail themselves of insurance benefits, enroll in a government program, purchase property, engage with law enforcement, or simply in getting caught cutting through your neighbor's lawn to get to your own house. Furthermore, law acts as *the* "boundary-setter for policy and ethical dilemmas"[206] in the United States; one that dictates, for better and for worse, how, when, and under what circumstances people ought to behave on the day-to-day or in special situations. Within the law, "we frame things in the question of duties and obligations that we expect of ourselves and other actors—balancing between public power and private rights"[207]; the language of law, indeed, is one of human conduct. For example, tracking first amendment law through time reveals consistently changing views of the populace toward protest, ideological pronouncements, and exchanges of ideas; understanding how the law of the right to privacy developed over time serves as a study in how "prevailing social attitudes [as] codify[ed] and enshrine[ed] … with a formal, official, and enforceable status."[208] In this way, the law "shapes social values by acting as a grand educator—forced under penalty of law to behave in certain ways." And, commensurately, to notice when people "get impatient with the law is behind the solidification of social and ethical consensus on a particular issue."[209]

The second reason, however, is even more important. Law is an exceptional tool for self-reflection and self-examination of one's values given its values-plural posture.[210] Law learning is not a "dogmatic assertion of beliefs held to be truths by academics that their students must accept as true," but "neither does it justify flimsy cynical relativism that exists in the popular culture of the modern world."[211] Law, as a subject-matter, "abides legitimate institutions, power dynamics, and ideas, but does not ascribe to be right and just. It is subject always to change based on learning and examination."[212]

Reflecting on this, one can easily channel Dewey's idealized learning environment. His chief complaint on contemporary iterations of character education, if you'll recall, was that traditional values-learning favored didacticism and explication.[213] Didactic approaches has no use in the study of reflective morality; through didactic methods, a child might learn what the conventions of morality or name specific, core aspirations morals but cannot develop any capacity to critically think or apply judgment in novel situations.[214] And they certainly cannot help one assess their own values independently! Indeed, Dewey ended up rejecting the idea that core values themselves were fixed and unchangeable—that they might change as society (or the person) changes—and so it was *crucial* that the individual be engendered with critical thinking skills to help assess morals and actively participate in that change-process. He had expounded that "our conceptions of moral education have been too narrow, too formal, and too pathological."[215] Moral education, to his mind, ought to cultivate students capable of facilitating a perpetually new, modern social order based on new critically assess values.[216]

Law precisely favors the reflective over the didactic. While law has universal values, which we discussed above, they are fluid and by no means delimiting—ever subject to change. The answer to *what* we stand for as a country is, indeed, an ongoing debate manifesting through the laws proffered by our institutions daily. By law learning, students see this, appreciate this, contend with this, relate to this, disagree with this, and grow by means of it. And, importantly, they can hold this education alongside the values they gain in other communities in which they take part. Ferris offers the example of the Roman Catholic who reserves an absolute value position on X, Y, and Z issues. He shows how the landscape of an education in law does not necessarily "threaten the monists' worldview and value system", but argues instead that "teaching value pluralism is not insisting that it is to be endorsed as a personal value."[217] In his words:

> [Law's] pluralist posture allows student to cultivate a rational discourse about values. It is the process of engaging in this discourse that generates the cognitive learning outcomes and development of reasoning abilities and the self-reflection leading to character formation and development of identity that a focus on values puts into the curriculum.[218]

What statement can be made about the systemic value-mindset as conceived of in *Roe v. Wade*? Where in *Masterpiece Cakeshop v. Colorado CRC* can we identify the balancing of interests between individual rights, religion, state interests; where does collective conscious fall and where does the system? None of these queries challenge the Roman Catholic's view; all of them help situate their view amidst a larger society-wide conversation on values-balancing. A conversation, indeed, that the citizen *must* involve themselves in or at least be aware is taking place as they go about squaring their dual identity as a Roman Catholic and member of the American civic community.

To put this idea another way, the subject matter of law espouses a plural posture, but the student does not "have to be informed by a personal commitment to pluralism" and this posture does not "threaten the sense of autonomy and independence of the student."[219] No, it *informs* that autonomy by pushing students to confront what they believe for themselves and what they hope for society; "the challenge in law will be to find some claims to goodness (that a value is good) and for rationality (that a way of reasoning or acting is objectively rational)."[220] As I have said before, this is *ideal* for democratic politics which is a necessarily pluralistic project. While the Roman Catholic student might stay secure in their faith, that law learning pushes them—through cases that urge "discussion, compromise, conciliation, and [explanation, defense, and] acceptance of difference"—to recognize the value of pluralism for political life and for others.[221] Ferris highlights that "pluralism [through law] acknowledges the need to accommodate rather than to convert the other in our public life."[222] Law is about seeing workable agreement on ideas through language and reason,[223] not trying to force assent to any one position[224]: good judgment, compromise, conciliation, and, even selfish self-advocacy, when a position is logically developed, is treated with primacy.[225]

Of course, law and law learning are also about getting to "truth," at least in terms of getting to what is "right" and "just." For, indeed, "without a respect for truth it is impossible for students to construct a realistic self-identity."[226] But even still where law education encourages students to seek the "truth," it is not done in a direct, didactic way but by way of reflection and discussion[227]; after all, "the notion of a single truth or a single standard of truth now seems hopelessly simpleminded." Ferris asserts that, rather, law engenders in students an appreciation in students for "expertise"—"over epochs, and with plenty of twists, human beings have established expertise. Indeed, we have developed collective ways to refine and improve our understanding that we constantly deploy."[228] We see our system consistently redefine truth and standards over long terms in court cases and in short terms by administrative agency decisions; the student in law learning places their choice of values, their plans for life, their perceptions of society in a dialogue with consistently changing notion of "expertise" which, in turn, opens them always to the potential for re-evaluation and re-configuration when new ideas present themselves.

When presented in this way, one might also note that a further benefit to law learning as a values-education is that anyone can participate in this education. This education "starts from the qualities and needs and abilities of the [student]" with the aim "to enhance the situation of each learner by creating new capabilities or enhancing existing ones."[229] This is especially important not *just* because it dovetails well with Nussbaum's Capabilities philosophy but speaks to the question of law learning's accessibility as a general civic education. Recall that, at the outset of the chapter, I discussed that when "the wide-eyed prospective 1L joins her classmates for her first day of law school, she likely comes to the bustling community of aspiring change-makers knowing no law." To learn law is about process, honing skills in rational argument, appreciating the ideal of legal decision-making—"the trial as a paradigm of rationality"; the understanding that "judgment is intended to identity the correct issues for a decision was made on the right issues in accordance with relevant evidence and law"[230]—a wealth of knowledge that *requires no front-work* or pre-requisite studies. In fact, the tools of law, from statutes to cases, implicate a world that *favors* identifying the correct issues for a decision was made on the right issues only in accordance with relevant evidence and law and *shuns* a decision based on the personal beliefs, or predispositions, or preferences of the decision-maker.[231] It is thus an eminently accessible means of studying our society by introducing you to the system, forcing prudent discussions and debates based on external ideas, values, questions, evidence, and—ancillary and simultaneously—urging the learner to introspectively examine one's self-identity and value-set in the context of societal-identity.[232]

To learn law is to study a system that seeks accommodation and compliance by carful and intelligent application of rules; it is a "diagnostic and creative" process,[233] equipped to accessible introduce students to "areas of social life that are prone to tensions, due to factors that may be internal or external to the law, and it generates the very norms it enforces in the attempt to resolve such tensions."[234] It is thus immensely valuable as a values-education, proffering an educational landscape by which students engage with the "the tensions of the entire culture," one in which "emergent power-patterns, ancient security-drives, religion politics, personality, and cross-purposed views of justice tangle in the open, that portion of the life will concentrate in the case of trouble and disturbance."[235] Yet, it does so in a way that invites perspective, diversity of opinion, and growth. Such an education would not just benefit, but is, indeed, necessary for *all* citizens needing to act "autonomously" while simultaneously entrenched in our legal institutions.

Notes

1 One main program that is worth distinguishing from is the 1970s "Street Law" movement. This movement (started at Georgetown in 1972) argues that they build civic agency and foster democratic culture by way of an education in "practical law," or the "the fundamental laws that affect a person's everyday life." Seán G. Arthurs, "Street Law: Creating Tomorrow's Citizens Today," 19 *Lewis Clark L. Rev.* 925 (2015); https://streetlaw.org/who-we-are/about/history/

> Street Law is about teaching high-school students how to have a voice and how to be better thinkers, communicators, and learners. Law is a perfect vehicle for helping students develop these cognitive and expressive skills while also gaining practical and relevant substantive knowledge.

The typical curriculum involves an education in crimes and their varied punishments, background on where "law" comes from, and studies in the exercise of rights. Street Law partner with schools, departments of education, and juvenile justice systems. In 1975, the published a textbook suited for grades 9–12. That book is currently in its 10th edition and taught in hundreds of schools nation-wide. This is a highly commendable program. But it is not the objective as conceived of in this proposal. It is technical in nature, where we seek to empower students in an elevated, intellectual discourse. It is preemptory in that it teaches "how to avoid problem with the law" rather than discussing "upon what values is the law founded and how can and should they be changed." *See* Arthurs, "Street Law," 946 (discussing that "discourse" in Street Law classrooms is about taking sides as plaintiff/defendant in cases to argue points. This is distinct from the even higher-order conversation about the values and ideas implicit in the laws themselves). Street Law is not about debate, counterarguments, and balancing of interests on values and system-wide levels, but about immersion and skills in discrete legal battles and settings. To be sure, Street Law serves an important function, but it is distinguishable.

2 This is congruent with Nussbaum's Capabilities Approach in terms of ensuring the development of key capabilities in which one could avail themselves to flourish but not expecting that they necessarily realize those capacities. But what about those critics—harkening back to our earlier chapters—who maintain that a civics

education ought to principally *for* the budding protester, that those who do not teach protest do not teach civics. This proposal equally serves those ends. Activism gains by understanding the powerful tools that move our system; indeed, by owning the system and understanding the values upon which it is predicated. We, as a country, do not have a tradition of changing our laws, our constitutional values, or our systems (beyond technical levels) very frequently. This means that legal values are often lagging to cultural values or novel political ideologies or stances, and that, if anyone is desirous of resolving a political question or remediating problematic institutions, they need to be able to do so on a higher more abstract level dealing in the language of law. Just so, when I say that law is essential to the citizen, I mean on this grander level. The claim is therefore not about discrete substantive knowledge, but skills in terms of the capacity for critical reasoning and discernment. These are good for protestors but, more importantly, good generally.

3 I have used this example in a previous article, Michael Broyde and Ariel Liberman, "Learning Law Young: Towards a More Robust, Impactful Civics Education Modeled Off of Jewish Law Learning," 52 *J. of Law & Educ.* 1 (2023).

4 Michael Broyde and Ariel Liberman, "Learning Law Young: Towards a More Robust, Impactful Civics Education Modeled Off of Jewish Law Learning," 52 *J. of Law Educ.* 1 (2023).

5 Selena Cheng, "Schools to add empathy, law-abidingness, diligence and 'loving China and Hong Kong' to moral education," Hong Kong Free Press (December 2021), ("As for the old guidelines, "understand the challenges and opportunities the motherland is facing today from rational, multi-angle and critical thinking", delete "critical thinking" and replace it with "understand and care about the country's society and economy from rational and multi-angles." Development, challenges and opportunities in various aspects such as safety, security, technology, etc.")

6 Selena Cheng, "Schools to add empathy, law-abidingness, diligence and 'loving China and Hong Kong' to moral education," Hong Kong Free Press (December 2021).

7 Selena Cheng, "Schools to add empathy, law-abidingness, diligence and 'loving China and Hong Kong' to moral education," Hong Kong Free Press, (December 2021).

8 Jack Chorowsky, "Thinking Like a Lawyer," 80 *U. Det. Mercy L. Rev.* 463, 464 (2003).

9 This list is borrowed from William M. Gibson. "Law Students: A Valued Resource for Law Related Education Programs." 25 *J. Leg. Educ.*, No. 2, 215–225 (1973).

10 To place these in Nussbaum's terms, I will trace the way in which law learning develops capabilities in practical reasoning, self-awareness, and political participation. Importantly, there are, of course, many more great results from this education. One that deserves at least a small mention is conferral upon the student a sense of self-worth, of *empowerment as an individual change-maker within the collective system.* A versatility and familiarity with mechanisms and processes, an understanding of the principles and values at work in the system, the substantive knowledge—all of this strengthens one's sense of self and elevates their impression of their potential impact on the system. This, we have seen, is especially true for students of marginalized backgrounds both from within and without the law school context. Carol Weinstein, "The Classroom as a Social Context for Learning," 42 *Ann. Rev. Psychol.* 493, 519 (1991). It also acknowledges the importance placed on values one acquires outside of school, and the necessity of engaging with them in the classroom. I will touch on this in the body of the text but suffice to say I am not alone in designing a way for which

privately held values can be lauded and engaged with productively in the classroom. *See*, e.g., Amy Gutmann, *Democratic Education* (Princeton, NJ: Princeton University Press, 1999) 77 (Gutmann discusses her principle of non-repression which "prevents society from restricting rational deliberation among competing conceptions of the good life.").

11 This is congruent, as well, with the Capabilities Approach's push for diverse understanding, multi-culturalism in the classroom, and plural opinion. It is, equally so, a part of Dewey and Kohlberg's conception of a proper moral education that does not indoctrinate toward specific values or belief-sets.

12 Graham Ferris, *The Uses of Values in Legal Education* (Cambridge: Insertia, 2015), 14.

13 Graham Ferris, *The Uses of Values in Legal Education* (Cambridge: Insertia, 2015), 14.

14 I note here that there is, indeed, a tension that exists between law as a "liberal education" and law as a "professional education." The ladder, indeed, focuses more on the education-for-employability aspect of a law school experience, and might critique the way in which I present this education for its philosophic and theoretical nature. However, as Ferris notes, "there is no contradiction from the human development point of view between enhancing choice and making students more employable" (2015, 14–18). The distinction between *ends* of a legal education speaks to a larger "shadow" in the higher education project, and one that I do not address for the purposes of this presentation. For, indeed, even if one considers that law school education is practical, they must also concede that it is theoretical. The two are not mutually exclusive.

15 Graham Ferris, *The Uses of Values in Legal Education* (Cambridge: Insertia, 2015), 14.

16 Consider, for instance, a few foundational texts in this area: *Educating for Justice: Social Values and Legal Education* (Jeremy Cooper & Louise Trubeck, eds.) (Hanover: Dartmouth, 1997); Duncan Kennedy, *Legal Education and the Reproduction of Hierarchy: A Polemic against the System* (New York: NYU Press, 2004); Elizabeth Mertz, *The Language of Law School: Learning to "Think Like a Lawyer"* (Oxford: Oxford University Press, 2007). And, more recently, John Inazu, *Learning to Disagree: The Surprising Path to Navigating Difference with Empathy and Respect* (Grand Rapids, MI: Zondervan, 2024).

17 *See e.g.*, Bethany Rubin Henderson, "Asking the Lost Question: What Is the Purpose of Law School," 53 *J. of Legal Education* 48 (2003); Jack Chorowsky, "Thinking Like a Lawyer," 80 *U. Det. Mercy L. Rev.* 463, 464 (2003).

18 Jack Chorowsky, "Thinking Like a Lawyer," 80 *U. Det. Mercy L. Rev.* 464 (2003).

19 Martha Nussbaum, *Not for Profit: Why Democracy Needs the Humanities* (Princeton, NJ: Princeton University Press, 2016), 48.

20 James Elkins, "Moral Discourse and Legalism in Legal Education," 32 *J. of Legal Education*, 11, 12 (1982); *see also* Angela Harris and Marjorie Shultz, "A(nother) Critique of Pure Reason: Toward Civic Virtue in Legal Education," 45 *Stanford L. Rev* 1173, 1176 (1993).

21 Angela Harris and Marjorie Shultz, "A(nother) Critique of Pure Reason: Toward Civic Virtue in Legal Education," 45 *Stanford L. Rev.* 1176 (1993) (referencing see Thomas C. Grey, Langdell's Orthodoxy, 45 *U. Pitt. L. Rev.* 1 (1983)).

22 James Elkins, "Moral Discourse and Legalism in Legal Education," 32 *J. of Legal Education*, 12 (1982).

23 James Elkins, "Moral Discourse and Legalism in Legal Education," 32 *J. of Legal Education*, 12 (1982) (discussing the problems with the "morality of rule veneration."). The debate currently rages as to whether Langdell's "purist" approach to law learning is optimal for the modern student. *See e.g.*, Angela Harris and Marjorie Shultz, "A(nother) Critique of Pure Reason: Toward Civic Virtue in Legal Education," 45 *Stanford L. Rev.* 1176 (1993) (discussing the purist approach as divorced from other subjects, from values, from larger social questions). We will see that *law learning*, as construed in this piece, takes a very different form than that that of Langdell's more scientific, deductive view into something altogether more liberal in terms of education.

24 Michael Swygert, "Striving to Make Great Lawyers—Citizenship and Moral Responsibility: A Jurisprudence for Law Teaching," 30 *B.C. L. Rev.* 803, 804 (1989) (quoting Oliver Wendell Holmes, The Use of Law Schools, in Collected Legal Papers, 37, 47–48 (1920)).

25 Jane Aiken, "Striving to Teach Justice, Fairness and Morality," 4 *Clinical L. Rev.* 1, 11 (1997).

26 Michael Swygert, "Striving to Make Great Lawyers—Citizenship and Moral Responsibility: A Jurisprudence for Law Teaching," 30 *B.C. L. Rev.* 806 (1989).

27 Concerns about the role and responsibility of the attorney as arbiter of justice or moral counsel often go to the forefront of courses in Legal Ethics and Professional Responsibility. *See* James Elkins, "Moral Discourse and Legalism in Legal Education," 32 *J. of Legal Education*, 12 (1982). And, indeed, there are those that think that the moral preoccupations of law are, realistically relegated to these fields alone. *See* Lee Modjeska, "On Teaching Morality to Law Students," 41 *J. of Legal Educ,* 71, 72 (1991).

28 Jane Aiken, "Striving to Teach Justice, Fairness and Morality," 4 *Clinical L. Rev.* 11 (1997).

29 James Elkins, "Moral Discourse and Legalism in Legal Education," 32 *J. of Legal Education*, 46 (1982).

30 Jane Aiken, "Striving to Teach Justice, Fairness and Morality," 4 *Clinical L. Rev.* 11 (1997).

31 Michael Swygert, "Striving to Make Great Lawyers—Citizenship and Moral Responsibility: A Jurisprudence for Law Teaching," 30 *B.C. L. Rev.* 807 (1989).

32 Jane Aiken, "Striving to Teach Justice, Fairness and Morality," 4 *Clinical L. Rev.* 12 (1997).

33 Michael Swygert, "Striving to Make Great Lawyers—Citizenship and Moral Responsibility: A Jurisprudence for Law Teaching," 30 *B.C. L. Rev.* 819 (1989).

34 Michael Swygert, "Striving to Make Great Lawyers—Citizenship and Moral Responsibility: A Jurisprudence for Law Teaching," 30 *B.C. L. Rev.* 819 (1989).

35 Jane Aiken, "Striving to Teach Justice, Fairness and Morality," 4 *Clinical L. Rev.* 7 (1997).

36 Graham Ferris, *The Uses of Values in Legal Education* (Cambridge: Insertia, 2015), 20.

37 Graham Ferris, *The Uses of Values in Legal Education* (Cambridge: Insertia, 2015), 20. Recall our earlier discussion on the purpose behind teaching the "rules of the game."

38 Graham Ferris, *The Uses of Values in Legal Education* (Cambridge: Insertia, 2015), 20.

39 Michael Swygert, "Striving to Make Great Lawyers—Citizenship and Moral Responsibility: A Jurisprudence for Law Teaching," 30 *B.C. L. Rev.* 803, 811 (1989).

40 This argument is made in Ronald Dworkin, "Hard Cases," 88 *Harv. L. Rev.* 1107 (1975). ("The sharp distinction between background and institutional morality will fade, not because institutional morality is displaced by personal convictions, but because personal convictions have become the most reliable guide he has to institutional morality.") Ronald Dworkin argued that judges rely on their own impression of community morality to decide "hard" cases in a way that promotes order consistent with our democratic principle. Attorneys, commensurately, rely on their understanding of community morality and sense of institutional values to frame legally consistent arguments and push similarly valued policy. *See generally*, Ronald Dworkin, "Hard Cases," 88 *Harv. L. Rev.* 1105 (1975). ("Individuals have a right to the consistent enforcement of the principles upon which their institutions rely. It is this institutional right, as defined by the community's constitutional morality, that Hercules must defend against any inconsistent opinion however popular.") Dworkin observes that the legal thinker in practice, over time, arrives at such a point where their "personal convictions have become the most reliable guide [to] institutional morality." Functionally, therefore, the moral pedagogy of law teaching takes the position that—through legal education—one is better positioned to anticipate institutional changes, address needs, and informedly exercise judgment on policies in a way always (at least subconsciously) aligned with the needs and values of the system.

41 There are, of course, many more great results from this education. One that deserves at least a small mention is conferral upon the student a sense of self-worth, of *empowerment as an individual change-maker within the collective system*. A versatility and familiarity with mechanisms and processes, an understanding of the principles and values at work in the system, the substantive knowledge—all of this strengthens one's sense of self and elevates their impression of their potential impact on the system. This, we have seen, is especially true for students of marginalized backgrounds both from within and without the law school context.

42 James Elkins, "Does Teaching Matter," 31 *St. Louis U. L. J.* 35, 41–43 (1986). Reinforcement of the belief in the good of the system is showcased especially in the prototypical law school ethics course. Among other more substantive objectives, the ethics course in a law school cultivates character, virtue, and values in newly minted legal professionals. Students engage with larger questions including the role of the lawyer within the system, expectations of the professional, and "professional socialization." The teacher, at once, instills a sense of duty and obligation towards both the profession and to act in the interest of justice. Implicit in this is an indoctrination into the idea that the two pieces go together; that by acting *through* the law as intended, one also works towards justice. Thus, to assess "competence" is to really judge whether a given attorney is holding themselves out in a way that helps further systemic goals and faith in the system as a whole. To teach the proper way of conducting oneself with a client is to perpetuate a certain type of behavior—a behavior favored by the system—until it becomes second nature. To be *ethical*, therefore, is built on a belief that the system in which one is acting and conforming is *right* and *correct*. *See* James Moliterno, "An Analysis of Ethics Teaching in Law Schools: Replacing Lost

Benefits of the Apprentice System in the Academic Atmosphere," 60 *Cin. L. Rev.* 87, 94 (1991).

43 James Elkins, "Does Teaching Matter," 31 *St. Louis U. L. J.* 43 (1986) ("By making a commitment to law and its failure, there is an expression of hope that the failure of law is not inevitable.").

44 *See e.g.*, Jessica Taft, "Is It Okay to Critique Youth Activists? Notes on the Power and Danger of Complexity," in Deborah Levinson, et al. (eds.), *Children and Youth as Subjects, Objects and Agents* (Cham: Springer, 2021). By contrast, some critics contend, youth activists are inclined towards institutional abolition, finding the system *too broken to fix*. While their passion is an excellent attribute, it is often construed as impulsive, "wowing," and obviates an inability, or, worse, resistance, to understanding the system, reflective of some immaturity, incapacity, and shallowness.

45 For a general bibliography on the moral obligation to obey the law, *see* John Hasnas, "Is There a Moral Duty to Obey the Law," 30 *Soc. Phil. Pol.* (2013); Kenneth Greenawalt, "The Natural Duty to Obey the Law," 84 *Mich. L. Rev.* 1 (1985).

46 Judith A. McMorrow, "Civil Disobedience and the Lawyer's Obligation to Obey the Law," 48 *Wash. Lee L. Rev.* 147 (1991). ("Lawyers are systemically part of the power structure, and the lawyer's intimate connection with the law may make the lawyer an even more effective symbol of civil disobedience.")

47 Judith A. McMorrow, "Civil Disobedience and the Lawyer's Obligation to Obey the Law," 48 *Wash. Lee L. Rev.* 147 (1991) (quoting Thomas Aquinas).

48 Robert M. Palumbos, "Within Each Lawyer's Conscience a Touchstone: Law, Morality, and Attorney Civil Disobedience" 153 *U. Pa. L. Rev.* 1057, 1062 (2005).

49 Judith A. McMorrow, "Civil Disobedience and the Lawyer's Obligation to Obey the Law," 48 *Wash. Lee L. Rev.* 147 (1991).

50 Judith A. McMorrow, "Civil Disobedience and the Lawyer's Obligation to Obey the Law," 48 *Wash. Lee L. Rev.* 147 (1991).

51 Emily Taylor Poppe, "New Legal Realism Goes to Law School: Integrating Social Science and Law through Legal Education," in *Research Handbook on Modern Legal Realism* (Shauhin Talesh, Elizabeth Mertz, and Heinz Klug, eds.) (Estonia: Edward Elgar, 2021), 191–207.

52 Emily S. Taylor Poppe, "New Legal Realism Goes to Law School: Integrating Social Science and Law through Legal Education," in *Research Handbook on Modern Legal Realism* (Shauhin Talesh, Elizabeth Mertz, and Heinz Klug, eds.) (Estonia: Edward Elgar, 2021), 191–207.

53 The approach itself was borne in many ways out of Jerome Frank's "clinical-lawyer schools" concept in the 1930s and the older legal realism movement in the 1920s and 1930s, is most seen in the context of clinical or experiential learning that is now widespread across law school curricula. For a full bibliography on this educational philosophy, Frank published two articles in 1933 calling for the creation of clinical lawyer-schools. See Jerome Frank, "Why Not a Clinical Lawyer-School?," 81 *U. Pa. L. Rev.* 907 (1933); Jerome Frank, "What Constitutes a Good Legal Education?," 19 *A.B.A. J.* 723 (1933). See Jerome Frank, "A Plea for Lawyer-Schools," 56 *Yale L. J.* 1303 (1947). For a discussion of Frank's ideas within the context of the history of clinical legal education, see George S. Grossman, "Clinical Legal Education: History and Diagnosis," 26 *J. Legal Educ.* 162, 166 (1973–1974).

54 Karl Llewellyn, *The Bramble Bush: The Classic Lectures on the Law and Law School* 5 (Oxford: Oxford University Press, 11th ed., 2008).
55 Brian Liter, "Legal Realism and Legal Doctrine," 163 *U. Pa. L. Rev.* 1985 (2015).
56 Elizabeth Mertz, "Inside the Law School Classroom: Toward a New Legal Realist Pedagogy," 60 *Vand. L. Rev.* 483, 505 (2007) (law does not convey abstract meaning in a legally created vacuum and thus cannot be understood without systematic study of the contextual molding that gives it foundation in particular cultures and societies).
57 Elizabeth Mertz, "Inside the Law School Classroom: Toward a New Legal Realist Pedagogy," 60 *Vand. L. Rev.* 483, 505 (2007). ("Like all human language, legal language is embedded in a particular setting, shaped by the social contexts and institutions surrounding it.")
58 Katherine Kruse, "Getting Real about Legal Realism," 56 N.Y.L. Sch. L. Rev. 295 (2011).
59 Duncan Kennedy,. "Legal Education and the Reproduction of Hierarchy," 32 *J. Leg. Educ.* 591–615 (1982).
60 Duncan Kennedy, "Legal Education and the Reproduction of Hierarchy," 32 *J. Leg. Educ.* 591–615 (1982).
61 Elizabeth Mertz, "Inside the Law School Classroom: Toward a New Legal Realist Pedagogy," 60 *Vand. L. Rev.* 483, 505 (2007).
62 Jerry L. Anderson, "Law School Enters the Matrix: Teaching Critical Legal Studies," 54 *J. Leg. Educ.* 201, 208 (2004); *see also* Carrie Menkel-Meadow, "Feminist Legal Theory, Critical Legal Studies, and Legal Education or the Fem-Crits Go to Law School," 38 *J. Legal Ed.* 61, 67 (1988) (criticizing how "In law school the student enters a world ordered in top-to-bottom ways that seem grossly ironic in a discipline whose mottos include 'Equality Under the Law.'").
63 Andrew Altman, "Legal Realism, Critical Legal Studies, and Dworkin," 15 *Philos. Public Aff.* 205, 216–235 (1988).
64 Carrie Menkel-Meadow, "Feminist Legal Theory, Critical Legal Studies, and Legal Education or the Fem-Crits Go to Law School," 38 *J. Legal Ed.* 68 (1988).
65 Carrie Menkel-Meadow, "Feminist Legal Theory, Critical Legal Studies, and Legal Education or the Fem-Crits Go to Law School," 38 *J. Legal Ed.* 68 (1988).
66 Martha Albertson Fineman, "Cracking the Foundational Myths: Independence, Autonomy, and Self-Sufficiency," 8 *Am. U. J. Gender Soc. Pol'y L.* 13, 18 (1999).
67 Martha Fineman, "The Nature of Dependencies and Welfare Reform," 36 *Santa Clara L. Rev.* 287 (1996).
68 Martha Fineman, "The Nature of Dependencies and Welfare Reform," 36 *Santa Clara L. Rev.* 287 (1996).
69 Martha Fineman, "The Nature of Dependencies and Welfare Reform," 36 *Santa Clara L. Rev.* 287 (1996).
70 Martha Fineman, "The Nature of Dependencies and Welfare Reform," 36 *Santa Clara L. Rev.* 287 (1996).
71 Richard Posner, "The Jurisprudence of Skepticism," 86 *Mich. L. Rev.* 849 (1988).
72 Henry Giroux, "Public Pedagogy and the Politics of Neo-Liberalism: Making the Political More Pedagogical," 2 *Policy Futures Educ.* 494–503, 500 (2004); *see also,* Ryan Peterson, *Legal Education, Art Before Science: Surrendering the Socratic Method Jeopardizes the Political Future* (Ames: Iowa State University, 2020), 3, where he articulates:

education is the means through which people immerse themselves in a common culture in order to refine their beliefs against the individual experiences of others. Education is not only the transference of information, [but] also a means of deconstructing social hierarchies and rebuilding political communities. Individuals in institutions of higher education are in a position to process information and develop skills by interacting with others with whom they would not normally engage. This process is a working model for democratic societies and advances politically desirable inspiration for democratic institutions.

73 The re-examination of "customs and priorities that traditionally favored core knowledge over the development of professional judgment" is the project of a series of law reform movements. *See* Mary Lynch, "An Evaluation of Ten Concerns about Using Outcomes in Legal Education," 38 *William Mitchell L. Rev.* 976, 1001 (2012). "*Best Practices*" called for law schools to "improve the preparation of their students for practice, clarify and expand their educational objectives, improve and diversify methods for delivering instruction, and give more attention to evaluating the success of their programs of instruction." "*Educating Lawyers* concluded that law schools in the twentieth century overemphasized the teaching of 'core knowledge' while underemphasizing direct training in professional practice and the development of professional identity."

74 Thomas Shaffer, "Learning the Law-Thoughts toward a Human Perspective," 51 *Notre Dame Law.* 951, 961 (1976) ("Few law teachers know of the contributions of such distinguished educational and psychological theorists of the learning experience as Jerome Bruner and Jean Piaget. Law teachers, even when they innovate, 'fly by the seat of their pants.'").

75 Richard E. Redding, "Where Did You Go to Law School? Gatekeeping for the Professoriate and its Implications for Legal Education," 53 *J. Legal Educ.* 594, 599 (2003).

76 *See* Mary Lynch, "An Evaluation of Ten Concerns about Using Outcomes in Legal Education," 38 *William Mitchell L. Rev.* 976, 1001 (2012). Notably, Lynch argues:

> It is not only faculty members who may conflate syllabus content with true learning. Students often express concerns that Professor Y didn't cover as much material as Professor X. These complaints may be targeted at those who integrate reform ideas into their course design. Law review literature suggests that first-year students, and law students in general, may have initial resistance to departures from their expectations of a "normal" doctrinal class with a final exam at the end.

77 Mary Lynch, "An Evaluation of Ten Concerns about Using Outcomes in Legal Education," 38 *William Mitchell L. Rev. 976*, 1001 (2012).

78 Thomas Shaffer, "Learning the Law-Thoughts toward a Human Perspective," 51 *Notre Dame Law.* 951, 961 (1976).

79 Thomas Shaffer, "Learning the Law- Thoughts toward a Human Perspective," 51 *Notre Dame Law*. 951, 961 (1976).

80 *See* Chapter 3.

81 For more information, *see* Judith Wegner, A Legal Education Prospectus: Law Schools and Emerging Frontiers: Reframing Legal Education's "Wicked Problems," 61 *Rutgers L. Rev*. 867, 871 (2009).

82 *See* Julie Spanbauer, "Using a Cultural Lens in the Law School Classroom to Stimulate Self-Assessment, 48 *Gonz. L. Rev.* 365 (2013).

83 Kim Forde-Mazrui, "Learning Law through the Lens of Race," 21 *J. L. Pol.* 27 (2005).

84 Martha Nussbaum, *Cultivating Humanity: A Classical Defense of Reform in Liberal Education* (Cambridge: Harvard University Press 1998), 293.

85 Martha Nussbaum, *Cultivating Humanity: A Classical Defense of Reform in Liberal Education* (Cambridge: Harvard University Press 1998), 19.

86 Martha Nussbaum, *Cultivating Humanity: A Classical Defense of Reform in Liberal Education* (Cambridge: Harvard University Press 1998), 293. She posits:

> [It does not produce] moral relativists—for ownership of one's mind usually yields the understanding that some things are good and some bad, some defensible and others indefensible. Nor will they scoff at the traditions that the older "liberal" education prizes: for they know that in tradition lies much that has stood the test of time, that should command people's respect.

87 Martha C. Nussbaum, *Creating Capabilities: The Human Development Approach* (Harvard: Belknap, 2011), 113–115

> Nations—reasonably democratic ones, at any rate—are systems of principles and laws that have their ultimate source in the people. They are thus important expressions of people's autonomy, that is, their entitlement to live under laws of their own choosing. Thus, key aspects of the Capabilities Approach, especially its respect for practical reason and political empowerment, lead it to accord the nation a central standing and to pursue a world in which national sovereignty is protected for reasonably democratic nations… . The nation then has a role that is securely grounded in the Capabilities Approach, because the approach gives central importance to people's freedom and self-definition. And most democratic nation, wisely and efficiently administered, can do well at securing for their people the capabilities on the list. Nonetheless, today's world contains inequalities in basic life chances that seem unconscionable from the standpoint of justice … If basic justice requires that a person's entitlements not be curtailed by arbitrary features, then justice is ubiquitously violated in the current world order, and the bare existence of the inequality is reason enough to do something about it.

88 Ryan Peterson, *Legal Education, Art Before Science: Surrendering the Socratic Method Jeopardizes the Political Future* (Ames: Iowa State University, 2020), 5.

89 For an example, we can think back to the *Heinz Dilemma* (Chapter 2, note 73), which asked whether Heinz should have broken into a laboratory to steal drugs for his wife in violation of law. A law case that poses an equally difficult moral dilemma, might be *Ward v. Wilbanks* which contemplates whether it is permissible to deny counseling services to a homosexual client based on a counselor's values. The case itself naturally urges the student to think on their own values and ideals, which is excellent and much like what goes on in the "dilemma discussions." But it has the added value of implicating more national questions of constitutional rights to free speech, free exercise of religion, freedom from retaliation for exercising First Amendment Rights, equal protection of the laws, due process, and freedom from establishment of religion. The outcome of the case gives the student insight into the country's position on these values, which is helpful as they consider their perspective and position.

Furthermore, law professors retain the power to embrace the moral role of legal education. Along with requiring students to read classic opinions such as *Roe v. Wade*, for example:

> law professors can pair such readings with feminist novels, short stories, and news articles related to the issue. The material for class can be used to enlighten students to broader political and social issues that exist. beyond the mere text of legal opinions. Untraditional sources could serve as an ally to minority students and could help the traditional white men in such a class to understand perspectives beyond their own personal experience."

Ryan Peterson, *Legal Education, Art Before Science: Surrendering the Socratic Method Jeopardizes the Political Future* (Ames: Iowa State University, 2020), 5.

90 C.L. Englund, "Using Kohlberg's Moral Developmental Framework in Family Life Education," 29 *Fam. Relat.* 80 (1980).

91 Chanah Tannenbaum, *Harnessing Lawrence Kohlberg for Tanakh Education* (HaYidion: The Prizmah Journal, 2011), www.prizmah.org/hayidion/ethics/harnessing-lawrence-kohlberg-tanakh-education

92 Chanah Tannenbaum, *Harnessing Lawrence Kohlberg for Tanakh Education* (HaYidion: The Prizmah Journal, 2011) www.prizmah.org/hayidion/ethics/harnessing-lawrence-kohlberg-tanakh-education

93 There are those, of course, who would criticize this education as, in fact, being wholly divorced from practicality: Thomas Shaffer, "Learning the Law-Thoughts toward a Human Perspective," 51 *Notre Dame Law.* 951, 961 (1976)

> This is a remarkable disposition if, in fact, the lawyer is concerned with justice. It invites the inquirer to guess that it is justice in the abstract, or justice as the product of law, rather than a personal sense of justice, that occupies the lawyer. It may be, too, that lawyers are too busy in the "administration of justice" to take much notice of their personal impact on clients. The study of law, insofar as it is task-oriented and fails to realize or conceptualize human experience, helps to insulate the student and practitioner from real people and from their experiences.

94 Recall, again, Kim Lane Scheppele's pronouncement to lawyers to take head of the "destruction of democracy by law."

95 Josu Ahedo Ruiz, et. al., "Updating the Proposal of 'Just Communities' for Democratic Civil Education," 13 *Ramon Llull J. Appl. Ethics*. 53–75 (2022).

96 Josu Ahedo Ruiz, et. al., "Updating the Proposal of 'Just Communities' for Democratic Civil Education," 13 *Ramon Llull J. Appl. Ethics*. 53–75 (2022).

97 Josu Ahedo Ruiz, et. al., "Updating the Proposal of 'Just Communities' for Democratic Civil Education," 13 *Ramon Llull J. Appl. Ethics*. 53–75 (2022).

98 There are, of course, criticisms levied against the Socratic method as being psychologically abusive, sexist, and much more. Indeed, many law schools find themselves moving from it. But, engaging with these criticisms is beyond the scope of this manuscript; moreover, it is the storied way in which a legal education was (and is) conducted and has many defenders amidst its detractors. For more information on challenges, *see* Williams, Susan H. "Legal Education, Feminist Epistemology, and the Socratic Method" 45 *Stan. L. Rev.* 1571, 1573 (1993); Kerr, Orin S. "The Decline of the Socratic Method at Harvard." 78 *Neb. L. Rev.* 113, 118 (1999).

99 Peter Preston, et al., *Politics, Education, Letters* (Springer, 1993), 225.

100 Ryan Peterson, *Legal Education, Art Before Science: Surrendering the Socratic Method Jeopardizes the Political Future* (Ames: Iowa State University, 2020), 5.

101 Peter Preston, et al., *Politics, Education, Letters* (Springer, 1993), 225.

102 I acknowledge, of course, that there are many detractors to the Socratic Method among even those who advocate for substantial legal education reforms. *See e.g.*, Jess M. Krannich, et al., "Beyond 'Thinking Like a Lawyer' and the Traditional Legal Paradigm: Toward a Comprehensive View of Legal Education," 86 *Denv. U. L. Rev.* 381, 384 (2009). One such critic argues that "the dominant or signature law school pedagogy reinforces a focus on the professor as the center of the classroom rather than focusing on the students' learning process." *See* Julie Spanbauer, "Using a Cultural Lens in the Law School Classroom to Stimulate Self-Assessment," 48 *Gonz. L. Rev.* 365 (2013)

> In many ways, a Socratic professor functions as a conductor or puppet master, carefully orchestrating the questions and arguments to guide the discourse in a preordained direction. A case method classroom therefore centers on the professor himself, and the students typically view the professor as holding the truth to the subject but rarely revealing it.

While interrogating this directly is beyond the scope of this piece, it is necessary to note that one of the reasons for criticism is owed the misapplication of this pedagogical technique in a performative style rather than the technique itself. *See* Julie Spanbauer, "Using a Cultural Lens in the Law School Classroom to Stimulate Self-Assessment," 48 *Gonz. L. Rev*. 365 (2013). ("The problem with the Socratic method as practiced in today's classroom lies in the teacher's complete failure to explain the purpose to first semester students combined with its formalistic roots.") It can, in my view, do quite a lot for a legal education.

103 Ryan Peterson, *Legal Education, Art Before Science: Surrendering the Socratic Method Jeopardizes the Political Future* (Ames: Iowa State University, 2020), 5 (quoting Arendt, The promise of politics. Schocken, 2009) (referencing Anthony Kronman, *The Lost Lawyer: Failing Ideals of the Legal Profession* (Harvard University Press, 1995)).

104 Ryan Peterson, *Legal Education, Art Before Science: Surrendering the Socratic Method Jeopardizes the Political Future* (Ames: Iowa State University, 2020), 5.

105 Martha Nussbaum, *Not for Profit: Why Democracy Needs the Humanities* (Princeton, NJ: Princeton University Press, 2016), 48. Now Nussbaum contends that Socratic pedagogy ought to be infused into every classes, not just the humanities. I agree. However, I also think that we can begin by reorienting civics education—which is principally tasked with developing the skills of the citizen. As a starting point, it is more accessible than total overhaul.

106 Martha Nussbaum, *Not for Profit: Why Democracy Needs the Humanities* (Princeton, NJ: Princeton University Press, 2016), 48.

107 Martha Nussbaum, *Not for Profit: Why Democracy Needs the Humanities* (Princeton, NJ: Princeton University Press, 2016), 48.

108 Martha Nussbaum, *Not for Profit: Why Democracy Needs the Humanities* (Princeton, NJ: Princeton University Press, 2016), 48.

109 Martha Nussbaum, *Not for Profit: Why Democracy Needs the Humanities* (Princeton, NJ: Princeton University Press, 2016), 48.

110 Martha Nussbaum, *Cultivating Humanity: A Classical Defense of Reform in Liberal Education* (Cambridge: Harvard University Press 1998), 293.

111 Martha Nussbaum, *Not for Profit: Why Democracy Needs the Humanities* (Princeton, NJ: Princeton University Press, 2016), 48.

112 Michael J. Broyde and Ira Bedzow, "Why We Should Teach Legal Reasoning Skills to Students," Education Week 2019, www.edweek.org/teaching-learning/opinion-why-we-should-teach-legal-reasoning-skills-to-students/2019/06

113 Taken from *A.C. v. Raimondo*, C.A. No. 18-645 WES 1, 7 (D. R.I. October 13, 2020).

114 For a representative scholarly discussion, *see e.g.*, Roberto Foa and Yascha Mounk, "The Signs of Deconsolidation," 28 *J. Democr.* 5 (2017) (discussing the generational rise of distrust, frustration, and disinterest in democracy).

115 Roberto Foa and Yascha Mounk, "The Signs of Deconsolidation," 28 *J. Democr.* 5 (2017).

116 Matthew S. Schwartz, "1 in 4 Americans Say Violence Against the Government is Sometimes Okay," NPR (2022), www.npr.org/2022/01/31/1076873172/one-in-four-americans-say-violence-against-the-government-is-sometimes-okay

117 Matthew S. Schwartz, "1 in 4 Americans Say Violence Against the Government is Sometimes Okay," NPR (2022), www.npr.org/2022/01/31/1076873172/one-infour-americans-say-violence-against-the-government-is-sometimes-okay

118 I acknowledge here, of course, the movements focused on the dismantling of systems that are deemed corrupted and venomous. Prison abolition is the most prevalent of such movements. I maintain that these are extreme solutions, albeit sophisticatedly theorized. *See e.g.*, Rachel E. Barkow, "Promise or Peril?: The Political Path of Prison Abolition in America," 58 *Wake Forest Univ. L. Rev.* 3 (2022):

> The mere existence of an abolition argument in the policy space might help lead people to embrace more fundamental changes and engage in a much-needed rethinking of a model of prisons that has been unchanged for hundreds of years that has been proven to fail. Put another way, with abolitionists in the mix, other reforms seem moderate by comparison.

The goal is not to defend a counter-stance to the abolition-school in this proposal, but suggest preliminarily that, as a nation of laws, the United States is (1) threatened for a myriad of reasons by extreme-thinking as opposed to solving within the existing system and (2) that the notion of legislating the abolition any major institution is far-fetched in a nation that has not changed its own Constitution substantively to reflect changing values in over a hundred years. They can thus be problematic as guiding theories, and we are not alone in thinking so. *See e.g.*, Carol Steiker and Jordan Steiker, "Entrenchment and/or Destabilization—Reflections on (Another) Two Decades of Constitutional Regulation of Capital Punishment," 30 *Minn. J. L. Inequal.* 211, 224 (2012) (noting that invoking the term abolition in the context of the death penalty brings connotations that "the decision to end the practice is morally compelled to the same extent as the duty to end slavery."); *see* Rachel E. Barkow, "Promise or Peril?: The Political Path of Prison Abolition in America," 58 *Wake Forest Univ. L. Rev.* 4

> there is the possibility that calls for abolition could lead to more harms than they prevent. This risk exists for two main reasons. First, because the rhetoric of abolition is absolutist, there is the risk that approach will frighten segments of the public who would otherwise support de-incarceration, even radical de-incarceration, but are not prepared to rule it out entirely.

It is also politically unpopular, in many cases, and therefore can be difficult to realize. *See* Rachel E. Barkow, "Promise or Peril?: The Political Path of Prison Abolition in America," 58 *Wake Forest Univ. L. Rev*. 5.

119 Just consider how many social movements and protests are led by lawyers who were mobilized in school to think critically about policy. Carrie Menkel-Meadow, "The Lawyer's Role(s) in Deliberative Democracy," 5 *Nev. L. J.* 347, 349–351 (2004) (this is distinct from movement lawyering which is a mixed bag in terms of lawyer participation).

120 The idea that an education fosters better dispositions and temperaments in activists is not novel. *See* Tricia Niesz, et al., "Social Movements and Educational Research: Towards a United Field of Scholarship," 120 *Teach. Coll. Rec.* 41 ("Educational processes and contexts are crucial to the ways in which social movements' ideas, identities and ideals are generated and promoted, taught and learned, contested and transformed". What the young have learned in school about the condition of our environment has been an important source of inspiration for their activism.)

121 Carrie Menkel-Meadow, "The Lawyer's Role(s) in Deliberative Democracy," 5 *Nev. L. J.* 349–351 (2004).

122 *See* Kenneth Rosen, "Lessons on Lawyers, Democracy, and Professional Responsibility," 19 *Geo. J. Legal Ethics* 155 (2006) ("A lawyer's fealty to democracy is obligated rather than aspirational."). Joseph Antoine Cantrell, Address at the Formal Opening of the New Law Library and Fiftieth Anniversary of the Foundation of the Georgetown Law School (December 4, 1920), in *Geo. L. J.*, 1920–1921, at 33, 35

> The American lawyer of today looks out upon a field crowded with problems which do not greatly differ from those of [the founder's] time. To meet such problems and to carry on our government as in the past we must grasp the three-fold principle of personal initiative, personal responsibility, and personal obligation, which it is the purpose of this School to instill.

123 This phrase is borrowed from what Nick Srnicek and Alex Williams, authors of the book *Inventing the Future: Postcapitalism and a World without Work.*

124 *See* Nathan Heller, "Is There Any Point to Protesting?," *The New Yorker* (2017), www.newyorker.com/magazine/2017/08/21/is-there-any-point-to-protesting. Srnicek and Williams are not the first to point out the inefficacy of such engagements. According to one scholar, "in a free and fair democracy, the normative protests of our time are unnecessary, aimless, counter-productive diversions from more virtuous, old-fashioned forms of political engagement, such as researching the issues, deliberating, and developing an argument before writing to Congress."

125 Nathan Heller, "Is There Any Point to Protesting?" *The New Yorker* (2017), www.newyorker.com/magazine/2017/08/21/is-there-any-point-to-protesting

126 Nathan Heller, "Is There Any Point to Protesting?" *The New Yorker* (2017), www.newyorker.com/magazine/2017/08/21/is-there-any-point-to-protesting
127 Brent Simpson, et al., "Does Violent Protest Backfire? Testing a Theory of Public Reactions to Activist Violence," 4 *Socius* 1–14 (2018). Consider one study where a protest by an anti-racist group against a white nationalist group, when turned violent, was shown to increase support for the white nationalist group.
128 *See generally*, R. Michael Alvarez, et al., "A Taxonomy of Protest Voting," 21 *Annu. Rev. Political Sci.* 135–154 (2018).
129 Barack Obama, "How to Make This Moment the Turning Point for Real Change," Medium (2020), https://barackobama.medium.com/how-to-make-this-moment-the-turning-point-for-real-change-9fa209806067
130 Barack Obama, "How to Make This Moment the Turning Point for Real Change," Medium (2020), https://barackobama.medium.com/how-to-make-this-moment-the turning-point-for-real-change-9fa209806067
131 Barack Obama, "How to Make This Moment the Turning Point for Real Change," Medium (2020), https://barackobama.medium.com/how-to-make-this-moment-the turning-point-for-real-change-9fa209806067
132 William M. Gibson. "Law Students: A Valued Resource for Law Related Education Programs," 25 *J. Leg. Educ.* No. 2, 215–225 (1973).
133 Graham Ferris, *The Uses of Values in Legal Education* (Cambridge: Insertia, 2015), 23.
134 Graham Ferris, *The Uses of Values in Legal Education* (Cambridge: Insertia, 2015), 23.
135 Graham Ferris, *The Uses of Values in Legal Education* (Cambridge: Insertia, 2015), 34.
136 Gallup Poll, "Supreme Court," https://news.gallup.com/poll/4732/supreme-court.aspx
137 Robert Barnes and Michael Karlik, "Roberts Says the Supreme Court Will Re-Open to the Public and Defends Legitimacy," The Washington Post (2022), www.washingtonpost.com/politics/2022/09/10/supreme-court-roberts-legitimacy/. On the day of the decision, many protesters called out "abort SCOTUS." Molly Olmstead, "What Protestors Said Outside the Supreme Court This Week," Slate (2022), https://slate.com/news-and-politics/2022/06/roe-dobbs-abortion-scotus-protests.html
138 Tara Leigh Grove, "The Supreme Court's Legitimacy Dillema," 132 Harv. L. Rev. 2240 (2019).
139 Tara Leigh Grove, "The Supreme Court's Legitimacy Dillema," 132 Harv. L. Rev. 2240 (2019).
140 Scott Cummings, "Rethinking the Foundational Critiques of Lawyers in Social Movements," 85 *Fordham L. Rev.* 2000 (2017).
141 Scott Cummings, "Rethinking the Foundational Critiques of Lawyers in Social Movements," 85 *Fordham L. Rev.* 2000 (2017).
142 In the context of movement lawyering, the individual is unconcerned with politics or policy, is clear-headed: they "engage with the implicit counterfactual embedded in each analysis: [are there] viable and more effective [legal or] nonlegal routes to the achievement of movement goals." Scott Cummings, "Rethinking the Foundational Critiques of Lawyers in Social Movements," 85 *Fordham L. Rev.* 2000 (2017).

143 Martha Nussbaum, *Not for Profit: Why Democracy Needs the Humanities* (Princeton, NJ: Princeton University Press, 2016), 48.

144 James Elkins, "Does Teaching Matter," 31 *St. Louis U. L. J.* 35, 41–43 (1986). *See* James Moliterno, "An Analysis of Ethics Teaching in Law Schools: Replacing Lost Benefits of the Apprentice System in the Academic Atmosphere," 60 *Cin. L. Rev.* 87, 94 (1991).

145 We see this in the context of budding lawyers learning law. James Elkins, "Does Teaching Matter," 31 *St. Louis U. L. J.* 43 (1986) ("By making a commitment to law and its failure, there is an expression of hope that the failure of law is not inevitable").

146 As I mentioned above, another perspective concerning one's relationship to authority is important has to do with—as we have discussed earlier—reinforcing the need to respect and obey the law. While in the next sub-section, we discuss how law learning paints the system as a reflection of higher normative principles and values—which is especially *apropos* of this discussion—here, in the case of *Dobbs* and shifting the perspective from villainizing the Court to seeing it as just one avenue for change to which we have access, we note that a young student who knows something about the law, who appreciates the complicated balancing that takes place in courts, the slow-moving evolution of law in legislatures, and the utility of each institution of authority, all while seeing the broader picture of how the system generally promotes order and fairness, is better predisposed to obey discrete positive rules even when they disagree with them.

147 I thank Professor Michael Broyde at Emory University School of Law for introducing me to the Jewish concept of "learning law young," and fostering a conversation that allowed me to develop the idea. The writing that follows is drawn from a collective effort of articulating the Jewish approach to 'learning law young' that we broached in an earlier article. Michael Broyde and Ariel Liberman, "Learning Law Young: Towards a More Robust, Impactful Civics Education Modeled Off of Jewish Law Learning," 52 *J. of Law Educ.* 1 (2023). Some similar phrasing might be seen in what follows, though the content is meant as background and will be contextualized differently in this manuscript.

148 To begin, it is important to note that the Jewish religious legal system explicitly rejects the clear separation of law and ethics. *See, e.g.*, Rabbi Dr. Isaac Herzog, *The Main Institutions of Jewish Law* (London: Soncino Press, 1939), 381, 381–386 (providing a general analysis of the moral claims in Jewish law as compared with those in English common law); *see also* Michael J. Broyde and Michael Hecht, "The Return of Lost Property According to Jewish & Common Law: A Comparison," 12 *J. L. & Religion* 225 (1995–1996) (looking at these same findings in a different context); Menachem Elon, *Jewish Law: History, Sources, Principles* (trans. Bernard Auerbach, 3 Volumes) (Philadelphia: The Jewish Publication Society, 1994).

149 Consider, for instance, the following custom: of the first things to teach Jewish children is how to read the biblical content concerning how God gave the law to Moses. *See* Shulchan Arukh Yoreh Deah 245:5, Sefaria.com, www.sefaria.org/Shulchan_Arukh%2C_Yoreh_De'ah.245?lang=bi. In this, the is urged to think, in his or her earliest stages, about a central Jewish narrative, about how Jewish community is organized, and where they fall in their history. Invariably, the child is

encouraged to develop a lifelong proclivity for questioning how one ought to act or live one's life in acknowledgment of the gift—the law—God bestowed upon the Jewish people through Moses. *See also* Michael Broyde, "Why Educate? A Jewish Law Perspective," 44 *J. of Cath. L. Stud.* 179 (2005).

150 *See, e.g.*, Oren Gross, "Venerate, Amend and Violate", 46 *Ariz. St. L. J.* 1151 (2015).

151 *See* Chaim Saiman, "Preface," in *Halakha: The Rabbinic Idea of Law* (Princeton, NJ: Princeton University Press, 2018), pp. ix–xii.

152 Richard Haass, *The Bill of Obligations: The Ten Habits of Good Citizens* (New York: Penguin Press, 2023), 135.

153 Richard Haass, *The Bill of Obligations: The Ten Habits of Good Citizens* (New York: Penguin Press, 2023), 135. This further emphasized by the fact Jewish Law specifically requires the creation of schools to perform such functions. *See* Michael J. Broyde, "Why Educate? A Jewish Law Perspective," 44 *J. of Cath. Leg. Stud.* (2005) (The Code also mandates that a Jewish school system be established in every community, stating that

> [e]very community is obligated to have an elementary school, and every community that does not have an elementary school should be shunned [until one is established] ... since the world only exists out of the merit of the discourse found when small children study.)

154 Louis Wirth, "Education for Survival: The Jews," 28 *J. of Sociol.* 682–691 (1943).

155 Elliot Dorff, "Judaism as a Religious Legal System," 29 *Hastings L. J.* 1331 (1978).

156 "After he finishes *Shacharit*, and before he goes to work, a person should set aside some time to learn Torah, preferably in the same place every day." Also, "if, for some reason, he must miss his daily Torah study, he should treat it like a 'debt' that he 'owes' and he should make it up that night." And also, "One should also set aside a fixed time to study Torah in the evening, preferably between the *Minchah* and *Ma'ariv* Prayer Services."

157 Rabbi Dovid Zauderer, "Talmud Torah: Setting Fixed Times for Torah Study," Torch, www.torchweb.org/torah_detail.php?id=668

158 *Mishnah Berurah* 155:2, available at Sefaria.com

159 Rabbi Dovid Zauderer, "Talmud Torah: Setting Fixed Times for Torah Study," Torch, www.torchweb.org/torah_detail.php?id=668

160 *See generally* Michael J. Broyde and Ira Bedzow, *The Codification of Jewish Law and an Introduction to the Jurisprudence of the Mishna Berura*, "Chapter II: History of Codification" (Boston: Academic Studies Press, 2014), 6–17.

161 Michael Broyde and Ariel Liberman, "Learning Law Young: Towards a More Robust, Impactful Civics Education Modeled Off of Jewish Law Learning," 52 *J. L. Educ.* 1 (2023); *see generally* Michael J. Broyde and Shlomo C. Pill, *Setting the Table: An Introduction to the Jurisprudence of Rabbi Yechiel Mikhel Epstein's Arukh Hashulhan* (Boston: Academic Studies Press, 2021).

162 *See* Michael Broyde and Ariel Liberman, "Learning Law Young: Towards a More Robust, Impactful Civics Education Modeled Off of Jewish Law Learning," 52 *J. L. Educ.* 1 (2023). *See generally* Michael J. Broyde, *Innovation in Jewish Law: A Case Study of Chiddush in Havineinu* (Jerusalem: Urim Publications, 2010).

163 Judith A. McMorrow, "Civil Disobedience and the Lawyer's Obligation to Obey the Law," 48 *Wash. Lee L. Rev.* 147 (1991) ("Lawyers are systemically part of the power structure, and the lawyer's intimate connection with the law may make the lawyer an even more effective symbol of civil disobedience.")

164 This channels, of course, Dewey and Kohlberg.

165 Robert M. Palumbos, "Within Each Lawyer's Conscience a Touchstone: Law, Morality, and Attorney Civil Disobedience," 153 *Penn. L. Rev.* 1057, 1062 (2005).

166 Taken from *A.C. v. Raimondo*, C.A. No. 18-645 WES 1, 7 (D. R.I. October 13, 2020).

167 I address a counterpoint to this in the next chapter. Namely, "is not law adversarial and thus instructive in adversity and argument and fighting as opposed to compromise?"

168 Sam G. Bratton, "Our Country Today," in 4 *ALA. L.* 66, 68 (1943).

169 I should say "is uniquely poised to embrace" a values-plural posture. One could, of course, contrive of an environment where an educator propounds a singular view of the law, the purpose of the law, the "right" perspective. This is not the case I draw attention towards here.

170 This has been done at length already. *See generally* Amalia Amaya and Ho Hock La (eds.), *Law, Virtue, and Justice* (New York: Hart Publishing, 2012).

171 A case on eminent domain injustice and property law, inculpating questions as well of community, social justice, social capital, and government mistrust all couched in a "fairness" discussion. 545 U.S. 469, 483–486 (2005).

172 Mentioned in passing in previous footnotes. *A.C. v. Raimondo*, C.A. No. 18-645 WES 1, 2 (D. R.I. Oct. 13, 2020) (now *A.C. v. McKee*, No. 20-2082 (1st Cir. 2022). *See A.C. v. Raimondo*, C.A. No. 18-645 WES 1, 7 (D. R.I. October 13, 2020).

173 Amy Gutmann, *Democratic Education* (Princeton, NJ: Princeton University Press, 1999), 39.

174 Amy Gutmann, *Democratic Education* (Princeton, NJ: Princeton University Press, 1999), 39. It follows, she argues, that "a society that supports conscious social reproduction must educate all educatable children to be capable of participating in collectively shaping their society."

175 Lawrence Kohlberg. "The Cognitive-Developmental Approach to Moral Education." 56 *Phi Delta Kappan* 670–677 (1975).

176 Robert Post, "Democracy and Equality," 603 *The ANNALS of the AAPSS (American Academy of Political and Social Science)*, 24–36 (2005).

177 Robert Post, "Democracy and Equality," 603 *The ANNALS of the AAPSS (American Academy of Political and Social Science)*, 24–36 (2005).

178 Robert Post, "Democracy and Equality," 603 *The ANNALS of the AAPSS (American Academy of Political and Social Science)*, 24–36 (2005).

179 *See* Marshall Knapp, "Social Values and Older Persons: The Role of Law," 7 *Maq. Elder's Advisor* 70 (2005).

180 Jane Aiken, "Striving to Teach Justice Fairness and Morality," 4 *Clinical L. Rev.* 1, 64 (1997).

181 Jane Aiken, "Striving to Teach Justice Fairness and Morality," 4 *Clinical L. Rev.* 1, 64 (1997).

182 Stephanie Wildman, "The Persistence of White Privilege," 18 *J. of L. and Pol'y* 245, 264 (2005); *see also* Thomas Morawetz, "Self-Knowledge for Lawyers," 68 *J. of Legal Educ.* (2018) (To be sure, this may not be the case concerning the current state

of a legal education in law schools. After all, future lawyers are asked to "implement the interests of clients, they are expected to put forth values and seek outcomes that they may not support, to construct versions of events and motives that may not accord with their sense of univocal truth." However, we are not focused on *law* for *lawyers*, but rather the use of law as a tool, in a pure form, for citizens).

183 *See* James R. Elkins, "Writing Our Lives: Making Introspective Writing a Part of Legal Education," 29 *Willamette L. Rev.* 45, 52 (1993)

> Learning law, practicing it as a lawyer, or teaching it, depends more than we have previously recognized on what we think and imagine of ourselves as persons. The continual exposure to law and legal thinking affects our inner world of images, emotions, and fantasies. Law and legal thinking, the talking and listening we do as lawyers, shape our view of the world and become a world view.

184 Catharine Pierce Wells, Improving One's Situation: Some Pragmatic Reflections on the Art of Judging, 49 *Wash. Lee L. Rev.* 323, 323 (1992); *see also* Benjamin N. Cardozo, *The Nature of the Judicial Process* 12–13 (New Haven: Yale University Press 1921)

> All their lives, forces which they do not recognize and cannot name, have been tugging at them—inherited instincts, traditional beliefs, acquired convictions … In this mental background every problem finds its settings. We may try to see things as objectively as we please. None the less, we can never see them with any eyes except our own.

185 Note: this is typically not done in the law school setting as we try and rid ourselves of any idea of the law as serving good or bad purpose sin the interest of more technical teaching. Jane Aiken, "Striving to Teach "Justice, Fairness, and Morality"" 4 *Clinical L. Rev.* 1–64 (1997) (Law is merely a process and there is no common good, no common goals toward which everyone is collectively working. "Many of us urge students to approach the law with a studied detachment to rid themselves of the emotion and personal experiences that may color their approach to a problem.").

186 This is something we have already subscribed to by reference to Habermas, though an in-depth discussion of this is beyond the scope of the proposal here. This line of discussion on "positive liberty" also finds support in, for example, Joseph Raz, *The Morality of Freedom* (1986); Habermas, *Justifications and Applications* (1994), and in many other places. Discussions on positive liberty implicate important questions of the law and its relationship to personal identity, responsibility, rights, and "living one's conception of the good life." These are all subjects I hope to explore more deeply in the future.

187 Jürgen Habermas, *The Theory of Communicative Action, Volume 1, Reason and the Rationalization of Society* (Boston, MA: Beacon Press, 1984); *Between Facts and Norms: Contributions to a Discourse Theory of Law and Democracy* (Cambridge: MIT Press, 1996). His larger chronological argument is that though common and civil law in democratic nations had emancipatory origins, through the gradual legalization of culture, law became a "micro-manager" of people's everyday lives, and this "formalization or textualization of everyday life replaces the social solidarity of the lifeworld that formerly was forged tacitly through uncodified norms

of communicative acts and reason." James Chriss, "Review essay view essay of Jurgen Habermas' Between Facts and Norms," Sociology & Criminology Faculty Publications (1998).

188 Jürgen Habermas, "Knowledge and Interest" 9 *Inquiry*, 285–300, 297 (1966). To Habermas, as a normative basis for his theory, humanity is autonomous by its nature.

> The concern with emancipation from quasi-natural authority is not just a vague idea that hovers before one's eyes: it can be *a priori* comprehended. What raises us above nature is indeed the only fact of which, due to its very nature, we *can* have knowledge: namely, language. The idea of autonomy is given to us with the structure of language. With the very first sentence the intention of a common and uncompelled consensus is unequivocally stated.

189 James Chriss, "Review essay view essay of Jurgen Habermas' Between Facts and Norms," Sociology & Criminology Faculty Publications (1998).

190 Jürgen Habermas, *Between Facts and Norms: Contributions to a Discourse Theory of Law and Democracy* (Cambridge: MIT Press, 1996), 109.

191 James Chriss, "Review essay view essay of Jurgen Habermas' Between Facts and Norms," Sociology & Criminology Faculty Publications (1998).

192 Ian Carter, "Positive and Negative Liberty", in N. Edward (ed.), *The Stanford Encyclopedia of Philosophy* (Spring 2022 Edition), https://plato.stanford.edu/archives/spr2022/entries/liberty-positive-negative/. For more information on how the law reflects this positive liberty, *see* Kai Moller, "Two Conceptions of Positive Liberty: Towards an Autonomy-Based Theory of Constitutional Rights," 29 *Oxf. J. of Legal Stud.* 757–786 (2009).

193 Ian Carter, "Positive and Negative Liberty", in N. Edward (ed.), *The Stanford Encyclopedia of Philosophy* (Spring 2022 Edition), https://plato.stanford.edu/archives/spr2022/entries/liberty-positive-negative/

194 Ian Carter, "Positive and Negative Liberty", in N. Edward (ed.), *The Stanford Encyclopedia of Philosophy* (Spring 2022 Edition), https://plato.stanford.edu/archives/spr2022/entries/liberty-positive-negative/. I can focus here on the liberal objection to "positive liberties and freedoms." Liberals might criticize legal expressions "positive liberty" on anti-paternalist grounds, "objecting that such measures will require the state to use resources in ways that the supposedly heteronomous individuals, if left to themselves, might have chosen to spend in other ways." If you'll recall, in the sphere of education, this was *precisely* what I found to be true in thinking through my initial manuscript project—people, if left to their own devices, can do insane things! Or, do nothing! The

> ideal of positive freedom might still conflict the liberal idea of respect for persons, one interpretation of which involves viewing individuals from the outside and taking their choices at face value. From a liberal point of view, the blindness to internal constraints can be intentional.

I agree, but this contends with the situation currently; again, I argue, consider the ramifications of a more rational and self-examining culture. People might think differently and will therefore be able to conduct themselves in different ways.

195 Ian Carter, "Positive and Negative Liberty", in N. Edward (ed.), *The Stanford Encyclopedia of Philosophy* (Spring 2022 Edition), https://plato.stanford.edu/archives/spr2022/entries/liberty-positive-negative/. (emphasis added).
196 Martha Nussbaum, *Cultivating Humanity: A Classical Defense of Reform in Liberal Education* (Cambridge: Harvard University Press, 1998), 49.
197 Martha Nussbaum, *Cultivating Humanity: A Classical Defense of Reform in Liberal Education* (Cambridge: Harvard University Press, 1998), 49.
198 Martha Nussbaum, *Cultivating Humanity: A Classical Defense of Reform in Liberal Education* (Cambridge: Harvard University Press, 1998), 49.
199 Graham Ferris, *The Uses of Values in Legal Education* (Cambridge: Insertia, 2015), 13. See the works also of Harry Frankfurt and Bernard Williams.
200 Bernard Williams, "Person, Character, and Morality," *in Moral Luck—Philosophical Papers* (1973).
201 Graham Ferris, *The Uses of Values in Legal Education* (Cambridge: Insertia, 2015), 13.
202 Graham Ferris, *The Uses of Values in Legal Education* (Cambridge: Insertia, 2015), 13.
203 Graham Ferris, *The Uses of Values in Legal Education* (Cambridge: Insertia, 2015), 13 (*quoting* Appiah, *The Ethics of Identity* (2005)).
204 Martha Nussbaum, *Cultivating Humanity: A Classical Defense of Reform in Liberal Education* (Cambridge: Harvard University Press, 1998), 49. Nussbaum declares this to be principally important, that all education ought to be suited to the pupil's circumstance and contexts. Learning law, rather than a universal curriculum, is a highly individualized experience given the way in which it invokes different things for different people. Yet, it *is* universal in that all are touched by the law.
205 Alexis de Tocqueville, *Democracy in America* (Chicago: University of Chicago Press, 2002), 270.
206 Marshall Knapp, "Social Values and Older Persons: The Role of Law," 7 *Maq. Elder's Advisor* 70 (2005).
207 Alexis de Tocqueville, *Democracy in America* (Chicago: University of Chicago Press, 2002), 270, 270.
208 Marshall Knapp, "Social Values and Older Persons: The Role of Law," 7 *Maq. Elder's Advisor* 70 (2005).
209 Martha Nussbaum, *Not for Profit: Why Democracy Needs the Humanities* (Princeton, NJ: Princeton University Press, 2016), 48. This only serves to further their capability for effective political participation and reasoning, as well.
210 Graham Ferris, *The Uses of Values in Legal Education* (Cambridge: Insertia, 2015), 13.
211 Graham Ferris, *The Uses of Values in Legal Education* (Cambridge: Insertia, 2015), 13.
212 Graham Ferris, *The Uses of Values in Legal Education* (Cambridge: Insertia, 2015), 13.
213 Xiandang Liu, "The Problem of Character Education and Kohlberg's Moral Education: Critique from Dewey's Moral Deliberation," 45 *Philos. Stud. Educ.* 136 (2014).
214 Graham Ferris, *The Uses of Values in Legal Education* (Cambridge: Insertia, 2015), 13.

215 Graham Ferris, *The Uses of Values in Legal Education* (Cambridge: Insertia, 2015), 13.

216 Xiandang Liu, "The Problem of Character Education and Kohlberg's Moral Education: Critique from Dewey's Moral Deliberation," 45 *Philos. Stud. Educ.* 136 (2014)

> For example, in traditional society, males have authority in leadership, females usually have the virtue of obedience. When we realize that value is unfair for the female, we critique the settled social order and begin to a new social order. In this way, Dewey holds that "the school has power to modify the social order.

217 Graham Ferris, *The Uses of Values in Legal Education* (Cambridge: Insertia, 2015), 75.

218 Graham Ferris, *The Uses of Values in Legal Education* (Cambridge: Insertia, 2015), 75.

219 Graham Ferris, *The Uses of Values in Legal Education* (Cambridge: Insertia, 2015), 68.

220 Graham Ferris, *The Uses of Values in Legal Education* (Cambridge: Insertia, 2015), 68.

221 Graham Ferris, *The Uses of Values in Legal Education* (Cambridge: Insertia, 2015), 75.

222 Graham Ferris, *The Uses of Values in Legal Education* (Cambridge: Insertia, 2015), 75.

223 Graham Ferris, *The Uses of Values in Legal Education* (Cambridge: Insertia, 2015), 23. Law is certainly about language and reason. As Ferris notes:

> the ability to locate weakness or error in an argument is a safeguard against being manipulated, misdirected, mistaken, or confused. The ability to construct, and recognize the need to be constrained by, valid arguments are fundamental to theoretical and practical reasoning.

Ferris also notes:

> [A legal education is not] merely logical competence (the manipulation of premises and conclusions), however, but one must also find the right expression for the thought, or proposal, or issue. The use of language and reason to ask questions, think about problems and decide what to do, is of immense importance in the law and in life. There is real value in being able to think and talk and write and figure and in being able to combine the primary symbolic systems we have developed for reasoning.

224 Graham Ferris, *The Uses of Values in Legal Education* (Cambridge: Insertia, 2015), 69. Ferris notes that the "idealism of perfectionism and the elegance of unitary explanations are both poor academic practice and bad politics."

225 Graham Ferris, *The Uses of Values in Legal Education* (Cambridge: Insertia, 2015), 69.

> In the public realm, the realm of law, we accept good judgment. Compromise need not be shamed or unprincipled. Compromise is the recognition of the legitimacy of the interests of the other. Conciliation need not be cowardly or based. Conciliation is the acceptance of the necessity of the other to the collective endeavor. Selfishness

need not be destructive of the common interests—the selfish assertion of one group is the political representation of that group.

226 Graham Ferris, *The Uses of Values in Legal Education* (Cambridge: Insertia, 2015), 30.

227 Graham Ferris, *The Uses of Values in Legal Education* (Cambridge: Insertia, 2015), 27.

228 Graham Ferris, *The Uses of Values in Legal Education* (Cambridge: Insertia, 2015), 30.

229 Graham Ferris, *The Uses of Values in Legal Education* (Cambridge: Insertia, 2015), 20.

230 Graham Ferris, *The Uses of Values in Legal Education* (Cambridge: Insertia, 2015), 20

231 I can compare this to Nussbaum's affection for Socrates. "Socrates demands only the sort of moral capacity that ordinary people have and use in their daily conduct. What he asks is that this capacity be trained and sharpened to realize itself more fully." Martha Nussbaum, *Cultivating Humanity: A Classical Defense of Reform in Liberal Education* (Cambridge: Harvard University Press, 1998), 26–27. So too is this the case for law learning. We ask only that you bring your rationality, no prior knowledge of systems.

232 Marc Galanter, "Why the Haves Come Out Ahead: Speculations on the Limits of Legal Change" 9 *Law Soc. Rev.* 95–160 (1974), 148. In addition to being accessible as a subject, it is also exceptionally inclusive:

> The legal system provides a way of accommodating cultural heterogeneity and social diversity while propounding universalism and unity; of accommodating base concentrations of private power while upholding the supremacy of public authority; of accommodating inequality in fact while establishing equality at law; of facilitating action by great collective combines while celebrating individualism... . It permits unification and universalism at the symbolic level and diversity and particularism at the operating level.

233 Graham Ferris, *The Uses of Values in Legal Education* (Cambridge: Insertia, 2015), 102.

234 Graham Ferris, *The Uses of Values in Legal Education* (Cambridge: Insertia, 2015), 102.

235 Graham Ferris, *The Uses of Values in Legal Education* (Cambridge: Insertia, 2015), 102.

5 A Critical Lens

Addressing Counterarguments

There are many positive attributes to an education in law learning; I have now discussed how the jurisprudential twists an educator applies to a law education transform the students' systemic perspectives in a law school setting and how this should inspire us in the civic context, as well as how—when even more broadly construed—law learning reconstructs one's relationship to authority and provides a forum for reflecting on one's own values in the context of larger socio-political conversations. This chapter further defends the benefits of a "learning law" project, but now by way of discussing anticipated criticisms—both practical and theoretical in nature—concerning the proposal.

Of course, the three criticisms below represent only a small cross-section of potential concerns.[1] These critiques arise, however, along a central throughline that is worth discussing outright: "law learning—if conceived as something derived from any current law school instruction—is *only* a one-dimensional professional training that is, in this proposal, being imbued with more value as a robust education than it rightly deserves credit for." In other words, the critic might assert that it is technical, functional, and practice-oriented rather than liberal and philosophical. And I'll be the first to admit that even when early legal scholars propounded that law education be conducted "in the grand manner,"[2] that never truly was the case at most legal institutions. Rather law school was meant more as an apprenticeship for practice, a "scientific occupation" even, and, by extension this proposal would necessarily be about providing professional training so as to have us create a "nation of lawyers." Nobody wants that, argues the critic.

Allow me to discuss this "professional versus liberal" education comment briefly before diving into the other varied criticisms. Indeed, this assailment has some merit in terms of legal education's training focus today,[3] but is wrong in terms of the outcome this yields for the civic project. What I am articulating here as a law learning curriculum is reconceived from training to be a lawyer. In the above, I have, at least ancillary, articulated a more liberal vision of law and legal education than "professional or practical training" that we see in today's graduate

DOI: 10.4324/9781003596523-8

legal education. The application of legal education to primary and secondary schools is something, indeed, more along the lines of what Harold Berman contemplated in 1986 (and before this at a Harvard conference in 1954) for law in undergraduate settings.[4] Berman explored how law can "enrich the minds of students[5] if it were taught"—not just as a separate course but integrated into other academic disciplines[6]—in college. The virtues he discussed were myriad; law obviates "a method of reasoning adapted to the reaching of decisions for action and to the establishing of frameworks or relationships"; it helps them become aware of the institutions in which they are presently, inextricably involved; it helps students to appreciate the role law has had as a part of the "tradition of western thought and action."[7] Law complements the politics students "to grasp more fully underlying premises" and the philosophy student needing "to understand better the nature of inductive and deductive reasoning, the relation of ends to means, and the meaning of justice."[8] And, of course, as I have touched on in this piece, by studying the law, "the student enlarges his own intellectual responsibility and his moral capacity to judge between competing claims and to strike a proper balance between rule and discretion."[9] Implicit in this, of course, is also that the student can "develop [their own] sense of justice and a capacity for responsible judgment."[10] For, in "studying the factors which enter the reaching of legal decisions and the making of legal rules, students can enlarge their own capacity to judge between competing claims and to apply general principles to the concrete circumstances of particular situations."[11]

Envisioning an education that puts at a premium the capability of attending to one's values (one's identity), the capacity for critical thinking, higher reasoning, and self-examination, but *all* done through the lens of law and its institutions, so as to educate for participating in legalistic national democracy as we have in America, is more along the lines of what I have in mind. That said, *I* am sure I did *not* gather that empowerment for introspection from *my own* law school education. Still, that's not the point. The point, rather, is that you *can* gain those skills and perspectives if the law curriculum taught for civics was constructed with that mind.

We have a problem today, Berman points out, in conceiving education as *either* professional *or* as liberal education. When, in fact, if properly conceived, they are a complement to one another: "all good professional education is characterized by a focus on the interaction of ends and means in reaching decisions."[12] We can, indeed, say that we should be educating students for the *profession* of citizenship, and to do so requires them to learn law. The study of law is, in fact, "closest to the subject matter of the liberal arts" as it instructs students in a "professional way of thought" while "deal[ing] with the problems of common men and are generally understandable. The decisions it makes, although they relate to individual persons or institutions, are made in a social setting."[13] The law, further "records not only the decisions it makes but [also] the reasons the individual judges thought they had for making them" which causes the students to be "directly in contact with reality."[14] All law, not just cases, articulate "reasons for and against particular legal solutions to particular social problems; and further, in all types of legal decision-making, the reasons that are offered must fall within a framework not only of logic and of values but also of tradition and of authority."[15]

This rhetoric reconceives the intersection of professional and liberal education in a way that is highly effective for the civic law learning project. Nussbaum complements this by way of articulating the job of the citizen in the context of the democratic experiment:

> our country has [already] embarked on an unparalleled experiment, inspired by these ideals of self-command and cultivated humanity … [we must now] hope to draw citizens toward one another by complex mutual understanding and individual self-scrutiny, building a democratic culture that is truly deliberative and reflective, rather than simply the collision of unexamined preferences.[16]

Under Berman's articulation, law is the *perfect* conduit for this work. Law, indeed, waits in the wings as a siloed graduate education that holds *so* much value to the student. An exploration of what an *empowering* education—for skills and for values—steeped in key educational philosophy—gives us guidelines as to *how* students ought to learn, *what* students ought to learn.

So, education in law is *not* synonymous with the proliferation of "lawyers" in the practical professional sense, and, no, in no way is law *just* one-dimensional training—even where it is siloed from other disciplines. Rather, the law is an example of an education that is *both* professional and liberal. It is a transformative and reconstructive education for students in the profession of citizenship. I want to bear this in mind as essential framing for the following criticisms of law learning, which all endeavor to get at the impact such an education would have on the citizen and the means of measuring it.

5.1 A Nation of Lawyers; Law Is Adversity, Selfishness, Dispassion, and Coldness

The concern for a "nation of lawyers" likely is owed to a certain checkered reputation we, as a profession, share and the notion that a legal education available to citizens everywhere would lead to engendering unsavory attitudes and qualities that are now relegated only to the lawyers. Now, I have argued that *law learning* is about building a new citizen, one who values self-reflection as well as patience, process, temperance, fairness, pluralism, and diversity of opinion, passionate advocacy, and debate. Furthermore, the classroom envisioned is one where students, through the catalyzing subject of law, come to reflect on their own principles through universal ideals that are implemented in our legal discourse and confront those who disagree with them in the spirit of collegiality, openness, and even compromise. This promises a level of not only moral awareness but also emotional maturity, patience, and resilience on the back of rationality, reasonableness, and awareness.[17] But is this really what law is about and can law learning really do this? The first criticism is about the qualities, attitudes and dispositions of the lawyer and concerns about the type of characteristics that, in reality, law learning would develop. The critic emphasizes the notion that law is about being adversarial[18] and is more interested in engendering competitive attributes than this whole spirited proposal lets on[19]; law study is about getting what *you want* more than compromise. And, even further, an education in law, by virtue of its emphasis on the analytical and rational, prizing critical thinking and reason, also favors distance and coldness. Indeed, it is oppositional to attributes like understanding, empathy, altruism, and compassion which has been implicit in our discussions to this point. I want to address both of these aspects to the first criticism in turn. Let us begin with this assailment that "adversarialism" and competitiveness are the real outcomes of legal education.

5.1.1 Adversarialism and Selfishness are More Likely than Compromise and Respectful Debate

The reputation the lawyer holds for adversarialism and selfishness—and legal education might have for engendering these qualities—is, at least in part, credited to her intimate understanding of our adversarial process. To be sure, "our legal system is based principally on an adversarial model that asks us to see the other side as "other"— as an opponent to be beaten or at least to be gotten the better of as we zealously represent our own side."[20]

Indeed, from the moment we start law school, it seems we learn to argue *against* someone; to explore all sides of the question, yes, but with the main purpose of finding missteps in another's position. It is incongruent, argues the critic, to impugn the study of American law with empathy, altruism, or even emotion—only cold, linear, competitive thinking. Even on paper, it seems that "the rule of law [is] intended to elevate the judicial system above personal pique and favoritism, displacing emotions with uniformity and predictability."[21]

The notion of the "adversarial system" in legal education as breeding competitive and hostile and selfish—albeit if rational and reasoning—students is worth addressing; it serves as a big obstacle in constructing the law the way that I have (as a subject favoring idea exchange, open plural discussion, and introspective self-examination). However, I maintain that it does not deal a death blow to the idea of a reconceived education supporting qualities of compromise, higher reasoning, and even empathy, altruism, compassion, and compromise (as we will see in the next section). In proving this, I want to start by exploring, first, the role and reception of the adversarial nature of law and its process in legal education. From where do we get this notion that law learning trains competitive people? Then, I want to understand how, on a more profound level as a part of a law learning education in our civic context, appreciation of the adversarial system—and criticism of it in the classroom space—might even enhance the development of qualities I have been discussing.

To be sure "conflict and conflicting notions of the good are inevitable for human beings."[22] It is more common for us to assume there is a basic value difference among us than that it is to establish universal notions of good or rightness. However, there are many ways to resolve conflict—for instance, cooperation, adaptation, negotiation, collaboration.[23] Many of these are embedded, for example, in Continental Europe's inquisitorial adjudicatory system where the decision-maker, rather than receiving packaged arguments upon which to decide a case, participates actively in the process of contending with facts and ideas to arrive to a more "truthful" conclusion.[24] But, in America, our adversarial adjudicatory system has been especially met with criticisms about its proclivity for exacerbating conflict.[25] It is charged that "the choice of [an adversarial] process will effect and limit the possible outcomes [in any conflict resolution process] to binary, stalemated, or impasse solutions."[26] Indeed, any "compromise" that might result is "unprincipled" on account of the goal being, always, for any lawyer, "like the payoff-maximizing game player, to gather as much of the goods or goodies for the client as possible."[27] There is no justice, fairness, or values of equity except with the greatest idealization, argues the critic.

In terms of education, the adversarial system is said to rigidify students' thinking; "the adversarial culture constrain[s] and cabin[s] our thinking unnecessarily by structuring it in polarized and oppositional terms."[28] To be sure, the adversarial nature of the law system contributes to the impression of the lawyer as always thinking in ways so "aggressively rational, linear, and goal-oriented," unaware of the "wishes, fears, beliefs, and defenses that motivate our actions."[29] I tend to agree; indeed, when taught to law students, the adversarial process might highly influence the cultivation of lawyers that are hot-headed and competitive and closed-minded. The ethos of adversarialism in law school might "constrain the way that students conceptualize their future roles and limits the 'possibility space' available to them for 'legal creativity', 'constructive lawyer[ing]' and 'peacemaking.'"[30] Part of the way adversarialism—and associated consequences—make their way into the attitude-shaping of the law student is through the special emphasis on the study of appellate materials (often to the detriment of studying other law materials like, for instance, administrative rules, scholarly articles, statutes, policies, and the like). As Molly Townes O'Brien writes:

> Rules are derived through the analysis of the rights of parties. Winners and losers are nominated. Wrongs are punished. In courses where appellate decisions are the primary teaching documents, law is predominantly the story of triumph and loss in the appellate courts. The task of the lawyer is to serve as an advocate for a client, to maximize that client's position and to win. The implicit messages of these stories are that the lawyer's central role is as an agent and advocate for a client whose interests are opposed to those of other parties and that real law emerges from the careful reasoning of appellate judges.[31]

This is, in no short order, a dark side of the *law-think* discussion in the previous chapter; *law-think*, our critic would argue, translates human conflict into abstract legal categories requiring dispassionate analysis and adversarial critique. Law students, therefore, begin to espouse these attitudes *en masse*; the structure of the learning of law through an adversarial lens "sharpens the mind in order the narrow it," pushing aside other "potentially important legal approaches including efforts to problem solve in light of the relevant social, political, or economic context," and discouraging "students from grappling with the moral values implicated by a problem."[32] It shoves aside more deliberative and collaborative approaches to problem-solving into the dominant frame of the appellate opinion, thereby "distorting their elaboration and marginalizing their value."[33]

Yet, while I do not dispute that any of this is a phenomenon in the larger project of training the next generation of lawyers, I am drawn to consider further O'Brien's particular emphasis on the conception of "the lawyer's central role [as] an agent and advocate for a *client* whose interests are opposed to other parties."[34] This in my view is key to distinguishing the above conversation with our conception of law learning. Indeed, it leads one to the realization that, perhaps, adversarialism in legal education might not be *the* poison that stunts critical thinking, inclusive dialogue, debate, and creativity that I have lauded as a part of learning law, but rather the professional "training" aspect, and, more specifically, the client-centric means of delivering legal education.[35] More than that, as Ann Shalleck highlights, it is the central focus on the "constructed client" in legal learning that really invites adversarialism to get in the way of other goals. This is a client that is unidentified, that lacks a world or context, and that exists in one-dimensionality only to serve one purpose: to have an interest and set the scene for advocacy.[36] The constructed client "wants something, but they have chosen the wrong means of obtaining it"; they come to the student's attention either knowing already what they want or are constrained and directed enough to fuel the student's competitiveness.[37] "Motivation and constraint are central" to the "constructed client"; but neglected are the "ambiguities and complexities of the client's actual situation, the multiplicity and confusion of goals that commonly characterize client behavior, even behavior that violates common norms of conduct."[38] "Students do not see the worlds that the clients come from, the institutions that shape the clients' lives, and the choices, or the conflicts, confusion, and uncertainty that some bring with them to the lawyer's office," and they certainly do not see the humanity in the opposition.[39] Rather, every case, every dispute centers around some anonymous client whose purpose is single-minded and absolute, who exists in a vacuum, and whose needs *you* must address or else be construed as failing.

Consider, for instance, an educator addressing a student in a law school class: they might ask, "if you represented the plaintiff, what would you argue in support of this rule?"; "what's the counterargument for the defendant?"; or "how would the plaintiff respond?"[40] Of course then the student would respond competitively, "my client is right because of X and the opposition is wrong because of Y," or else "my cause is just and consistent with the law and the other has no merit." In this way, because we are focused on clients and causes rather than ideas and relationships and larger questions, our adversarialism shines through. While "philosophers may seek the truth," "lawyers seek to achieve their client's interests and to 'win,' which may entail simply obfuscating the other side's case-as in the 'creation' of reasonable doubt in the criminal case-or leaving out important facts if they are deemed harmful."[41] Even where the particular use of the adversarial model can be defended—and we will offer some virtues that commend the adversarial system in due time—as a procedure of truth-finding in other settings, it does not pass muster in legal settings as a genuine exercise in knowledge.[42] Especially in the law school setting, where students are constantly judged against one another,[43] the need to defend this "clients" interest exacerbate differences and conflict in ways that justify our critics concern that the "adversarial nature of law" cannot be overcome. Indeed, even the Socratic method, if applied in a law school setting where students are vigorously trying to defend the interest of a client against, say, a professor who takes the opposing position, proves little more than a confrontation between a "hapless novice and an imperious authority."[44] And, further, when applied in a vacuous conversation about a case devoid of emotional and cultural context, the Socratic method can be conceived of as perpetuates the notion that "presumed objectivity of the law is from the white, middle-class perspective" and that there are no alternative means of understanding or reasoning a legal question.[45]

With all this said, it is worth noting the distinction between a legal education, as I have constructed it, and legal training as an apprenticeship or as a lawyer representing a client. We can recall Berman's cross-fertilization of liberal education with the professional education discussed above. Law learning broadly construed, or, more aptly, when a student puts themselves "in the position of judge"—unbiased, intellectually engaged— rather than advocate, is not a matter of "training in techniques; it is rather, as Lon Fuller put it, 'a kind of vicarious experience which [is] in part a substitute for the kind of experience in practical affairs that [enriches] philosophical study.'"[46] It is a *law learning* without advocacy that I have proposed—at least no advocacy confined to defending a "constructed client." No, instead *you* are the client; democracy is the client. And this shift is rather simply conducted, even with the adversarial system being what it is and featuring as heavily in any law learning experience as it must.

Many have already proposed the reconstruction of graduate legal education bearing this observation in mind, and those conversations might paint a helpful picture of the inspiration from which we might draw for the civic classroom featuring law learning. One way, for instance, would be to reconceive the "constructed client" in the law learning process. Shalleck herself advocates for reconceptualizing the client to better complement the "relationship between individuality and community in the law," saying that "the discourse about civic virtue needs to reclaim clients as they are situated in the world to make them part of the dialogue of the law."[47] In other words, by humanizing the "client" in a given case, understanding more deeply context and socio-cultural milieus giving rise to conflict, coloring motivations, detailing descriptions of the particular situations of clients and how that relates to broader social phenomenon, one begins to reinterpret emergent conceptions of legal institutions, problems, and obligations "toward civic values or republican notions of community."[48] This, in turn, generates a whole different disposition on a case and attitude toward learning and modifies the learning outcome from selfish, zealous advocacy to understanding and fairness and justice. As Shalleck articulates:

> discussion about civic virtue cannot change legal discourse if clients continue to be used to supply somewhat different motivations that prefigure the ends of this altered legal thought. Within the language of civic discourse, clients are citizens who come in contact with the law in ways that cause them to seek lawyers. It is critical that their experience shape the discussion.[49]

The study of law—at least in terms of the civic project—*without* client-centeredness is something altogether different from the adversarial "legal training." Of course, such an education does still involve the adversarial system as subject matter. In an appellate opinion, there are two sides and there are positions. Yet, the reception of these cases shifts. The student—free from expectations of zealous advocacy—can come to appreciate the law, and indeed the adversarial system, more philosophically. And to be sure, the adversarial system, when studied and criticized in a classroom environment, is predicated on reasoning and values that could complement so many of the ideas previously discussed in these pages, separate from its self-evident competitiveness element. Many have argued, for example, for the superiority of this system in finding the truth (in terms of fact-finding),[50] engendering a procedure that reduces the citizen's desire for self-help and leads to a more ordered society,[51] fairness, rationality, un-biasedness,[52] and its prizing of being highly individualistic (in terms of responsibility and individual dignity), "[giving] control and responsibility to the individuals who are most interested in the result and takes advantage of their self-interest in complete and creative argument."[53] This is important to note: "adjudicatory systems reflect the values that members of society share," and, for us, "individualism is our most prominent."[54] While I *in no way* case a judgment on the merits of the adversarial system, I must concede that, when it comes to its role in law learning for civic students, it is a valuable conduit for bringing this theme to the fore for a general citizen, even if only to criticize its *failure* to meet the values that have been attributed to it.

If, as I suggest at the beginning of this chapter, we endeavor to provide a transformative and reconstructive professional *and* liberal education for students in the profession of citizenship, then these values—the adversarial system's values—ought to be studied and explored. And, when they are critiqued, students will come to understand that a certain of amount "winning" and self-interest is contemplated in the general civic education project. They are certainly not the only thing—for if "consequentialist justifications were all that motivated us, democratic theorists tell us, we would not vote since we know that one vote almost never makes a difference in an election"[55]—but they are a part of a mixed motive:

> people vote (at least some of them some of the time) for things that would actually be costly for them—such as tax measures to build prisons, schools, and other public facilities—*and* because of the "we-feeling" generated by group participation.[56]

In other words, they want to "win" on things they care about, and they want everyone to "win" according to their values. We need both individualistic and communitarian interests, in balance, for the purposes of our democracy.

In this way, we begin conceiving of the adversarial aspect of law in a much more creative way, indeed promising a much more creative education on the subject as well for students. The adversarial system, rather than just preaching and engendering competitiveness and a "winning" mentality, also instructs us that "new explanations must be found, new defenses created, and new causes of action and new transactional forms [must] be discovered. Some adversarial creativity may even be exercised in the spirit of law avoidance."[57] Carrie Menkel-Meadow proposes that, in engendering creativity and critical thinking as opposed to selfishness and myopic views of the law, especially when instructing in typical appellate cases, educators might ask a series of questions in law cases to "push students to look for multiple possibilities and directions that the case could have taken, before it hardened into its appellate form."[58] One might ask:

> What are the "real" issues between the parties? What were the parties trying to accomplish? Who else is, or was, involved in the transaction, dispute or underlying issue? How else might the parties have dealt with or managed their problem aside from the lawsuit at hand? What other solutions, proposals

> or resolutions of their matter would have been possible? Answering these questions allows students to see how much more might be at stake than what the court fixes on; that other people may be involved and that other resources might have been mobilized to deal with the problem.[59]

And these guiding questions serve us incredibly well in our re-conception of the civic classroom devoted to law learning. No client loyalty; only deliberation, our preoccupation with institutional awareness, gaining the capability to balance multiple interests and ideas, and proffering an education that opens the doors for cooperative learning, perspective taking, values debate, and even empathy training. "Morality is not only cognitive, but affective, not only individualistic, but relational, and not based only on rules, but on variations that are context dependent." Importantly, "these can enhance the ability of our students to be more sensitive to others and particularly inviting of important counterpoints and diverse opinions."[60] All of this, to be sure, can be done even in light of the natural adversarial process in which cases and disputes are adjudicated, the natural proclivity for conflict and the push to take sides.

5.1.2 An Education in Critical Thinking and Rationalism Means Coldness and Ruthlessness

Now, this is all fine and well, continues our critic, but education in law is *still* analytical and rational, prizing critical thinking and reason. Classical legal education (and social tradition) has long held that the cultivation of rationality is indelibly at odds with emotions[61] and, thereby, compassion, empathy, love, and understanding are foreign to the law-trained mind. Part of the concern, therefore, with "creating a nation of lawyers" is that we are educating in a way that does not prioritize love and emotion, but cold, analytical, technical rationalism.[62]

I concede that lawyers have received—perhaps rightfully—a reputation "as cold, dispassionate, uncaring, overly logical, fact-driven, aggressive, competitive, ruthless, and even amoral."[63] Statistics have shown the pre-law student, law student, and lawyer to be "uniformly less interested in people, in emotions, and interpersonal concerns"; they "display an orientation toward rights and justice, logic, thinking, and rationality without regard to their personal values" and do not "consider interpersonal harmony or humanistic concerns in making decisions."[64] And, I would agree, a nation that pushes forward a civic education that promises these qualities in students would not be a good thing. However, as I will show, a position which argues that legal education *necessarily* places rationality and emotions *in opposition* relies on some antiquated conceptions about law, law education, and legal reasoning,[65] and, indeed biology.[66] A re-conception of graduate legal education that bridges the reasoning–emotion dichotomy has been well-argued for by a school of legal (and multi-disciplinary) theorists in the field of "law and emotion," so as to show that, indeed, critical thinking and reasoning—even if treated as prime in law learning—are *only benefited* by the integration of emotions and the valuing of empathy, compassion, understanding, and more humanistic qualities. In other words, I can sketch, at least superficially here, a view of law and law learning that balances the relationship between reason and emotion more appropriately than our critic suggests in light of current understanding.[67] This is quite helpful in understanding what *law learning*, in this proposal, might more look like both in terms of what students and learn and what characteristics are prized.

I will go about this explanation in two stages. To begin, we might discuss the relationship between law and emotions, beginning with its rootedness in biological and psychological research on the relationship between reasoning and emotion, and then continuing by way of studying how this relationship has long been historically dichotomized in legal education and the problems that have resulted. I will then explore how legal theorists have proposed re-envisioning and re-integrating the law learning project—even with its rationalism and emphasis on critical appraisal and logical reasoning—to keep emotions in mind, as well as carve out space for altruism and compassion in service of the law training project. These comments, we will see, provide a good theoretical foundation for thinking about our *law learning* civic classroom environment (indeed, echoing a lot of the qualities and classroom environment components we have already discussed in this piece). Finally, upon laying out that background, I want to reflect more generally on the fact that this *law learning* proposal should be considered merely a starting point in terms of curricular reforms. Far from being taught in a vacuum, *law learning* should be conceived as a complementary education to other instruction, like that in social, emotional, and ethical learning, to best educate students for robust citizenship. While I show that *law learning* is not at odds with emotional education, I do not make the claim that it is the best form of it.

Contrary to centuries-old conceptions of the dichotomous relationship between reason and emotion, new work in the field of cognitive psychology has substantially reformulated our understanding of the connection between these two "rich realms of human experience,"[68] a connection that has inspired a whole school of "law and emotion" legal theorists concerned with the way in which emotion is siloed out in the law school classroom.[69]

One of the chief architects of this breakthrough in scientific understanding, Antonio Damasio, challenged the notion of "pure reason" on biological levels:[70]

> reason may not be as pure as most of us think it is or wish it were, [] emotions and feelings may not be intruders in the bastion of reason at all: they may be enmeshed in its networks, for worse *and* for better.[71]

In his somatic-marker hypothesis, Damasio theorized and proved that "instead of facing the infinite array of conceivable logical thoughts and actions in every situation, some *nonconscious affective process* rejects many potential courses of action automatically, dramatically reducing the scope of decision alternatives."[72] If this process—the ability to *emotionally* experience potential outcomes in a given decision—is impaired, we can spend hours on the simplest matters. Fascinatingly, this shows the limit to "pure reason" on biological levels; our "non-conscious affective process [our emotions] interact constantly with the environment to direct our attitudes and behaviors."[73]

Now, to be sure, Damasio does concede that "emotions and feelings can cause havoc in the processes of reasoning under certain circumstances."[74] This is in line, indeed, with the long-standing general belief that, as I will further below, served in the legal community to support the earliest pushes for rationalism and deductive, scientific approaches to solutions and legal reasoning training in the law academic.[75] But Damasio observes that *so too* is the "absence of emotion and feeling no less damaging [than too many emotions or the wrong emotions], no less capable of compromising the rationality that makes us distinctly human and allows us to decide in consonance with a sense of personal future, social convention and moral principle."[76]

Indeed, "certain aspects of the process of emotion and feeling are indispensable for rationality."[77] Critically, Damasio continues, this knowledge of the relationship between reasoning and feelings should not "make us less inclined to empirical verification,"[78] nor "diminish our determination to control external circumstances to the advantage of individuals and society, or our resolve to develop, invent, or perfect the cultural instruments with which we can make the world better."[79] However, the time has arrived to cast aside the preconception of feelings as invoking the images of "self-oriented concern, of disregard for the world around, and of tolerance for relaxed standards of intellectual performance" and toward an understanding that "strengthening of rationality probably requires that greater consideration be given to the world within."[80]

This is a remarkable breakthrough, especially given a tradition of belittling and ostracizing emotion both in terms of gender norms and professional demeanor. Turning to the landscape of "law and emotion" theory, scholars have, since the 1990s, seized on biology as a means of recreating the legal culture around rationality and emotion, and, more importantly for our purposes, re-envisioning the role of *emotion in connection with law-think*, in the law school classroom. They have done so, first, by critiquing prevailing ideologies of rationality and "pure" reason as the law classroom's *raison d'etre* in many ways, including both the "chilling" effect that such an obsession has on intellectual discourse and rationalism's reliance on false narratives of objectivity in the law. I will discuss both below. First, however, I believe it is worth noting again that just the fact that these conversations have taken place—indeed a whole field developed exploring the intersection of "law and emotions" and legal education—demonstrates an acknowledgment, on the part of the law academy, of two things relevant to our critic's concern: (1) yes, legal education can be, and has been, cold on account of its rationalism and dichotomization from emotions, but (2) that legal education can and has (in some cases) innovated. This, at the outset, should assuage our reader that *law learning*, as constructed in this proposal, mindful of the law and emotion discussions already taking place in the graduate school context, has the theoretical foundation needed to not fall into the trap of producing cold, dispassionate, unfeeling, and uncaring citizens.

Harris and Shultz, in a seminal "law and emotions" article, offer the following thoughtful description of the "dominant ideology" of "pure reason" and its relationship to emotions:

> Law legitimates official coercion. It designs institutions and processes for the resolution of conflict. It prescribes norms for conduct. It expresses and effectuates social ideals of fairness and justice. These functions—central in our society—cannot help but evoke strong emotions. Moreover, legal rules and institutions incorporate our deepest concerns about culpability and desert, free will and responsibility, equality and freedom. These ideals are generally agreed upon at the highest levels of abstraction, but their implementation is deeply problematic. Given these realities, it seems that emotion could not possibly be eliminated from the domain of the law. **We speculate that it is precisely because of the threat unrestrained emotion poses to the "rule of law" that the dominant ideology has been so pervasive.** Because law stands at the fulcrum of deeply consequential, deeply emotional, never-ending struggles, it must seek a basis for fairness and disinterest. The attempt to isolate and suppress emotion in law serves at least two purposes. First, it provides habits and aspirations that increase lawyers' ability to resist the temptations inherent in their societal function. Second, it increases their credibility and the legitimacy of lawyers' social role. Thus, legal institutions and professionals' separate reason from emotion and exalt reason as a way of warding off a fundamental fear that law itself is inseparable from the passions of "politics." In this way, the dream of law becomes the dream of pure reason.[81]

Their challenge to "pure reason" was, indeed, one to a "long intellectual tradition that dichotomized reason and emotion," reflective of "the historic view of law as a quasi-science: a process of deducing, from a framework of legal principles, the rule to be applied to a particular case."[82] But, founded in new research and understanding, like that of Damasio, the early theorists minced no words in claiming that the "pure reason" attributed to legal-decision-making, in practice and in the classroom, was patently fictious; *law-think*, specifically, was already "enriched and refined by the operation of emotions because they direct attention to particular dimensions of a case, or shape [one's] ability to understand the perspective of, or the stakes of a decision for, a particular party."[83] To try and excise that emotional component, one would produce "legal judgements that are shallow, routinized, evaluative, and even irresponsible."[84] Nevertheless, commitment to this picture of rationality was, and to a certain extent remains, steadfast often leading to a chilling effect on intellectual discourse, both in terms of classroom and student dynamics and in terms of the caliber of ideas and substantive conversation being held.

In terms of classroom experience, one would not be hard-pressed to deny that favoritism toward dispassionate rationality led to many issues,[85] an especially important one for our purposes being stifled conversation. Rationalizing classroom discussions made them dry and sterile[86]; where rationalization was unchallenged by emotion, legal analysis became an abstract exercise that not only bred boredom but was both "technically precious and practically irrelevant," "intellectually shallow and uninvolving."[87] This was problematic as students were ill-equipped to face hard choices or deal in gray areas. This is where students might learn to argue for and against, and they could not place their arguments in a broader philosophical or moral context, lapsing into apathy or taking blindly neutral positions where personal judgment was required. According to Harris and Shultz:

> law students became passive receptacles of knowledge; personal experience and the light it sheds seems irrelevant to legal thought. When teaching is simply the exercise of getting students to jump through logical hoops, day after day, week after week, it becomes mind-numbing and devoid of intellectual interest.[88]

In other words, patent rationality yields only tools of the system rather than change-makers or critics.

This, of course, also comes through in terms of the development of ideas themselves in the law school setting. Where to "think like a lawyer" meant to be *only* "incisively rational, logical, analytical, and especially, dispassionate,"[89] the dominant ideology being unchallenged, "fairness and neutrality [become] encoded as 'objectivity,' and 'objectivity' is narrowly understood as 'rationality'."[90] In other words, divorcing emotion or devaluing personal feelings on issues reinforces existing hierarchies of all sorts. This becomes plain in the context of the (problematic) "winners" and "losers" ideology propagated in the law school classroom, as I have already discussed above. If you will recall, every legal structure or decision creates "winners" and "losers," but, when seen through the lens of a culture of hyper-rationality, "winners," more than just favoring the competitive, become those that are "comparatively dispassionate in discussing existing arrangements unless or until those arrangements are seriously threatened." "Losers" are those that "get emotionally agitated by what they perceive as unjust disadvantage."[91] Now, this is certainly problematic were we to adopt legal education to *law learning* in civics; a community of citizens, after all, would hardly be benefited by this "winner" mentality. Such a disposition goes against a culture of acceptance and tolerance, social justice, and empathy, not to speak of the way in which it exacerbates adversarialism, conformity, and competitiveness. In the law school setting, compounded with the already problematic client-centric, advocative nature of the classroom, "pure reason" ideology yielded—and still yields—students with toxic characteristics—that of a "hired gun, able to argue anything on behalf of anyone," but "untouched by her own fervor."[92] All this to say, a hyper-prizing of rationalism at the expense of all others is a bad look for this proposal. Fortunately, theorists have proposed new solutions bridging the analytical, critical thinking focus with emotional appreciation. This only builds a more robust thinker; as Martha Nussbaum notes, curricular innovations ought to favor emotions in tandem with law discussions as they produce conversations "more reliable in deliberation than [those featuring only] detached intellectual judgments, since emotions embody some of our most deeply rooted views about what has importance, views that could easily be lost from sight during sophisticated intellectual reasoning."[93]

One key solution has been broadening the potential ways of conceiving of tradition, law, ideas, and substance in more humanistic ways in the classroom.[94] Harris and Shults, for instance, propose that to get a class engaged, willing to challenge "preconceived notions, to question received wisdom, and to consider threatening new ideas," it is prudent to "get them to talk about what they really *think and believe* about whatever we're studying."[95] Integrating case discussions with "life experiences, agendas, and beliefs of people [that] vary widely," promise that "emotional friction will be enmeshed in any genuinely meaningful exchange."[96] Another theorist, borrowing from John Dewey's philosophy, proposed integrating emotions by way of an experimental-learning model including role-playing practices in the classroom, more individual-centered discussions surrounding cases, and posing legal questions in the context of moral discussions, to let students connect with materials and avoid falling into the rationalist trap producing passivity of students, lack of independent thinking, absorbing ideology, and obedience. Still others have proposed imbuing the classroom environment with a sense of uncompromising trust and respect and openness so as to encourage students—when learning law, facts, and contexts—to "submit feelings to reflection" in group settings, which "allows some choice about which feelings to reinforce as worthy and which to try to discard."[97] Naturally all of these suggestions include the use of a variety of different legal sources—not just cases, but also court transcripts, statutes, narratives, articles, policies, rules, and ordinances—so as to ensure a robust understanding of legal materials, and, of course, "leavening [] reasoned analysis with intuition and empathy, with purposes and values, enable[ing] us to move beyond mere comprehension toward wisdom."[98]

Importantly, "infusing rationality with emotion … renders visible the fact that, whatever its aspirations, law is never neutral or objective."[99] Thus, emotions act as a guide to those contemplating what constitutes a "just and moral world,"[100] and help introduce a "fellow feeling"[101] in classrooms that promote respect and robust exchange. This is especially *apropos* of this proposal for *law learning* in the civic context. These solutions—as well as the before-heard critiques in the realm of graduate legal education—provide us excellent intellectual fodder for considering a *law learning* environment that is predicated on bridging the connection between law and emotions. To tap into one's emotions, while studying law and thinking on law matter, will augment and strengthen the student's ability for self-reflection, understanding, curiosity, and compassion. It provides a compass for justice and moral decision-making, integrity and purpose, and allows for a culture that supports the "golden rule,"[102] and thereby even altruism.[103] In environments like this, students develop a whole different perspective on law and their positions on key issues; consider that:

> reflective people want to satisfy themselves that their judgments and decisions will withstand serious scrutiny. They also want to satisfy other people, whose interests are affected by what they do, that they are acting out of tested conviction and with integrity. So, they try to explain their convictions in a way that displays reflection, sincerity, and coherence, even when they have no hope of converting others to those convictions.[104]

Beyond a doubt, learning law requires an empathetic understanding of the interests of others and *gains* by way of being able to put ourselves in others' shoes. As Susan Bandes writes:

> [emotions both] have independent epistemic validity, and they are inextricably intertwined with reasoning—both moral and legal. Indeed, the passion for justice—and all the emotions that feed it, including moral outrage, moral shock, empathy, and compassion—are prominent among the motivations that draw so many of us to the law.[105]

Yet, in remarking as such, I do not mean to suggest that law learning alone can cultivate emotional maturity, develop empathy, or compassion alone—only that it is not at odds with doing so. The interjection I propound for civics—to best realize the vision of a robustly trained and empowered student turned robust citizen—ought to be accompanied by other educational reforms that develop emotional maturity and strength of character. Just as, for Damasio, a "comprehensive understanding of the human mind requires an organismic perspective,"[106] so too, indeed, must the student be immersed in all manner of ideas and constructions and thoughts and educations. Efforts toward ensuring student access to social and emotional learning,[107] for instance, or purpose-driven leadership education, are perfect complements to *law learning focus* on values and skills training for the democratic project. Whereas law, law debate, and legal reasoning are optimal for the exchange of varied ideas and values-pluralism, refinement in things like tolerance and acceptance can and should still be augmented with these important ideas.

Nevertheless, it *is* important to note that law and legal reasoning are not, by their nature, cold and dispassionate nor do they necessarily produce cold and dispassionate people. If we are cognizant of the general aim toward cultivating acculturated, thoughtful, and open citizens desirous of seeing both others and the nation flourish, *law learning* is a powerful tool in that mission.

5.2 Law Learning Is Too Vague for Tangible Metrics for Success

Given this proposal's theoreticality and broad scope, our critic might continue their assailment by suggesting that, while such a civic education might be ideal, it can hardly ever be realized.[108] They might further offer that, even if this proposal were to overhaul the current landscape of civic education coursework, *what* are the actual expected outcomes of *law learning*? *How* can they be measured? And *what* are some tangible benchmarks for student success? It is to these latter questions I want to turn next.

I have proposed that *law learning* is about self-examination and self-reflection; it is about the inculcation of key values while also embracing values-pluralism and the strengthening of one's identity and perspectives by way of engaging with diverse views through the universally touching subject of law. However, "self-examination" and "self-reflection" are, to be sure, very abstract notions and are hard to assess in the classroom—not least because they are skills engendered through mental processes that take place internally over time. In conceiving of potential benchmarks for *law learning* students and actual, articulable assessment goals, I am called, rather, to pivot away from thinking on these intellectual skills and more outwardly toward our vision of the "citizen"[109] and the project of citizenship *writ large*. For, after all, "every conception of citizenship education presupposes a theory of democracy—which in turn requires a theory of society—that should be made explicit as a central theme of deliberation and reflection in the curriculum."[110] I have, earlier, engaged the notion of the *deliberative* citizen in referencing Habermas' notion of communicative action and discourse theory of law and democracy as a framing mechanism for the value of *law learning*. I think this is an exceptional place to start in conceiving the assessment metrics of this new form of civics, specifically calling to mind Habermas' social, citizenship, and ethical theories specifically as they relate to education for *deliberative* citizenship.[111] The *deliberative* citizen—who we can assess—would also be developing the internal skills and conducting the introspective work I have prized above—which we would be hard-pressed to assess.

Recall that Habermas' *discourse* theories on law and democracy, his ideas on communicative action, and, by extension, his notion of citizenship, are founded on the value of "abstract, legally mediated solidarity between strangers. This form of social integration, which first emerges with the nation-state, is realized in the form of a politically socializing *communicative context*."[112] His vision is of individuals—autonomous, rational, active, civically competent—coming together, *participating* in "self-determining discourse communities" whose "debates in democratic public spaces are crucial for both social integration and legitimation of law."[113] Thus, Habermas' citizen (and ours) is naturally an "active, competent, ethical participant in reasoned conversations about issues of common concern."[114]

Another way of saying this is that the citizen, to participate in this discourse, must be *deliberative* and thoughtful. To Habermas, "deliberation" as a process of civic participation envisions "the possibility of collective, mutual learning that over time can change individual preferences and attitudes in constructive ways."[115] Indeed, his is a theory that prioritizes not just participation in political process but *quality* of participation. To vote mindlessly, to read current events without understanding, and to know of institutions only on descriptive levels, is all an affront. This perspective lends itself, of course, to civic curricula like *law learning* that place particular importance on "learning critical competencies necessary for active and reflexive citizenship."[116] For, after all, deliberation, Habermas formulates, is a dialogue grounded in the "*unforced force of the better argument*." Implicit in this is the idea that citizens *must learn to argue better*, that "public discourses find a good response only under circumstances of broad [engagement and] participation."[117] In this way, "deliberative policy and decisions in the institutionalization of procedures" promises "intersubjectivity on a higher level"[118] by means of integrating voices on lower levels.

This requires cultivation of citizens not just with intelligence or substantive understanding but a citizenry capable of active conversation about important moral, social, and civic ideas; it requires one to "live educationally."[119] In terms of outcomes, objectives, and measurable benchmarks, this means we must effectively gauge students' proclivities and abilities for *learning* and *growing*—the internal skills of the learner—not just measure *what* they learned (and, thereby, we can gauge self-reflection and self-examination, critically assessing, and rationally principled). A life-long learner[120] if you will. To achieve an "emancipatory educational model" to cultivate the life-long learner, "requires understanding the learner as person with agency, situated in layered networks of social relationships, and with a particular life story and set of aspirations."[121] There are key internal skills for the learner that are essential.[122] Adaptability, for instance, "a sense of the person's ability to learn and to change"—and the assurance that the student learns that "learning itself is learnable" is absolutely central.[123] One notes that this is already built into the construction of *law learning*, which focuses squarely on *how* individuals approach problems through critical lenses rather than on substantive material acquisition. It is about reasoning by analogy and constantly exposing yourself to brave new ideas and frontiers. Indeed, for this reason, it makes sense that the lawyer is regarded as something of a forever-and-continuous student. Aside from this, however, other equally important qualities include an awareness of the students' own "critical curiosity needed for learning,"[124] as well as a propensity for "meaning making," or an interest in looking for "links between what they are learning and what they already know."[125] In this way, the life-longer is a more *resilient* individual, capable of grappling with complexity, engaging headfirst in challenging situations, and much less likely to find themselves "dependent on others and show[ing] greater fragility when the learning gets difficult."[126] They also become a more *aware and attentive* citizen, observant of many different relationships in which they are embedded as a member of society, relationships from which they can draw to learn and relationships that require challenging and innovating for the sake of equity and justice. "They come to see that as learners they are neither completely independent nor totally dependent. Rather, they come to recognize the balance of interdependence with others around them, working collaboratively, sharing thoughts, doing their share in common learning tasks."[127] In all these ways, the life-long learner is an active agent, a protagonist with an "emancipatory energy," developing an aptitude and competence for learning that carries them to consistently "acquire the skills, strategies and knowledge management necessary for making the most of learning opportunities over a lifespan in the public domain."[128]

This means that students must be able to "assess their assumptions about the accessibility, objectivity and meaningfulness of the world to which their conversations refer"; they must appreciate that any "conversation partners, even or especially those that seem different, are reasonable people," and they must be able to "express their positions and reasons in a sincere, authentic yet critical fashion."[129] This cultivates *deliberativeness* and thereby associated qualities.[130] These qualities and attributes can be affirmatively assessed in *law learning* civic classrooms, in my view, in three broadly conceived ways.

The first measurement concerns *communication skills*. Conversations and words, indeed, "carry the weight that helps constitute, reproduce, and transform society."[131] A discursive theory of democracy must prize conversation as *the* apparatus by which "better understandings of the world and more appropriate social norms for human flourishing"[132] are founded, assessed, and enacted. More importantly for our purposes, communication skills—exhibited through constructive debate and argument—both lay bare students' internal thought processes—contradictions, reflections, logics, principles—and can be readily measured. Consider, as a superficial comparison, the way in which debate and argument are featured in the Tibetan Monastic Education System. By way of intense discussion, two students nuanced positions on ideas, demonstrate understanding of topics, and strengthen scaffolded reasoning. Their confrontation on an issue opens one up to logical critique by the other student eager to prove a point, the interaction pushes one to demonstrate knowledge on their feet (literally, as they are standing when speaking!). One's demeanor *while* arguing, furthermore, showcases underlying qualities of appreciation, respect, and curiosity for their counterpart, as well as demonstrates meditation and reflection on their own ideas enough to articulate them—temperament necessary for the embrace of plural ideas, values, and principles in a democratic society.

Indeed, communication skills test recognition of diverse voices and ideas in different settings, and abilities to convey *their* ideas succinctly in a way others are able to receive and comprehend them (which in turn proves understanding and reflection on one's position). The educator could look for this; the benchmark is met where competence—in terms of the substance of lessons—and literacy—in terms of the reception of others' ideas—come through in how they speak. Students can work, by way of self-examining their ideas and forging their own perspectives, to *show* deliberation by way of their interjections and a "communication which [reflects respectively] sharing and contesting different ways of apprehending the world and ideas from different standpoints."[133] Importantly:

> learning to [communicate,] cooperate and collaborate with others—activities which in turn intensify the formation of habits of careful listening and deliberate, thoughtful speaking. Such habits position students to communicate responsibly about their experiences within the school, the classroom and the larger world. They equip them to deliberate about what they are doing and why they are doing.[134]

Tomas Englund captures this idea in his notion of "deliberative communication," where the classroom serves as a space in which "different opinions and values can be brought face to face, with an endeavor to ensure that each individual takes a stand listening, deliberating, seeking arguments, and evaluating." Students are evaluated on this by way of how they discuss, disagree, and agree. And to be sure, a hallmark of the classroom will be, amidst the divergent views, "a collective effort to find values and norms that everyone can agree upon."[135] Whether they are capable of this—both in receiving information and communicating positions or ideas back—is necessary as a part of being a competent participatory citizen in the discourse of democracy.

A second aptitude or benchmark is a bit more abstract, but nevertheless measurable: namely, the demonstration of *capacity and interest in cultivating common ground.*[136] This ability to find paths of concordance—if not agreement—is an important concept implicating values of respect, justice, toleration, unity, and empathy. The *common ground* is the "optimal" discursive situation where "there is a situated common frame of reference and where the fundamental conditions for understanding and respect are at hand or can at least be developed in due course."[137] Where students are able to get to this place, especially in conversations concerning law that implicate simultaneously facts and values, and do so in a respectful, poised way, they are, in no short order, cultivating tools *essential* for the politically, socially, and conscientiously autonomous citizens. Getting to this place is an act of great personal effort, both in terms of literally demonstrating a commitment to connection with others, but also to avoid entrenchment in extremist, intolerant, non-cogent, and problematic viewpoints.

Whereas above, in stressing communication skills, I placed importance on measuring how students—through words—process different views, articulate arguments, listen and reflect, and promote "tolerance and respect for the concrete other,"[138] here I am more interested in the assessing students' commitment to "collective will formation," an interest in "endeavoring to reach consensus or at least temporary agreements" *in spite of* differences.[139] This *does not* mean rational minds cannot disagree; this *does not* mean that criticism is unwelcome. Common ground rather connotes forging for and appreciation of new paths, of comradery, and of investment in "solving problems or shedding light on them from different points of view."[140] Importantly, it is "the kind of agreement aimed for is not mere accord or *de facto* consensus, but an agreement based on rational conviction. It is not simply the agreement one feels with likeminded souls, but rather enjoins participants actively."[141] Such a benchmark ensures that disputations are contained to the relevant and the teleological; students cognizant of this aim espouse qualities of consideration, seriousness, delicacy, and humility. They are free to criticize authorities or traditional views but do so in constructive, thoughtful ways, asking: what is the point of the argument? It is at this stage—measured by this benchmark—that the Roman Catholic student might while staying secure in her faith, challenge themselves to think about societal considerations implicated in cases on abortion or end-of-life matters in the spirit of "discussion, compromise, conciliation, and [explanation, defense, and] acceptance of difference." They might become interested in recognizing the value of pluralism for political life and for others, even if it goes against their traditions.[142] Or not! Though the aim is a "collective search for common frames of reference," the classroom is also a place to reflect on what students "are not agreed upon and why."[143] Yet, though *common ground* might not always be achieved, the benchmark is satisfied where students of divergent minds act fairly toward each other in the spirit of respect and deference.[144] "While acknowledging that we are destined to disagree, deliberative democracy also affirms that we are capable of deciding our common destiny on mutually acceptable terms."[145]

And, indeed, this folds well into the final benchmark: a *capacity and interest in respecting free and rational choices*; or, respecting the reality that, in deliberation and discussion, the conversation may result in a conclusion that there can be no agreement. At that juncture, the educator might watch and consider: are students seeking other angles? Is the nature of this disagreement logical, or is it a product of stalwart positioning and frustration? This is a question of demeanor in discussion, the capability of dealing with conflict, and, on a deeper level, the capability of attention to note precisely *what* one disagrees with in the viewpoint of another. Importantly, "the dimension of conflict and confrontation (of different views) is substantially central to, and constitutive of, deliberative communication."[146] This means *both* examining "openly conflicting views" and also "relatively minor difference, which are seen in deliberative communication as crucial to investigate and possible to resolve."[147] In *free and rational choice*, I endeavor to capture both an "equality" component and "substantive assessment" component. In terms of equality, it is important to ensure that students, when arguing or debating a specific point of law or values, treat another as coming from a place of equal merit[148]; essential, indeed, is this for our socio-cultural milieu today which, far too often, features exclusion of voices on the basis of haphazard equality judgments. And, in terms of "substantive assessment," the students *must* examine for themselves a good argument based on convictions, or, more appropriately use of good reasons "and not by using rhetoric, lies, deception or coercion."[149]

This dovetails importantly with our previous conversation concerning the integration of rationality and emotion in a *law learning* setting. Habermas' notion of discourse—and our education for "deliberation"—requires the integration of emotion—manifest through "the personal and autobiographical, as well as the cultural community stories, which shape the way students understand the world, experience social interactions and express their personal meanings"[150]—into conversations about law, social policy, democratic values, principles, and legal frameworks and ideas. It requires them to bring in their *own values* and perceptions to the classroom to create the most robust and comprehensive "process of knowledge creation." While this idea is of course contrary to the notion of the value-neutral curriculum that has become synonymous with the education project,[151] it is *essential*. Indeed, "the interdependence of intellect and affect in meaning-making and the co-construction of knowledge is a profoundly important factor in the engagements of students" inculcating a capacity to make meaning that is lasting, well-absorbed, and, importantly, differently associated for each student.[152] There is only so much one will gain from the study of law without the added benefit of personal interjection as they develop an understanding of their society.[153] Moreover, such a multi-dimensional education promises the development of emotional intelligence, awareness of self-identity, and maturity.

One can see this especially helpful, for instance, in a situation where the student has to contend with an extremist view (which of course can happen in today's climate): a position beyond-the-pale; extreme; fundamentalist; anti-democratic; heretical. My position is that where a student interjects such a position in the classroom, it *is* worthy of inclusion in the conversation and challenged for its linkage to rational bases of argument and subject to the demands of proof. The school *must* serve the critical function of *clarifying* positions for students, values, and views of the individual student learned by socialization at home or in church or elsewhere can be challenged at school in unique ways in constructed, safe environments.[154] This is how one measures the growth of reasoning skills—by way of being able to distinguish bad or venomous ideas from those we simply disagree with. Yet, while the "extremist" can have their day—so long as they are open to being disproven, debated, and critiqued (as with all ideas)—a critical judgment pro-exclusion must be made where students *do not* want to defend, where the idea limits choice or denies humanity, where the idea promises violence or is of little intellectual value.[155] Part of this calculus—discerning rational ideas in disagreement verses harmful and valueless interjection—necessarily calls upon affect, emotional, or personal reflection through students' lived experiences. And this should be welcome! This is, after all, how the larger deliberative democratic community operates. Furthermore, this is not a new interjection. Indeed, it is a very democratic argument—an argument of non-repression and non-discrimination—that has been propounded by scholars as illustrious as Amy Gutmann. So long as a view can be rationally deliberated, and does not operate exclusively, then it ought to be accommodated and tolerated.[156]

As Dewey had envisioned it: a deliberative education is characterized by mutual, free, and open communication within and between groups. Ideas that are at opposite ends of the spectrum ought to be welcomed to the extent they can be. After all, for a society to become like a community in this sense—and thus for a classroom to represent it with justice—"a community must be constitutive of the shared self-understandings of the citizens embodied in their institutional arrangements, not simply an attribute of certain of the participants' plan of life."[157] This is read, of course, in two ways. Neither can the extremist monopolize or alienate, nor can a few push aside ideas with which they disagree. The goal of cultivating a discursive democracy, replete with deliberative citizens, "cannot be realized by a person pursuing his or her own private interests, but only as a joint enterprise in an intersubjective, shared practice."[158]

5.3 The Questionable Value of Higher Reasoning Skills in Today's World

While the above concern was somewhat granular, a final comment levied by our critic focuses on the broader implications of this proposal: the valuation of law as the *best* option for grounding civic education, and, by extension, the primacy with which we have treated this idea of higher reasoning and critical thinking. In other words: is higher reasoning really so important?

I cannot say for sure if law is the *best* option for ground civic education, only that it is a *strong* option for the reasons I have discussed above in this proposal. Whether one abides by Martha Nussbaum's proposal that history, philosophy, and the liberal arts ought to serve as the grounding force for citizenship education,[159] or else Amartya Sen's focus on economics for the perpetuation of capabilities and the achievement of freedom,[160] or even others' placement of philosophy as a core subject for cultivating robust, engaged individuals, *the substance is less important than the skills-and-capabilities-focus* of a classroom, and in this an innovated *law learning* program excels.

Recall that the capabilities approach, from which we draw significant philosophy, prioritizes the improvement of access to the *tools* people use to live fulfilling lives. Nussbaum assesses societies for their "basic decency and justice"; indeed, she asks: "what is each person able to do and to be?"[161] This mentality is focused on *choice* or *freedom*; the hallmark of good societies is promoting for their people a set of opportunities or "substantial freedoms" which people then may or may not exercise: the choice is theirs. This is thus respect for people's powers of self-definition.[162] The civic education in *law learning*, as has been constructed above, offers the tools for the realization of such societies. Its curriculum and subject matter are both about offering knowledge, skills, values, and understanding that enable a young person—more than morally, but also practically and intellectually—to think in new ways and develop agency in society; *to flourish consistently and to grow*—specifically in America's legalistic environment and democratic culture. Part of the reason *law learning* can be credited with all of this is its emphasis on criticality and higher-reasoning ability, whose importance is, in my view, self-evident.[163] But, for the sake of our critic, let us briefly explore the way in which higher-reasoning skills have become *supremely and urgently* needed in today's day and age.

In a recent interview, Yuval Noah Hariri made the following comment:

> for most of history, information was rare. I mean, the main job of the education system was just to provide people with the basics … . Now, it is the other way around. We are flooded by [an] enormous amount of information that we cannot handle. The main job of the education system is not to provide information. We don't need more information. We need *the ability to sift through the information to tell the difference between reliable and unreliable information.*[164]

He warns that "information isn't the truth"; "lies are also information, fiction and fantasies are also information. Most information in the world is not about the truth, it's not about anything."[165] And, of course, he is not the first to comment on this modern phenomenon,[166] nor on the counterpart notion of "information overload."[167] This information age, argues many, presents unparalleled promise for the assurance of human convenience and wellbeing but also great challenges—even threatens—some of our most steadfast institutions. For us, principally concerning might be the potentiality of information to undermine our democratic milieu and threaten core values of privacy, autonomy, personal decision-making, and the "erosion of trust in and control over our democratic institutions."[168] Karl Manheim and Lyric Kaplan note that technology and the dissemination of information are frequently used *offensively* "to 'silently [taken] over democracy' through the use of behavioral advertising, social media manipulation, bots and trolls."[169] This is not just in America but globally.[170] "Since 2010, political parties and governments have spent more than half a billion dollars on the research, development, and implementation of psychological operations and public opinion manipulation over social media."[171] Indeed, to study the landscape of information available to individuals is not just inculcating questions "false" versus "truth" but also about the threat to institutions and to justice.

And, of course, this preoccupation with threat is even further compounded by the increasingly sophisticated character of artificial intelligence ("AI").[172] AI "added more than effectiveness to the 'info wars,' but elevated them to a whole new dimension." As fake news competes with the real-world news in the popular discourse—increasingly personalized, believable—it often crowds it out such that people get inured to facts altogether. "Facts become denigrated as information sources for cognitive processing. Lacking facts for decision-making, we turn to emotional cues such as authenticity, strength of assertion, feelings and beliefs."[173] In other words, not knowing what to believe, we stop relying on real ideas and more "what we heard," "how we feel," "who *we* choose to trust," without verifying or assuring the veracity of claims. This is very disquieting; the landscape is open wide to already-polarized Americans succumbing to influence, manipulation, confusion, and radicalization with every novel, computer-generated attack or any peer-pressuring colleague convinced about something and ready to spread the news. And it is not going anywhere; we *rely* on it, indeed, increasingly in all areas of the economy and even political and cultural life. At the highest echelons of government, the question has become: "how will we use AI to solve a problem," and not the more critical and thoughtful: "what problem are we trying to solve, why, and how will we solve it?"[174] In other spheres, AI has tremendously impacted areas of employee hiring, organization and task management, and more. Just in July 2023, New York State, in fact, passed the broadest law yet on the books regulating AI in the form of "Automated Employment Decision Tools" in the use of promotion and hiring processes,[175] which serves as a testament to the integration of AI into mainstream work and social life.

But this, like the production of fake news or the "information overload," presents even greater challenges to the individual and to our socio-political milieu. AI—in both its predictive and generative forms—*and our reaction to it*—is worth reflecting on seriously given its absolute integration into our social lives and, yes, our democratic systems. It should be studied, indeed, through a multi-disciplinary lens, viewed "not just as a neutral tool or instrument, but a [means] of mutual co-shaping between technologies and societies, politics, and cultures in which it is embedded."[176] And to do so should make us both excited and nervous. Hariri noted:

> [Generative AI is] the first technology ever that we invented that can actually make decisions by itself, and therefore it takes power away from us, and it is increasingly making more and more decisions about our lives, whether to give us a loan, whether to accept us to a job, or to university. Even sentences in court are increasingly influenced or even given by AI. We increasingly don't even understand how the AI reaches its decisions.[177]

And this explainability is only the starting point. A great source of inquiry and criticism for AI concerns biases by way of the data sets that products necessarily rely on, and the exacerbation of discriminatory ideology and proclivity already systemic in the human society that feeds AI data. As Kate Crawford and Meredith Whittaker discuss:

> when data reflects biases of either form, there is the risk that AI systems trained on this data will produce models that replicate and magnify those biases. In such cases, AI systems would exacerbate the discriminatory dynamics that create social inequality and would likely do so in ways that would be less obvious than human prejudice and implicit bias.[178]

This is all to say that, based on the data set that a specific AI program is basing its algorithm upon, the program might produce answers, ideas, and information that is problematic to its fundamental core—based on gender biases, racism, and unjust ideas. *Nevertheless, we rely on it,* whether that is because of convenience or ignorance our future is squarely involving AI.

As AI systems gradually take on more and more important roles in more important decision-making fora, the transition will begin undoubtedly have an impact on who gets offered crucial opportunities and who is left behind. "*This brings questions of rights, liberties, and basic fairness to the forefront.*"[179] Dovetailing this notion of bias are concerns over unreliability and the increasing *distrust* in AI programs and the systems that produce them.[180] Thinkers have noted:

> despite sophisticated techniques to teach algorithms from data sets, there is no ground truth available to check whether the results match reality … we do not have proof that [an AI] outcome is correct in terms of an underlying factual basis, rather than inferences from indirect or arbitrary factors.[181]

This has frustrating impacts. Consider, for example, the increasing use of "risk scoring"—the use of algorithmic tools to predict and judge the probability of an individual's re-arrest or repeat offenses—in the judicial decision-making in the criminal justice context.[182] Risk Assessment Instruments are based on little more than mathematic probability,[183] and yet they are favored as quick ways to decide on granting or denying defendants *freedom* (i.e. parole or pretrial release) and inform the dispensation of justice. Critics assail these tools on grounds of discriminatory datasets, lack of individualization, questions of true impact, and lack of transparency. There are implications, furthermore, of exacerbating racism, elitism, and more on the back of these mysterious datasets. Dwork and Minow ask pointedly:

> what is the meaning of the probability of nonrepeatable event? Is what we perceive as randomness in fact certainty, if only we had sufficient contextual information and computing power? Inferences about the future when predicated on limited or faulty information may create an illusion of truth, but illusion it is.[184]

Importantly, AI "can nudge and change what people want, know and value"; this leads us to nervously conclude that "sustainability of our democratic governance systems, our social institutions, and our personal life fixtures, is far from assured."[185] So what is there to be done? Or, to go back to an earlier comment: how can we reflect on changes needed for the human piece of the larger AI narrative? We might continue thinking about the "risk-scoring" subject to get an idea. As a matter of ethical obligations, commentators contend, judges ought to be settled with a "daunting checklist"[186] for "assess[ing], in the application [of technologies], whether justice is being served while being mindful of the personal biases that these tools are designed to counteract."[187] In the famous 2016 Wisconsin COMPAS case, the judge had noted that "the justice system must keep up with the research and *continuously assess* the use of tools."[188] Judges, specifically, must *always* retain the responsibility to exercise "that human trait and obligation to provide justice through judgement."[189] But more than just judges, I contend, *all of us* as citizens must retain powers of judgment, discernment, analytical thinking, and criticality; education *must* provide us the tools to navigate a world where we will be consistently challenged discern truth from fiction, right from wrong, justice from injustice.

The project of a critical thinking education is to prime the student to "engage consistently with uncertainty"; in the classroom, students who learn to problem-solve are inundated with scenarios featuring "incomplete information pertaining to the situation," an unknown "ideal resolution" to the problem, and unclarity as to "how to transform a problematic situation into an acceptable situation."[190] Critical thinking has been lauded as one of four key 21st-century skills, along with communication, collaboration, and creativity, though it lacks emphasis in curricula generally and in civic education curricula specifically.[191] The capabilities of "re-examining, reasoning, reflection," permeate across all four of these interrelated skills leading to higher order thinking skills that, simply put, make us better than the robots.[192] Through reasoning, we question assumptions, evaluate alternatives, and even develop "motivation along with an inquisitive disposition." And these are all teachable aptitudes; *law learning* prioritizes them by way of the exploration of unsettled matters of law and complex social and political discussions. Where AI perpetuates falsities or produces solutions based on problematic assumptions, it is not our substantive knowledge of a given area of expertise that will serve as a bulwark, but our critical thinking and capacity for discernment and assessment.

This notion of needing to engender a measure of criticality in our citizens is not new. We bore witness to it before in the context of the Puritan educational project, where empowerment of the citizen—for the unified purpose of ensuring the survival, both spiritual and physical, of a new community—took the form of literacy. Through religious rhetoric, Massachusetts Bay Colony began working as a unit, ever-diligently, toward attaining their proverbial true "brotherhood of all believers" bonded with accessible education, command of central texts and ideas, and openness to re-assessment of institutions and principles. Their aim was an *empowering* education for religious and public life. *Well, critical thinking education is our modern-day literacy education.* We face down a socio-cultural milieu inundated with information at our fingertips, though most of its OS lies, and one where, at least in the dimension of civics, new technologies both revolutionize and challenge our perceptions of storied institutions and ideas. To effectively participate (indeed, even to have the capability of doing so) in this new political environment and new society requires an education in ethics and morals and skills. *Law learning* is all of these things.

Notes

1 Others can either be dispensed with quickly or require *too* much engagement so as to become distracting. One in the latter category, for instance, could be about my discussion—sequestered in the footnotes—concerning the jurisprudential and political views assumed to support a call for the need of implementation a learning law process, i.e., the view of democracy, deliberation, and law's function as a medium of norms, the involved nature of the citizen. I have thought hard about in situating the proposal in this context to emphasize the potentially beneficial way in which citizens are empowered to participate in the process of "communicative action,' to use Habermas' term. This requires a chapter all its own! Another critique, for instance, in the former category, that can be dispensed with quickly might consider the values-plural posture of law learning. By inviting self-examination and criticism of one's own values *and* more universal "American" values—perhaps, for instance, "justice," "fairness," "process" and more—and by offering an education that puts all values in the limelight for critique, one could argue that this is necessarily going to disrupt traditions and that the ripples of re-evaluation are boundless. Aren't some things too ingrained and true to be reconsidered? Is this not a problem? Especially in an education where students are begged to reconsider preconceived notions, challenge ideologies, and confront cross-cultural or universal moral standards, traditions *will* necessarily be abandoned the political system will be overhauled, storied processes departed from. Yes is my answer; the valuation of the political and social conversation is a central value for the legal curriculum, the re-evaluation of one's own principles is also subject to the scrutiny of this education, discourse over fiat—which inevitably leads to

change—is prime. This does not, however, mean all tradition will change, that there are *no* universal values, and that there is *no* truth. As Nussbaum articulates, "what is excellent in our own traditions will survive the scrutiny of [self-examination]." Martha Nussbaum, *Cultivating Humanity: A Classical Defense of Reform in Liberal Education* (Cambridge: Harvard University Press, 1998), 49. *Not everything will change on account of scrutiny*; indeed, all I argue for is the development of good judgment and the invitation to hear arguments from all sides, even those groups who are disagreeable, groups who are greedy, or groups retaining beliefs that afront your own. In this way, our conception of the "good" and the "valuable" changes. It is where rational interaction takes place, common interests can be identified; persuasion and compromise are easier if common interests can be identified, if the participants are able to empathically understand the views of opponents. Law is about, most vitally, engaging with the other rather than reacting with disgust toward the other. This in no way can change tradition in ways that are problematic.

2 Oliver Wendell Holmes, "The Use of Law Schools," in *Collected Legal Papers* (Minola: Dover, 2007), 37, 47–48.

3 In the future, I would like to address this phenomenon in the landscape of higher legal education, which is a move, to my mind, in the wrong direction.

4 Harold J. Berman, "Law in the University," 10 *Legal Stud. F.* 53 (1986). He argues that law should not just be a class you take but incorporated as "an integral part of the teaching of other disciplines-history, political science, sociology, economics, philosophy, and others" but that this "cannot happen until professors in those other disciplines are themselves exposed to some sort of basic education in law."

5 Harold J. Berman, "Law in the University," 10 *Legal Stud. F.* 53 (1986).

6 This could be a next step in the context of our primary and secondary school civics discussion as well. While I would advocate for reconstructing civic education classes—which already exist and are a disservice to students—with learning law, a more effective way of empowering students would be integrate law—and thereby the civic and philosophical questions it propounds—in all classes. This also along the lines of what Nussbaum advocates (in terms of philosophy) and Dewey (in terms of values education).

7 Harold J. Berman, "Law in the University," 10 *Legal Stud. F.* 53 (1986).

8 Harold J. Berman, "Law in the University," 10 *Legal Stud. F.* 53 (1986).

9 Harold J. Berman, "Law in the University," 10 *Legal Stud. F.* 53 (1986).

10 Harold J. Berman, "Law in the University," 10 *Legal Stud. F.* 53 (1986). There is a difference, Berman contended, between "a 'concept' of justice," and a "sense of justice"—law study contributes to the latter, "apply[ing] concepts of justice to specific situations [and] relating concepts or theories of justice to particular circumstances." The student of law is

> continually confronted with concrete problems to which pre-existing concepts give conflicting solutions. In testing the solutions against the theories and the theories against the solutions, he can learn how concepts of justice are created in the very process of application.

11 Harold J. Berman, "Law in the University," 10 *Legal Stud. F.* 53 (1986).

12 Harold J. Berman, "Law in the University," 10 *Legal Stud. F.* 53 (1986).

13 Harold J. Berman, "Law in the University," 10 *Legal Stud. F.* 53 (1986).

14 Harold J. Berman, "Law in the University," 10 *Legal Stud. F.* 53 (1986).
15 Harold J. Berman, "Law in the University," 10 *Legal Stud. F.* 53 (1986).
16 Martha Nussbaum, *Cultivating Humanity: A Classical Defense of Reform in Liberal Education* (Cambridge: Harvard University Press, 1998), 294.
17 And this is certainly supported, as it has been showing that—though law is castigated as a cold and unfeeling profession, lawyering requires significant amount of emotion intelligence, "self-awareness, self-management, social awareness, and relationship management skills," on the part of the lawyer. *See* David J. Arkush, "Situating Emotion: A Critical Realist View of Emotion and Nonconscious Cognitive Processes for Law and Legal Theory," 2008 *BYU L. Rev.* 1275; Neil Hamilton and Verna Monson, "The Positive Empirical Relationship of Professionalism to Effectiveness in the Practice of Law," 24 *Geo. J. Legal Ethics* 137 (2011).
18 For more background on the adversarial system, *See* Model Rules of Professional Conduct, Rule 1.3 ("a lawyer should act with commitment and dedication to the interests of the client and with zeal in advocacy upon the client's behalf."); *see generally Talks on American Law: A Series of Broadcasts to Foreign Audiences by Members of the Harvard Law School Faculty* (Harold Berman (ed.)) (New York: Vintage Books) (1961).
19 A chief thinker in the 1990s—upon whom I rely deeply—on the pitfalls of the adversarial process, the connection between lawyering and deeper ideals of altruism, justice, and fairness in lawyers, and the conception of empathy and justice in conflict was Carrie Menkel-Meadow. *See generally* Carrie Menkel-Meadow, "From Legal Disputes to Conflict Resolution and Human Problem Solving: Legal Dispute Resolution in a Multidisciplinary Context," 54 *J. Legal Educ.* 7–29 (2004); Carrie Menkel-Meadow, "Is Altruism Possible in Lawyering?" 8 *Ga. St. U. L. Rev.* 385–419 (1992); Carrie Menkel-Meadow, "Aha? Is Creativity Possible in Legal Problem Solving and Teachable in Legal Education?" 6 *Harv. Negot. L. Rev.* 97–144 (2001).
20 Carrie Menkel-Meadow, "Is Altruism Possible in Lawyering?" 8 *Ga. St. U. L. Rev.* 385 (1992).
21 Randall Kaiser, "The Emotionally Attentive Lawyer: Balancing the Rule of Law with the Realities of Human Behavior," 15 *Nev. L. J.* 442 (2015).
22 Carrie Menkel-Meadow, "From Legal Disputes to Conflict Resolution and Human Problem Solving: Legal Dispute Resolution in a Multidisciplinary Context," 54 *J. Legal Educ.* 7 (2004).
23 Carrie Menkel-Meadow, "From Legal Disputes to Conflict Resolution and Human Problem Solving: Legal Dispute Resolution in a Multidisciplinary Context," 54 *J. Legal Educ.* 7 (2004).
24 Sward, Ellen E., "Values, Ideology, and the Evolution of the Adversary System," 64 *Ind. L. J.* 301–355 (1989).
25 Sward, Ellen E., "Values, Ideology, and the Evolution of the Adversary System," 64 *Ind. L. J.* 301–355 (1989); *see also* Jerold S. Auerbach, *Justice without Law* (Oxford: Oxford University Press, 1983), 144–46; Jerome Frank, *Courts On Trial: Myth and Reality in American Justice* (Princeton, NJ: Princeton University Press, 1949), 80–102; Kenneth J. Arrow, "Information Acquisition and the Resolution of Conflict," in *Barriers To Conflict Resolution* (Kenneth Arrow, et al., eds.) (New York: Norton, 1995), 259, 270.

26 Carrie Menkel-Meadow, "From Legal Disputes to Conflict Resolution and Human Problem Solving: Legal Dispute Resolution in a Multidisciplinary Context," 54 *J. Legal Educ.* 7 (2004).
27 Carrie Menkel-Meadow, "From Legal Disputes to Conflict Resolution and Human Problem Solving: Legal Dispute Resolution in a Multidisciplinary Context," 54 *J. Legal Educ.* 7 (2004).
28 Carrie Menkel-Meadow, "Aha? Is Creativity Possible in Legal Problem Solving andTeachable in Legal Education?" 6 *Harv. Negot. L. Rev*. 97–144 (2001).
29 Randall Kaiser, "The Emotionally Attentive Lawyer: Balancing the Rule of Law with the Realities of Human Behavior," 15 *Nev. L. J.* 442 (2015).
30 Carrie Menkel-Meadow, "The Lawyer as Problem Solver and Third-Party Neutral: Creativity and Non-Partisanship in Lawyering," 72 *Temple L. Rev.* 785, 786 (1999).
31 Molly O'Brien, "Facing Down the Gladiators: Addressing Law School's Hidden Adversarial Curriculum," 37 *Monash U. L. Rev.* 40, 47 (2013). Importantly, there is a large contingency of scholars and associated scholarship challenging this in the legal education space, endeavoring to transform the teaching of law students by way of exposing how the law school curricula supports adversarialism. Carrie Menkel-Meadow was a chief proponent of this.
32 Susan Sturm and Lani Guinier, "The Law School Matrix: Reforming Legal Education in a Culture of Competition and Conformity," 60 *Vand. L. Rev.* 515 (2019).
33 Susan Sturm and Lani Guinier, "The Law School Matrix: Reforming Legal Education in a Culture of Competition and Conformity," 60 *Vand. L. Rev.* 515 (2019).
34 Molly O'Brien, "Facing Down the Gladiators: Addressing Law School's Hidden Adversarial Curriculum," 37 *Monash U. L. Rev.* 40, 47 (2013).
35 For more information on the role of the client in the legal education framework, *see* Ann Shalleck, "Constructions of the Client within Legal Education," 45 *Stanford L. Rev.* 1732 (1993); Pierre Schlag, "The Problem of the Subject," 69 *Tex. L. Rev.* 1627 (1991).
36 Ann Shalleck, "Constructions of the Client within Legal Education," 45 *Stanford L. Rev.* 1732 (1993).
37 Ann Shalleck, "Constructions of the Client within Legal Education," 45 *Stanford L. Rev.* 1732 (1993).
38 Ann Shalleck, "Constructions of the Client within Legal Education," 45 *Stanford L. Rev.* 1732 (1993).
39 Ann Shalleck, "Constructions of the Client within Legal Education," 45 *Stanford L. Rev.* 1732 (1993).
40 Ann Shalleck, "Constructions of the Client within Legal Education," 45 *Stanford L. Rev.* 1732 (1993).
41 Carrie Menkel-Meadow, "The Trouble with the Adversary System a Postmodern, Multicultural World," 38 *Wm. Mary L. Rev.* 5–44 (1996).
42 Carrie Menkel-Meadow, "The Trouble with the Adversary System a Postmodern, Multicultural World," 38 *Wm. Mary L. Rev.* 5–44 (1996).
43 Susan Sturm and Lani Guinier, "The Law School Matrix: Reforming Legal Education in a Culture of Competition and Conformity," 60 *Vand. L. Rev.* 515 (2019); Molly O'Brien, "Facing Down the Gladiators: Addressing Law School's Hidden Adversarial Curriculum," 37 *Monash U. L. Rev.* 40, 47 (2013) ("While the stereotypic law school

'paper chase' may be out of date, the competitive, cut-throat mood of the law school has not necessarily softened over the years.").

44 Molly O'Brien, "Facing Down the Gladiators: Addressing Law School's Hidden Adversarial Curriculum," 37 *Monash U. L. Rev.* 40, 47 (2013).

45 Susan Kuo, "Culture Clash: Teaching Cultural Defenses in the Criminal Law Classroom," 48 *St. Louis L. J.* 1297–1311 (2004).

46 Harold J. Berman, "Law in the University," 10 *Legal Stud. F.* 53 (1986).

47 Ann Shalleck, "Constructions of the Client within Legal Education," 45 *Stanford L. Rev.* 1732 (1993).

48 Ann Shalleck, "Constructions of the Client within Legal Education," 45 *Stanford L. Rev.* 1732 (1993).

49 Ann Shalleck, "Constructions of the Client within Legal Education," 45 *Stanford L. Rev.* 1732 (1993).

50 Ellen Sward, "Values, Ideology, and the Evolution of the Adversary System," 64 *Ind. L. J.* 301–355 (1989).

51 Ellen Sward, "Values, Ideology, and the Evolution of the Adversary System," 64 *Ind. L. J.* 301–355 (1989).

52 Ellen Sward, "Values, Ideology, and the Evolution of the Adversary System," 64 *Ind. L. J.* 301–355 (1989).

53 Ellen Sward, "Values, Ideology, and the Evolution of the Adversary System," 64 *Ind. L. J.* 301–355 (1989).

54 Ellen Sward, "Values, Ideology, and the Evolution of the Adversary System," 64 *Ind. L. J.* 301–355 (1989).

55 Carrie Menkel-Meadow, "Is Altruism Possible in Lawyering?" 8 *Ga. St. U. L. Rev.* 385 (1992).

56 Carrie Menkel-Meadow, "Is Altruism Possible in Lawyering?" 8 *Ga. St. U. L. Rev.* 385 (1992).

57 Carrie Menkel-Meadow, "Aha? Is Creativity Possible in Legal Problem Solving andTeachable in Legal Education?" 6 *Harv. Negot. L. Rev.* 98 (2001).

58 Carrie Menkel-Meadow, "Aha? Is Creativity Possible in Legal Problem Solving andTeachable in Legal Education?" 6 *Harv. Negot. L. Rev.* 98 (2001).

59 Carrie Menkel-Meadow, "Aha? Is Creativity Possible in Legal Problem Solving andTeachable in Legal Education?" 6 *Harv. Negot. L. Rev.* 98 (2001).

60 Carrie Menkel-Meadow, "Is Altruism Possible in Lawyering?" 8 *Ga. St. U. L. Rev.* 385 (1992).

61 This was at least the case with classical legal education, argues Angela Harris and Marjorie Shultz, "A(nother) Critique of Pure Reason: Toward Civic Virtue in Legal Education," 45 *Stan. L. Rev.* 1773 (1993) ("The phrase 'thinking like a lawyer' means suppressing or denying one's feelings and personal experience while putting forth a 'cold' analysis of the 'facts.').

62 Angela Harris and Marjorie Shultz, "A(nother) Critique of Pure Reason: Toward Civic Virtue in Legal Education," 45 *Stan. L. Rev.* 1773 (1993) (criticizing that virtue in the endeavor of law study requires banishing emotion from the conversation).

63 Susan Daicoff, "Lawyer, Know Thyself: A Review of Empirical Research on Attorney Attributes Bearing on Professionalism," 46 *Am. U. L. Rev.* 1338 (1997).

64 Susan Daicoff, "Lawyer, Know Thyself: A Review of Empirical Research on Attorney Attributes Bearing on Professionalism," 46 *Am. U. L. Rev.* 1338 (1997).

65 Harris and Shultz's piece—which identified the error in this judgment and emphasized the role emotions play in legal thought and decision-making—gave rise, however, to a whole community of legal scholars preoccupied with the intersection of law and emotions. *See, e.g.*, Heidi Feldman, ed., "Symposium on Law, Psychology, and the Emotions," 74 *Chi.-Kent L. Rev.* 1423, 1426–1429 (2000). This field has challenged the predominant construction of "legal thought as a professionally instilled cognitive process, which could be powerfully unsettled by affective response." *See* Kathryn Abrams and Hila Keren, "Who's Afraid of Law and the Emotions?" 94 *Minn. L. Rev.* 517 (2010) (providing a thorough background of the field, including references to Martha Minow, Martha Nussbaum, Judith Resnick, and more); *The Passions of Law* (Susan A. Bandes Ed.) (New York: NYU Press, 1999), 311.

66 Even outside the confines of law and law study and law practice, the very idea of the separation of rationality and emotion is criticized has been long criticized. Indeed, emotion *only* helps reasoning on biological levels. *See* Antonio Damasio, *Descartes' Error: Emotion, Reason, and the Human Brain* (New York: Penguin Books, 1994), 191–96.

67 To be sure, whether or not this reconceptualization of the legal curriculum in graduate schools has actually taken root is beyond the scope of this piece. *See., e.g.*, Kathryn Abrams and Hila Keren, "Who's Afraid of Law and the Emotions?" 94 *Minn. L. Rev.* 517 (2010)

> mainstream legal academics have often greeted [the integration of emotions into the curriculum] with ambivalence. They have not predictably viewed it as a resource for addressing questions within their substantive fields. It is often treated as a novel academic pastime rather than an instrument for addressing practical problems.

Rather, my goal is to show that it *merely can be incorporated*, and, in so doing, join my voice in acclaiming that it ought to be. This is another area of interest of mine that can be explored later on.

68 To use Nussbaum's language, Martha Nussbaum, *Love's Knowledge: Essays on Philosophy and Literature* (1990), 40.

69 *See, e.g.*, David J. Arkush, "Situating Emotion: A Critical Realist View of Emotion and Nonconscious Cognitive Processes for Law and Legal Theory," 2008 *BYU L. Rev.* 1275 (2008); Eric Posner, "Law and the Emotions," 89 *Geo. L. J* 1977 (2001) (who makes specific mention of Damasio's work).

70 Antonio Damasio, *Descartes' Error: Emotion, Reason, and the Human Brain* (New York: Penguin Books, 1994), xvi.

71 Antonio Damasio, *Descartes' Error: Emotion, Reason, and the Human Brain* (New York: Penguin Books, 1994), xvi.

72 Antonio Damasio, *Descartes' Error: Emotion, Reason, and the Human Brain* (New York: Penguin Books, 1994), 171–174; *see also* David J. Arkush, "Situating Emotion: A Critical Realist View of Emotion and Nonconscious Cognitive Processes for Law and Legal Theory," 2008 *BYU L. Rev.* 1275 (2008) (for a view of this in terms of law study and legal theory).

73 Antonio Damasio, *Descartes' Error: Emotion, Reason, and the Human Brain* (New York: Penguin Books, 1994).

74 Antonio Damasio, *Descartes' Error: Emotion, Reason, and the Human Brain* (New York: Penguin Books, 1994), xvi.

75 Angela Harris and Marjorie Shultz. "A(nother) Critique of Pure Reason: Toward Civic Virtue in Legal Education," 45 *Stan. L. Rev*. 1773 (1993).
76 Antonio Damasio, *Descartes' Error: Emotion, Reason, and the Human Brain* (New York: Penguin Books, 1994), xvi.
77 Antonio Damasio, *Descartes' Error: Emotion, Reason, and the Human Brain* (New York: Penguin Books, 1994), xvi.
78 Antonio Damasio, *Descartes' Error: Emotion, Reason, and the Human Brain* (New York: Penguin Books, 1994), 246.
79 Antonio Damasio, *Descartes' Error: Emotion, Reason, and the Human Brain* (New York: Penguin Books, 1994), 246.
80 Antonio Damasio, *Descartes' Error: Emotion, Reason, and the Human Brain* (New York: Penguin Books, 1994), 246.
81 Angela Harris and Marjorie Shultz. "A(nother) Critique of Pure Reason: Toward Civic Virtue in Legal Education," 45 *Stan. L. Rev*. 1773 (1993).
82 Abrams and Keren, "Who's Afraid of Law and the Emotions?" at 517; Angela Harris and Marjorie Shultz. "A(nother) Critique of Pure Reason: Toward Civic Virtue in Legal Education," 45 *Stan. L. Rev*. 1773 (1993); *See* Chapter 4 discussing the departure from Christopher Columbus Langdell and the traditional view of a legal education as a scientific process of deduction. Indeed, Harris and Shultz offer a critique of the original conception of legal education. Langdell explicitly assimilated the study of law to the practice of science. Legal reasoning, in his view, was a deductive process by which one derived right and wrong answers from principles inherent in the written opinions of appellate judges His exhortations to treat law as a science had the practical effect of encouraging universities to incorporate law schools and the ideological effect of reinforcing educators' convictions that emotions were irrelevant to legal knowledge and learning.
83 Angela Harris and Marjorie Shultz. "A(nother) Critique of Pure Reason: Toward Civic Virtue in Legal Education," 45 *Stan. L. Rev*. 1773 (1993).
84 Angela Harris and Marjorie Shultz. "A(nother) Critique of Pure Reason: Toward Civic Virtue in Legal Education," 45 *Stan. L. Rev*. 1773 (1993).
85 Another was the issue of gender dynamics. Studied had been conducted on how "women are more comfortable with acknowledging and expressing their emotions in conversation than men. If this is true, then to the extent that emotions are banned from the classroom, women will tend to be disadvantaged as participants in debate." Angela Harris and Marjorie Shultz. "A(nother) Critique of Pure Reason: Toward Civic Virtue in Legal Education," 45 *Stan. L. Rev*. 1773 (1993).
86 Angela Harris and Marjorie Shultz. "A(nother) Critique of Pure Reason: Toward Civic Virtue in Legal Education," 45 *Stan. L. Rev*. 1773 (1993).
87 Angela Harris and Marjorie Shultz. "A(nother) Critique of Pure Reason: Toward Civic Virtue in Legal Education," 45 *Stan. L. Rev*. 1773 (1993).
88 Angela Harris and Marjorie Shultz. "A(nother) Critique of Pure Reason: Toward Civic Virtue in Legal Education," 45 *Stan. L. Rev*. 1773 (1993).
89 Angela Harris and Marjorie Shultz. "A(nother) Critique of Pure Reason: Toward Civic Virtue in Legal Education," 45 *Stan. L. Rev*. 1773 (1993). This was spurred on by the prevailing image of law as "blindfolded justice," colored (and to a certain extent still does color) the mission of legal education; the blindfold "shut[s] out persons and passions that might inappropriately influence [justice's] inward deliberation."

90 *See, e.g.*, Jeanne L. Schroeder, "Subject: Object," 47 *U. Miami L. Rev.* No. 1, 42 (1992) ("Really, Really True Objectivity V. Wishy-Washy Subjectivity"). See Martha Minow and Elizabeth V. Spelman, "Passion for Justice," 10 *Cardozo L. Rev.* No. 37, 45 (1988).

91 Angela Harris and Marjorie Shultz. "A(nother) Critique of Pure Reason: Toward Civic Virtue in Legal Education," 45 *Stan. L. Rev*. 1773 (1993).

92 Angela Harris and Marjorie Shultz. "A(nother) Critique of Pure Reason: Toward Civic Virtue in Legal Education," 45 *Stan. L. Rev*. 1773 (1993).

93 *See* Martha Nussbaum, *Love's Knowledge: Essays on Philosophy and Literature* (Oxford University Press, 1990), 40.

94 Angela Harris and Marjorie Shultz. "A(nother) Critique of Pure Reason: Toward Civic Virtue in Legal Education," 45 *Stan. L. Rev*. 1773 (1993). To Harris and Shultz, "once discussion is broadened, traditions about what matters, what's interesting, and what's correct will all be deeply controversial. Emotion as well as reason should play an essential role in the resulting effort to integrate traditional commitments with new perspectives."

95 Angela Harris and Marjorie Shultz. "A(nother) Critique of Pure Reason: Toward Civic Virtue in Legal Education," 45 *Stan. L. Rev*. 1773 (1993).

96 Angela Harris and Marjorie Shultz. "A(nother) Critique of Pure Reason: Toward Civic Virtue in Legal Education," 45 *Stan. L. Rev*. 1773 (1993).

97 There are many initiatives. For representative examples, *see*, *e.g.*, Carrie J. Menkel-Meadow, "When Winning Isn't Everything: The Lawyer as a Problem Solver," 28 *Hofstra L. Rev.* 905 (2000); John Montgomery, "Incorporating Emotional Intelligence Concepts into Legal Education: Strengthening the Professionalism of Law Students," 39 *Toledo L. Rev.* 324 (2008).

98 Angela Harris and Marjorie Shultz. "A(nother) Critique of Pure Reason: Toward Civic Virtue in Legal Education," 45 *Stan. L. Rev*. 1773 (1993).

99 Angela Harris and Marjorie Shultz. "A(nother) Critique of Pure Reason: Toward Civic Virtue in Legal Education," 45 *Stan. L. Rev*. 1773 (1993).

100 Carrie Menkel-Meadow, "Is Altruism Possible in Lawyering?" 8 *Ga. St. U. L. Rev.* 385 (1992).

101 Carrie Menkel-Meadow, "Is Altruism Possible in Lawyering?" 8 *Ga. St. U. L. Rev.* 385 (1992).

102 Neil Duxbury, "Golden Rule Reasoning, Moral Judgment, and Law," 84 *Notre Dame L. Rev.* 1529 (2009).

103 Carrie Menkel-Meadow, "Is Altruism Possible in Lawyering?" 8 *Ga. St. U. L. Rev.* 385 (1992).

104 Neil Duxbury, "Golden Rule Reasoning, Moral Judgment, and Law," 84 *Notre Dame L. Rev*. 1529 (2009) (quoting Ronald Dworkin, *Justice in Robes* (Cambridge: Harvard University Press, 2008), 80).

105 Susan A. Bandes, "Feeling and Thinking Like a Lawyer: Cognition, Emotion, and the Practice and Progress of Law," 89 *Fordham L. Rev.* 2427 (2021).

106 Antonio Damasio, *Descartes' Error: Emotion, Reason, and the Human Brain* (New York: Penguin Books, 1994), xvi.

107 Such programs are incredible, and I am deeply familiar with them. *See, e.g.*, Center for Contemplative Science, SEE Learning, https://seelearning.emory.edu/. They do not, however, educate for citizenship or for versatility with democracy but are

approaches to compassionate dispositions and perspectives on the world. We need the pair.

108 I imagine that the reasons for suggesting this are myriad and probably similar to the practical critiques levied at the capabilities approach to development. But, as this is intended as a theoretical proposal, and having made a conscientious decision *not* to propose specific curricula or articulate a way for realizing *law learning* based on practical considerations and appealing to policy stakeholders, I address the resourcing-question in a footnote so as not to distract from the larger critique. From a resource perspective, some might say that "law learning" is an unsustainable way of going about civic education, requiring re-training of teachers, more money, and institutional expenses, and much more government legwork. And to be sure, they might not be wrong. Berman, in offering his suggestion that law be taught at the undergraduate level, did opine that teachers needed to be educated in law before law learning could properly be integrated into an undergraduate curriculum. He proposed that

> what are needed, then, are law courses for the professors of the liberal arts—one or two courses specially designed to give them sufficient background to enable them to bring legal subjects, legal materials, and legal insights into their teaching and writing in their fields of special interest.

This does cost money and is a drain on time. But, in his view, law education needed to be integrated, at the outset, into *all* classes, not just added piecemeal as courses to an "already overcrowded menu of offerings" or else they "can hardly achieve the intellectual and moral integration that is needed to fulfill the underlying purposes of higher education." Harold J. Berman, "Law in the University," 10 *Legal Stud. F.* 53 (1986). My proposal is already in a different place. Already, we have a national commitment—consistently renewed—to the development of civic education and the strengthening of citizenship skills through this coursework. This is made manifest by an existing infrastructure of civic courses and teaching already integrated into the curriculum of schools nationwide. There are no additional courses needed. Even aside from the fact that there is money, interest, and attention already aligned, the issue of educating civics teachers in law is very easily solved. Indeed, we have a great resource for the education of civics teachers in *law learning* at our fingertips: our communities of lawyers and legal practitioners around the nation could help in terms of facilitating access to civics teachers and offering input in terms of curriculum. This is not the first time someone has proposed mobilizing bar associations, law communities, legal academics, law clinics, and lawyers to educate children. *See, e.g.*, a multitude of "community lawyering" articles including, Margaret Berry, "Teaching Social Justice Lawyering: Systematically Including Community Legal Education in Law School Clinics," 18 *Clinical L. Rev.* 401 (2012); William Quigley, "Revolutionary Lawyering: Addressing the Root Causes of Poverty and Wealth," 20 *Wash. U. J. L. Pol'y* 101 (2006); William Simon, "Introduction: Lawyers and Community Economic Development," 95 *Calif. L. Rev.* 1821, 1823 (2007); Scott Cummings, "The Pursuit of Legal Rights – And Beyond," 59 *UCLA L. Rev.* 506 (2012); Jennifer Gordon, "Concluding Essay: The Lawyer Is Not the Protagonist: Community Campaigns, Law, and Social Change," 95 *Calif. L. Rev.* 2133 (2007). With a little organization, these highly educated individuals could partner with civic learning organizations to cultivate curricula and strengthen civic academics. In short, our options are many, and there is no practical point where one needs to start from scratch in implementing "law learning." This, to my mind, does great credit to the idea of realizing such an innovation. However, a harder question will be the reorientation of the civic curriculum toward a more Kohlbergian and Deweyan approach to interactive learning based in collaborative pedagogy rather than didactic or lecturer-style work to which we are accustomed. Indeed, an effective *law learning* education relies on the use of "participatory pedagogies—including a focus on the quality of dialogue, student voice, contextual knowledge and relevance to students' lives and narratives." Clarence Joldersma and Ruth Crick, "Citizenship, Discourse Ethics, and the Emancipatory Model of Lifelong Learning," in *Habermas, Critical Theory, and Education* (Routledge, 2010), 137.

109 *See* Section 2.3.

110 Raymond Morrow, "Habermas and Civic Education," in Richard Desjardins and Susan Wiksten (eds.), *Handbook of Civic Engagement and Education* (London: Routledge, 2002), 28–41.

111 Luckily, there are a great many resources connecting Habermas' deliberative democracy to civics education, from which I'll borrow some general benchmark ideas. *See, e.g.*, Tomas Englund, "The Educated, Deliberative Citizen: Constituents for a Normative Model," 8 *Nord. J. Stud. Educ. Policy*, 149–155 (2022). And, interestingly, Englund and others also refer to the works of Martha Nussbaum and John Dewey who introduce the deliberative perspective on schools and education. For a full bibliography of individuals who consider a "deliberative" approach to civic education and learning outcomes, *see* James Bohman, *Public Deliberation: Pluralism, Complexity And Democracy* (Cambridge: MIT Press, 1997); *Deliberative Democracy: Essays On Reason and Politics* (Bohman and Rehg, eds.) (Cambridge: MIT Press, 1996); Amy Gutmann, *Democratic Education* (Princeton: Princeton University Press, 1999); Martha Nussbaum, *Cultivating Humanity: A Classical Defense of Reform in Liberal Education* (Cambridge: Harvard University Press, 2000); *Habermas, Critical Theory and Education* (Mark Murphy and Ted Fleming, eds.) (London: Taylor & Francis Group, 2009).

112 Habermas, Jürgen, "Citizenship and National Identity: Some Reflections on the Future of Europe," in Ronald Beiner (ed.), *Theorizing Citizenship* (New York: State University of New York Press, 1995), 255–282.

113 Tomas Englund, "The Educated, Deliberative Citizen: Constituents for a Normative Model," 8 *Nord. J. Stud. Educ. Policy*. No. 2, 149–155 (2022). Habermas also lays out a framing for discourse ethics as a principle that opens up a space to develop community in a more ethical way.

114 Habermas, Jürgen, "Citizenship and National Identity: Some Reflections on the Future of Europe," in Ronald Beiner (ed.), *Theorizing Citizenship* (New York: State University of New York Press, 1995), 255–282.

115 Tomas Englund, "The Educated, Deliberative Citizen: Constituents for a Normative Model," 8 *Nord. J. Stud. Educ. Policy*. No. 2, 149–155 (2022).

116 Tomas Englund, "The Educated, Deliberative Citizen: Constituents for a Normative Model," 8 *Nord. J. Stud. Educ. Policy*. No. 2, 149–155 (2022). Englund also refers to the cultivation of "well-established deliberative attitudes and a society that rests on the idea of deliberative democracy as a long-term project." This is also quite

concordant with the *law learning* project that also envisions long-term change and shifting of perspectives and attitudes. It is also important to highlight the intersection of "deliberativeness" with the "practical reasoning capability of Martha Nussbaum." As Englund connects the two,

> the method by which most everyday practical problems get solved has been variously called "deliberation" or "practical reasoning". It is an intricate and skilled social process whereby, individually or collectively, we identify the questions to which we must respond, establish grounds for deciding on answers and then choose among the available solutions.

Training for one, indeed, promises training in the other necessarily. Tomas Englund, Toward a Deliberative Curriculum, 1 *Nord. J. Stud. Educ. Policy*, 48–56 (2015).

117 Tomas Englund, "The Educated, Deliberative Citizen: Constituents for a Normative Model," 8 *Nord. J. Stud. Educ. Policy*, 149–155 (2022).

118 Tomas Englund, "The Educated, Deliberative Citizen: Constituents for a Normative Model," 8 *Nord. J. Stud. Educ. Policy*, 149–155 (2022).

119 Tomas Englund, "The Educated, Deliberative Citizen: Constituents for a Normative Model," 8 *Nord. J. Stud. Educ. Policy*, 149–155 (2022). It is important to note that, per Habermas,

> according to discourse theory, the success of deliberative politics depends not on a collectively acting citizenry but on the institutionalization of the corresponding procedures and conditions of communication, as well as on the interplay of institutionalized deliberative processes with informally developed public opinions.

Habermas, *Between Facts and Norms: Contributions to a Discourse Theory of Law and Democracy* (Cambridge: MIT Press, 1996), 298. This, in other words, argues for the necessity of systemic change as any education change. I agree but also acknowledge Gutmann's comment that "any effort to make democracy more deliberative, the single most important institution outside government is the educational system." *See* Amy Gutmann and Dennis F. Thompson, *Democracy and Disagreement* (Cambridge: Harvard University Press, 1998).

120 Joldersma and Crick note that the term "life-long learner" has been mobilized, most frequently to denote those with economic facility, with a "focus directly on improving the knowledge, skills and other competencies directly required for employability." They co-opt the notion, arguing that "citizenship education requires a model of lifelong learning with emancipatory dimension." After all, "if learning is to provide competencies for active and ethical citizenship, it cannot do so with a learning model geared only to supplying the skills and knowledge for the economy." I agree with this idea and borrow from its rhetoric. Clarence Joldersma and Ruth Crick, "Citizenship, Discourse Ethics, and the Emancipatory Model of Lifelong Learning," in *Habermas, Critical Theory, and Education* (Routledge, 2010), 137.

121 Clarence Joldersma and Ruth Crick, "Citizenship, Discourse Ethics, and the Emancipatory Model of Lifelong Learning," in *Habermas, Critical Theory, and Education* (Routledge, 2010), 137.

122 When I speak about these skills, I do not mean to say that life-long learner *must always* be realizing them. Indeed, it is enough to say, as Martha Nussbaum would

point out, that they have the *capability* of doing so. They have the *capability of attention* or the *capability of* resilience. These, of course, are all dovetailing and complementary to capabilities of practical reason and political participation.

123 Clarence Joldersma and Ruth Crick, "Citizenship, Discourse Ethics, and the Emancipatory Model of Lifelong Learning," in *Habermas, Critical Theory, and Education* (Routledge, 2010), 137.

124 Clarence Joldersma and Ruth Crick, "Citizenship, Discourse Ethics, and the Emancipatory Model of Lifelong Learning," in *Habermas, Critical Theory, and Education* (Routledge, 2010), 137.

> They are more likely to ask their own questions, try to uncover assumptions, and struggle towards the truth. Those who are not aware of their own curiosity are more likely to remain passive with respect to that which they do not know or understand.

125 Clarence Joldersma and Ruth Crick, "Citizenship, Discourse Ethics, and the Emancipatory Model of Lifelong Learning," in *Habermas, Critical Theory, and Education* (Routledge, 2010), 137. ("This includes connections to the resources of the lifeworld the student inevitably brings to the educational task. The connections function as a way to make meaning in their learning."). This also dovetails well with our early conversation on law and emotions, which begs us to invite student perspectives into the classroom so as to ensure an open discussion that encourages reflection on personal experience.

126 Clarence Joldersma and Ruth Crick, "Citizenship, Discourse Ethics, and the Emancipatory Model of Lifelong Learning," in *Habermas, Critical Theory, and Education* (Routledge, 2010), 137.

127 Clarence Joldersma and Ruth Crick, "Citizenship, Discourse Ethics, and the Emancipatory Model of Lifelong Learning," in *Habermas, Critical Theory, and Education* (Routledge, 2010), 137. In terms of awareness, they also "become interested in becoming more knowledgeable and more aware of themselves as learners, including their own particular strengths and weaknesses as learners." They will more likely venture into trying out different approaches to learning to see what happens. They become more reflective and better at self-evaluation, asking meta-cognitive questions and talking about their own learning processes.

128 Clarence Joldersma and Ruth Crick, "Citizenship, Discourse Ethics, and the Emancipatory Model of Lifelong Learning," in *Habermas, Critical Theory, and Education* (Routledge, 2010), 137.

129 Clarence Joldersma and Ruth Crick, "Citizenship, Discourse Ethics, and the Emancipatory Model of Lifelong Learning," in *Habermas, Critical Theory, and Education* (Routledge, 2010), 137.

130 *See also* Amy Gutmann, *Democratic Education* (Princeton, NJ: Princeton University Press, 1999).

131 Clarence Joldersma and Ruth Crick, "Citizenship, Discourse Ethics, and the Emancipatory Model of Lifelong Learning," in *Habermas, Critical Theory, and Education* (Routledge, 2010), 137.

132 Clarence Joldersma and Ruth Crick, "Citizenship, Discourse Ethics, and the Emancipatory Model of Lifelong Learning," in *Habermas, Critical Theory, and Education* (Routledge, 2010), 137.

133 Thomas Englund, "Educational Implications of the Idea of Deliberative Democracy," in Mark Murphy and Ted Fleming (eds.), *Habermas, Critical Theory and Education* (London: Taylor & Francis Group, 2009), 19–32.
134 David Hansen and Carmen James "The Importance of Cultivating Democratic Habits in Schools: Enduring Lessons from Democracy and Education," 48 *J. Curric. Stud.* 94–112 (2016).
135 Thomas Englund, "Educational Implications of the Idea of Deliberative Democracy," in Mark Murphy and Ted Fleming (eds.), *Habermas, Critical Theory and Education* (London: Taylor & Francis Group, 2009), 19–32.
136 Further elaboration on this notion of an "emancipatory education" is described by Joldersma and Crick.
137 Thomas Englund, "Educational Implications of the Idea of Deliberative Democracy," in Mark Murphy and Ted Fleming (eds.), *Habermas, Critical Theory and Education* (London: Taylor & Francis Group, 2009), 19–32.
138 Thomas Englund, "Educational Implications of the Idea of Deliberative Democracy," in Mark Murphy and Ted Fleming (eds.), *Habermas, Critical Theory and Education* (London: Taylor & Francis Group, 2009), 19–32.
139 Thomas Englund, "Educational Implications of the Idea of Deliberative Democracy," in Mark Murphy and Ted Fleming (eds.), *Habermas, Critical Theory and Education* (London: Taylor & Francis Group, 2009), 19–32.
140 Thomas Englund, "Educational Implications of the Idea of Deliberative Democracy," in Mark Murphy and Ted Fleming (eds.), *Habermas, Critical Theory and Education* (London: Taylor & Francis Group, 2009), 19–32.
141 Thomas Englund, "Educational Implications of the Idea of Deliberative Democracy," in Mark Murphy and Ted Fleming (eds.), *Habermas, Critical Theory and Education* (London: Taylor & Francis Group, 2009), 19–32.
142 Graham Ferris, *The Uses of Values in Legal Education* (Cambridge: Insertia, 2015), 75.
143 Thomas Englund, "On Moral Education through Deliberative Communication," 48 *J. Curric. Stud.* 58–76 (2015).
144 Thomas Englund, "On Moral Education through Deliberative Communication," 48 *J. Curric. Stud.* 58–76 (2015).
145 Amy Gutmann and Dennis F. Thompson, *Democracy and Disagreement* (Cambridge: Harvard University Press, 1998).
146 Thomas Englund, "On Moral Education through Deliberative Communication," 48 *J. Curric. Stud.* 110 (2015).
147 Thomas Englund, "On Moral Education through Deliberative Communication," 48 *J. Curric. Stud.* 110 (2015).

> Consensus is no doubt necessary, but it must be accompanied by dissent. Consensus is needed on the institutions constitutive of democracy and on the "ethico-political" values informing the political association—liberty and equality for all—but there will always be disagreement concerning their meaning and the way they should be implemented. In a pluralist democracy such disagreements are not only legitimate but also necessary.

148 Habermas would agree

> that nobody who could make a relevant contribution may be excluded; that all participants are granted an equal opportunity to make contributions; that the participants must mean what they say; that communication must be freed from external and internal coercion so that the "yes" or "no" stances that participants adopt on criticize-able validity claims are motivated solely by the rational force of the better reasons."

149 Thomas Englund, "Educational Implications of the Idea of Deliberative Democracy," in Mark Murphy and Ted Fleming (eds.), *Habermas, Critical Theory and Education* (London: Taylor & Francis Group, 2009), 19–32.

150 Clarence Joldersma and Ruth Crick, "Citizenship, Discourse Ethics, and the Emancipatory Model of Lifelong Learning," in *Habermas, Critical Theory, and Education* (Routledge, 2010), 137.

151 Clarence Joldersma and Ruth Crick, "Citizenship, Discourse Ethics, and the Emancipatory Model of Lifelong Learning," in *Habermas, Critical Theory, and Education* (Routledge, 2010), 137.

152 Clarence Joldersma and Ruth Crick, "Citizenship, Discourse Ethics, and the Emancipatory Model of Lifelong Learning," in *Habermas, Critical Theory, and Education* (Routledge, 2010), 137.

153 Clarence Joldersma and Ruth Crick, "Citizenship, Discourse Ethics, and the Emancipatory Model of Lifelong Learning," in *Habermas, Critical Theory, and Education* (Routledge, 2010), 137.

> If students are asked to connect in ways that bear little resemblance to their existing cognitive and emotional inner landscapes, then their capacity to develop personally meaningful understandings as they engage in the learning process is limited. But the ability to bridge lifeworlds is precisely a central competence needed for active participation in public discourse.

154 Thomas Englund, "Educational Implications of the Idea of Deliberative Democracy," in Mark Murphy and Ted Fleming (eds.), *Habermas, Critical Theory and Education* (London: Taylor & Francis Group, 2009), 19–32.

155 Thomas Englund, "On Moral Education through Deliberative Communication," 48 *J. Curric. Stud.* 110 (2015).

> In situations where teachers know that, in their school class, they have students who represent and are able to argue for anti-democratic and racist attitudes and values, deliberation may not be the answer in the short run. Rational arguments, as we know from experience, are not always enough. In such situations, it may be necessary for the teacher to work with a long-term aim of building relations and attempt to create the preconditions for moral deliberation, in parallel with referring to current norms, laws and rules.

In this way, I also diverge from Guttman's position on exclusion of extreme material in a conversation. *See, e.g.*, Amy Gutmann, *Democratic Education* (Princeton, NJ: Princeton University Press, 1999), 104 (where she contends that schools ought to be prevented—by the principle of non-repression—from entertaining, as a subject of discussion, something like "creationism." The principle is violated by the indirect imposition of the religious views of some on all children in the guise of science.). I, and others, would disagree. *See, e.g.*, Jonathan Marks, "Democratic Education (Review)," 86 *Mich. L. Rev.* 1140 (1988). Creationism could ostensibly be taught as an alternative to evolution, *so long as* it is proffered in a way that students could both develop and exercise "reasoning skills necessary for each child to make a choice." This would likely also apply to a variety of positions on legal cases or social issues that others would find "extreme" or oppositional necessarily.

156 Amy Gutmann, *Democratic Education* (Princeton, NJ: Princeton University Press, 1999), 122 ("on this argument, [schools] should accommodate children who refuse to salute the flag, but not those who refuse to sit next to blacks (assuming both refusals are based on principle rather than mere preference.").

157 David Hansen and Carmen James "The Importance of Cultivating Democratic Habits in Schools: Enduring Lessons from Democracy and Education." 48 *J. Curric. Stud.* 94–112 (2016).

158 Thomas Englund, "Educational Implications of the Idea of Deliberative Democracy," in Mark Murphy and Ted Fleming (eds.), *Habermas, Critical Theory and Education* (London: Taylor & Francis Group, 2009), 19–32.

159 *See, e.g.*, Martha Nussbaum, *Cultivating Humanity: A Classical Defense of Reform in Liberal Education* (Cambridge: Harvard University Press, 2000).

160 *See, e.g.*, Amartya Sen, *Development as Freedom* (New York: Vintage, 1999).

161 Martha C. Nussbaum, *Creating Capabilities: The Human Development Approach* (Harvard: Belknap, 2011), 18 ("The approach takes each person as an end, asking not just about the total average well-being but about the opportunities available to each person.").

162 Martha C. Nussbaum, *Creating Capabilities: The Human Development Approach* (Harvard: Belknap, 2011), 18.

163 And, to my understanding, the current educational landscape should reflect the placement of storied importance on critical thinking in today's public educational environment. *See, e.g.*, Constance Kamii, "Toward Autonomy: The Importance of Critical Thinking and Choice Making," 40 *Sch. Psychol. Rev.* 382–388 (2022). This is not even to say about the importance placed on critical thinking in our historic education project, as we have discussed in Chapter 3.

164 Yuval Noah Hariri in conversation with The Jordan Harbinger Show, "Peering into the Future of Humanity" (Episode 848). www.jordanharbinger.com/yuval-noah-harari-peering-into-the-future-of-humanity/

165 Yuval Noah Hariri in conversation with The Jordan Harbinger Show, "Peering into the Future of Humanity" (Episode 848). www.jordanharbinger.com/yuval-noah-harari-peering-into-the-future-of-humanity/

166 For more information, *see, e.g.*, Mario Perez-Montoro, *The Phenomenon of Information: A Conceptual Approach to Information Flow* (Scarecrow Press, 2007).

167 Defined as the condition by which a person (or system) cannot process by all communication resulting in the rendering of that person or system as ineffective. For more information, *see, e.g.*, Jonathan Haber, *Critical Thinking* (Cambridge: MIT Press, 2020) (discussing information overload in the context of education).

168 Karl Manheim and Lyric Kaplan, "Artificial Intelligence: Risks to Privacy and Democracy," 21 *Y. J. L. Technol.* 138 (2019); *see, e.g.*, Dan Patterson, How AI

Is Creating New Threats to Election Security, *CBS NEWS* (November 6, 2018, 11:50 AM); Trent J. Thornley, "The Caring Influence: Beyond Autonomy as the Foundation of Undue Influence," 71 *Ind. L. J.* 513, 524 (1996).

169 Karl Manheim and Lyric Kaplan, "Artificial Intelligence: Risks to Privacy and Democracy," 21 *Y. J. L. Technol.* 138 (2019) (quoting the Vyacheslav Polonski, How Artificial Intelligence Silently Took over Democracy, World Econ. Forum (August 9, 2017)).

170 Karl Manheim and Lyric Kaplan, "Artificial Intelligence: Risks to Privacy and Democracy," 21 *Y. J. L. Technol.* 138 (2019). "A 2018 report by the Computational Propaganda Research Project found evidence of manipulation campaigns in 48 countries, where 'at least one political party or government agency us[ed] social media to manipulate public opinion domestically'" (Samantha Bradshaw and Philip N. Howard, "Challenging Truth and Trust: A Global Inventory of Organized Social Media Manipulation," Computational Propogranda Research Project, Oxford University, 3 (2018)).

171 Samantha Bradshaw and Philip N. Howard, "Challenging Truth and Trust: A Global Inventory of Organized Social Media Manipulation," Computational Propogranda Research Project, Oxford University, 3 (2018).

172 "Artificial intelligence signifies a variety of technologies and tools that can solve tasks requiring 'perception, cognition, planning, learning, communication, and physical actions,' often learning and acting without oversight by their human creators or other people." Cynthia Dwork and Martha Minow, "Distrust of Artificial Intelligence: Sources & Responses from Computer Science & Law," 151 *Daedelus* 310 (2022); *see also* Jonathan Michael Spector and Shanshan Ma, "Inquiry and Critical Thinking Skills for the Next Generation: From Artificial Intelligence Back to Human Intelligence," 6 *Smart Learn. Environ.* 2 (2018) (defining AI as "label machines (computers) that imitate human cognitive functions such as learning and problem solving, or that manage to deal with complexity as well as human experts.").

173 Karl Manheim and Lyric Kaplan, "Artificial Intelligence: Risks to Privacy and Democracy," 21 *Y. J. L. Technol.* 138 (2019).

174 Hila Mehr, "Artificial Intelligence for Citizen Services and Government," Research report for Harvard University (2017).

175 "NYC Law Promises to Regulate AI in Hiring, But Leaves Crucial Gaps," Axios (July 6, 2023).

176 Inga Ulicane, "Power and Politics in Framing Bias in Artificial Intelligence Policy," 40 *Rev. Policy Res.* 665–687 (2023).

177 Yuval Noah Hariri in conversation with The Jordan Harbinger Show, "Peering into the Future of Humanity" (Episode 848). www.jordanharbinger.com/yuval-noah-harari-peering-into-the-future-of-humanity/

178 Kate Crawford and Meredith Whittaker, "The AI Now Report. The Social and Economic Implications of Artificial Intelligence Technologies in the Near-Term." AI Now Institute, New York University (2016).

179 Inga Ulicane, "Power and Politics in Framing Bias in Artificial Intelligence Policy," 40 *Rev. Policy Res.* 665–687 (2023).

180 Cynthia Dwork and Martha Minow, "Distrust of Artificial Intelligence: Sources & Responses from Computer Science & Law," 151 *Daedelus* 310 (2022).
181 Cynthia Dwork and Martha Minow, "Distrust of Artificial Intelligence: Sources & Responses from Computer Science & Law," 151 *Daedelus* 310 (2022)
182 Alex Chohlas-Wood, "Understanding Risk Assessment Instruments in Criminal Justice," Brookings Institute (June 19, 2020).
183 Cynthia Dwork and Martha Minow, "Distrust of Artificial Intelligence: Sources & Responses from Computer Science & Law," 151 *Daedelus* 310 (2022); *see also* Julia Dressel and Hany Farid, "The Accuracy, Fairness, and Limits of Predicting Recidivism," 4 *Sci. Adv.* (2018) (showing that laypeople predict recidivism as accurately as a widely used actuarial RAI tools).
184 Cynthia Dwork and Martha Minow, "Distrust of Artificial Intelligence: Sources & Responses from Computer Science & Law," 151 *Daedelus* 310 (2022).
185 Cynthia Dwork and Martha Minow, "Distrust of Artificial Intelligence: Sources & Responses from Computer Science & Law," 151 *Daedelus* 310 (2022).
186 Michael Arkfield, "A Call to Action: Litigating and Judging Artficial Intellgience," American Bar Association (2020), www.americanbar.org/groups/judicial/publications/judges_journal/2020/winter/a-call-action-litigating-and-judging-artificial-intelligence-cases/
187 Michael Arkfield, "A Call to Action: Litigating and Judging Artficial Intellgience," American Bar Association (2020), www.americanbar.org/groups/judicial/publications/judges_journal/2020/winter/a-call-action-litigating-and-judging-artificial-intelligence-cases/
188 *State of Wisconsin v. Eric L. Loomis*, 371 Wis. 2d 235, at 242 (2016).
189 *See* Frederic Lederer, "Here There Be Dragons: The Likely Interaction of Judges with the Artificial Intelligence Ecosystem," 59 *Jud. J.* 12 (2020); *see also* Zichun Xu, "Human Judges in the Era of Artificial Intelligence: Challenges and Opportunities," 36 *Appl. Artif. Intell.* (2022) (highlighting the importance of sound decision-making on the part of human judges for the purposes of bettering the data-set upon which AI relies).
190 Jonathan Michael Spector and Shanshan Ma, "Inquiry and Critical Thinking Skills for the Next Generation: From Artificial Intelligence Back to Human Intelligence," 6 *Smart Learn. Environ.* 2 (2018).
191 Jonathan Michael Spector and Shanshan Ma, "Inquiry and Critical Thinking Skills for the Next Generation: From Artificial Intelligence Back to Human Intelligence," 6 *Smart Learn. Environ.* 2 (2018).
192 Jonathan Michael Spector and Shanshan Ma, "Inquiry and Critical Thinking Skills for the Next Generation: From Artificial Intelligence Back to Human Intelligence," 6 *Smart Learn. Environ.* 2 (2018).

6 Combatting Apathy; Combatting Fracturing

I began this project by expressing a concern over apathy in our citizenry. Pressing and noteworthy, of course, is the lack of substantive knowledge about civic and political institutions; alarming, indeed, is the paucity of resources combatting polarization. But I was especially struck by this lack of care. The phenomenon, to my mind, is borne out of an educational failure; this proposal therefore deals in education. A more *civically minded* American populace requires that citizens of all ages *know* about our institutions but also feel *vested* in them, *care* about outcomes, and feel *empowered* to deal with them and through them. I have argued in the above that teaching law to students in primary and secondary schools—that is, higher reasoning skills through *law learning*—serves this purpose by developing civic temperament, civic values, and critical-mindedness in the next generation. To learn law and legal reasoning is a greatly empowering education that crucially emphasizes an intersecting acquisition of political capabilities and democratic virtues. This, all while complementarily encouraging self-examination and reflection, honing, and redefining our sense of self-identity and personally held beliefs. Such an education is a *formational* one; to educate children in law, to let them wrestle constructively with the important texts, values, and ideas that make up our constitutional democratic system, placing them in conversation with their own, for all the reasons discussed above, will breed a generation more *connected* to the democratic project and *capable* of resolving our divisive issues years hence.

In support of a *law learning proposal*, I began by first surveying the existing civic education landscape. The problems that contemporary iterations of civic education face—and consequently the answers to why it is not producing a civically literate citizenry—either in terms of knowledge or investment—began at the definitional levels: there is no clear conception of the attributes of the citizen we are trying to cultivate nationally or best practice as to how to do the educating. The *descriptive* nature of civic curricula and the utter lack of preoccupation for developing skills or perspectives that promote the capability of political participation are, frankly, a discredit to the storied civic project. With that in mind, we began our redesign and proposed reforms. In

DOI: 10.4324/9781003596523-9

philosophically grounding this new proposal, I emphasized a new definition of the citizen, the value in studying *law* as an epistemological tool, and the importance of such an education in terms of values-formation. Laws, indeed, are important exemplifiers and tools for normalizing and strengthening norms and values; to learn them is an *empowering* education especially for a legalistic nation where innovation *needs to be bottom-up*, by people, reforming with a mind toward the highest levels of change. The law learning project teaches legal reasoning and institutional awareness as *the* tools for the citizen to speak America's language of law. Meanwhile, the values-plural posturing of *law learning* promises a challenging moral-learning environment that pushes students to think on their deepest values in service of the balance between autonomy and social needs.

This proposal, I argued, was nothing new philosophically; *law learning* is an outgrowth of an older vision for the public-school civics program, a "game" that sought to *empower and cater toward the individual student*, rooting back to the colonial schooling enterprise. Anything short of a civic learning experience that challenged and developed the whole of the person, to my mind, represents *bad game teaching* and a complete misunderstanding of the *common field*. My curricular proposal offsets a loss of criticality, directedness, versatility with self-examination that were once so sacrosanct in early education but were left in the dust with Mann's common school. I called, indeed, for us to look back to our oldest view of the "common field of the educational game": to engender an "education for the empowered citizen"; the "rules and tools for this game" lay in the values-plural teaching approaches of Dewey and Kohlberg and the Capabilities Approach of Martha Nussbaum and in reconceiving the classroom to let values organically emerge (in their diversity!) in discursive settings that emphasize only equality, critical inquiry, and rational deliberation as frameworks for child education—all cross-cultural and uniform. This is as essential for children as it is for adults, lest children—being already encumbered by the ideas of their parents—grow up not to challenge them or think for themselves (whether this leads to agreement or disagreement) and thereby move our democracy forward. As Amy Gutmann articulates:

> rational deliberation remains the form of freedom most suitable to a democratic society in which adults must be free to deliberate and disagree but constrained to secure the intellectual grounds for deliberation and disagreement among children. Adults must therefore be prevented from using their present deliberative freedom to undermine the future deliberative freedom of children.[1]

A civic education is this prevention; *law learning* is civics at its most effective. There are surely benefits, and of course critiques (a cross-section of which I have addressed), but in the end suffice to say: something must be done, such change to education, and especially civics, is of prime importance in today's pressing, modern world.

Having said all of this, what I would like to offer in this concluding reflection is further articulation concerning the way in which *law learning* impacts apathy. This can be most plainly seen by reflecting on this proposal in light of the "values-neutral classroom" project. What I encourage is the invitation of substantive discussions and pedagogical initiatives that aggravate values-neutrality, inviting and encouraging children to bring *their whole selves* to the classroom. Doing so is *essential* to developing a child's feeling of *autonomy* by way of senses of self, identity, morality. The *law learning* classroom takes these innermost beliefs—cultivated by the family, by one's church, by one's community—and puts them in conversation with democratic values and societal ideas manifested through law in order to forge connection and buy-in. It does so *out of respect and veneration for pluralism*, an interest in providing common rhetoric, building democratic relationships that are complimentary rather than competitive with personal principles, and developing children's communication skills—precisely these abstract values issues—that are absolutely necessary for effective political and societal participation. The curriculum brings children together to discuss mutually important issues, critique the system, contend with differing perspectives, and resolve disputes.

Charles Glenn, in his assailment of the values-neutral classroom, precisely argues this point; schools today fail to teach students *conviction*. He articulates:

> schools today love to talk about differences of color, of sexual identities and preferences, and of trivial customs, but not convictions—these must remain unexpressed in the public-school contexts of the bland leading the bland, and thus youth are often persuaded that deep-rooted beliefs play no part in defining a worthy life.[2]

And, where they do, schools overstep the family, "presume[ing] to provide [children] with a distinctive worldview" that is superficial and contingent, that avoids, in the interest of "social unity and progress," conversations on controversies, even insofar as an account of the nature of a "flourishing life."[3] Tolerance, though a major (if not, the only) hallmark of the public education experience, is simply "nonjudgmental relativism," and not genuine respect or understanding. The school of today, to Glenn, "risks negating or at best minimizing the benefits that children gain from becoming self-fulfilled individuals who can choose from among various visions of the good life under the guidance of their family and cultural community."[4] And to be sure, democratic citizenship will suffer.

"There is no values-free form of education," argued Martha Nussbaum, and the heart of my proposal agrees.[5] This is meant both in terms of what we inculcate through civic education about societal values, and also the project of engaging with ideas brought from home. Children develop—at the youngest ages[6]—ideas and convictions that need to be honed, critiqued, framed, connected with the system. This is so important; we must support and guide them in this natural process. Where we face problematic ideas, we must ensure children feel comfortable criticizing them, coming to compromise, coming to see other points of view. We must treat this project with primacy. In effect, the devotion I request in this proposal emblemizes my interest in reconceiving all citizens, especially children, as consequential, active participants in our institutions, almost as *lawgivers*[7] themselves, restructuring our educational programming to produce actors with ideas of value who will move our democracy forward *by way of their convictions*. Doing so looks like, foremost, fostering classroom environments in which students, at younger and younger ages, can hold debate in tolerant, respectful, and inclusive ways that do not diminish their individuality or (even divergent) foundational beliefs. In the words of Amy Gutmann, "[citizens] are born within complex social contexts, and they become human agents by interacting with other people within culturally loaded contexts."[8] Democracies and democratic education should "recognize important cultural contributions of different groups," tolerating them even where they "might offend some people's sensibilities but that do not violate anyone's rights to civic equality."[9] From this, we can see how, though "no values are culturally neutral in the sense of being equally conducive or acceptable to all cultures," some "can be defended from the vantage point of many—even if not all—cultures that are common in and across democracies."[10] And even if not, deliberative democracy can make a virtue out of the necessity of such disagreement.[11]

Implicit in all of this is, of course, a respect for multiculturalism, but also equal respect for conscience, for political position, for ideology. In effect, this conceives of a sense of larger belonging and connection on the basis that we *are all* citizens with conviction, bridged by this shared calling, rather than simply disconnected on account of our beliefs. And the classroom is the place to discover all of this! The values-neutral classroom stands in opposition to this idea; it presupposes a "narrow focus on knowledge, together with an adjustment of different schools to different social groups, with no agenda to changing the social structure and promoting social mobility through education."[12] It is a static education; it is an affront to the project of pluralism shrouded in political sensitivity. *Empowerment*, for our purposes, takes the form of presenting a difficult question, expressing differing views, and dialoguing critically with the expectation that the results will not be stringently enshrined beliefs or ideas, right or wrong dispositions, but yield a respectable myriad of dispositions and roundtable discussion. Law learning *informs* perspectives rather than indoctrinates; indeed, one studies the system from without rather than from within. We combat, in turn, superficial understanding that leaves one vulnerable to political sway; we develop the individual to a place of true *autonomy*, above manipulation, to a level of at once entrenched in our system, stalwart in self-identity, and critical of information.

As Scheppele denoted, "citizens need to be trained as constitutionalists—to understand the point of constitutionalism, to recognize threats to self-sustaining democracy, and *to care about defending liberal values*."[13] This book articulated how a *law learning* does just this as a necessarily values-education with civic elements; it unites citizens with the common rhetoric that empowers them to operate in a legalistic nation like America, serves as starting point for generating future leaders interested in innovation, invited debate and self-examination by reference to judgments and social policy issues engaged with in cases and statutes, and, when inserted into the curriculum of diverse classrooms with students embracing differing political, religious, cultural, and social identities, as those that exist already in public schools,[14] leads to important identity-building and relationship-strengthening lessons through respectful, tolerant, and discursive discussions *we need to be having*. It teaches calculative and reflective temperament, appreciation for tradition, and respect for others; it is the sort of education, when properly conceived, that empowers students to connect with systems, see their worth and value as change-makers, *want to act*, and build relationships with that in mind. In turn, beneficiaries of this education in the next generation might be more inclined to care and effectively better civic projects, to put stock in conversations that are now seen as "not one's problem." This goes farthest toward Dewey's vision that "a democratic society requires that citizens have a personal interest in social relationships and control, and the habits of mind which secure social changes without introducing disorder."[15] This is an education that pushes us to care, and, eventually to dialogue, critique, and, if the occasion calls for it, *to intentionally resist.*

Notes

1 Amy Gutmann, *Democratic Education* (Princeton, NJ: Princeton University Press, 1999), 45.

2 Charles Glenn, "Civic Norms and Distinctive Convictions: Finding the Right Balance," in Pickard et al. (eds.), *The Impact of Education on Character Formation, Ethics, and the Communication of Values in Late Modern Pluralistic Societies* (Leipzig: Evangelische Verlagsanstalt, 2022), 68.

3 Charles Glenn, "Civic Norms and Distinctive Convictions: Finding the Right Balance," in Pickard et al. (eds.), *The Impact of Education on Character Formation, Ethics, and the Communication of Values in Late Modern Pluralistic Societies* (Leipzig: Evangelische Verlagsanstalt, 2022), 68.

4 Charles Glenn, "Civic Norms and Distinctive Convictions: Finding the Right Balance," in Pickard et al. (eds.), *The Impact of Education on Character Formation, Ethics, and the Communication of Values in Late Modern Pluralistic Societies* (Leipzig: Evangelische Verlagsanstalt, 2022), 68.

5 Though, in reflecting on Glenn, I am not in agreement, necessarily, with his use of the conviction argument to support school choice or voucher programs. I agree more with Amy Gutmann's position that "voucher plans attempt to avoid rather than settle

our disagreements over how to develop democratic character through schooling." Amy Gutmann, *Democratic Education* (Princeton, NJ: Princeton University Press, 1999), 68.

6 Recall, again, our discussion at the outset of Chapter 1 featuring the New Jersey children. When the teacher saw young children building a wall and she asked the students what they were doing, the boys proudly responded, "we're building a wall to keep the Mexicans out!" Unsure of what to do—herself also disquieted—the teacher posed a question to the whole of the class: "why do some people want to keep other people out?" One child responded as follows: "because sometimes you just want to be alone or with your best friends, and so you have to say no to some people." Another said, "because you have to stay safe, and you don't know if strangers could be dangerous." And finally, one of the boys building the wall offered, "Because the Mexicans will take our jobs." This shows political integration at early ages, but also a propensity for picking up on values-conversations.

7 This phrase is used by Habermas and Amy Gutmann to describe the varied ways for the bottom-up production of law in democracy. Habermas, Jürgen, *The Inclusion of the Other: Studies in Political Theory* (Cambridge: MIT Press, 1996).

8 Amy Gutmann, "Educating for Individual Freedom and Democratic Citizenship: In Unity and Diversity There Is Strength," 1 *J. Eth. Ref.* 20 (2021).

9 Amy Gutmann, "Educating for Individual Freedom and Democratic Citizenship: In Unity and Diversity There Is Strength," 1 *J. Eth. Ref.* 20 (2021).

10 Amy Gutmann, "Educating for Individual Freedom and Democratic Citizenship: In Unity and Diversity There Is Strength," 1 *J. Eth. Ref.* 20 (2021).

11 Amy Gutmann, "Educating for Individual Freedom and Democratic Citizenship: In Unity and Diversity There Is Strength," 1 *J. Eth. Ref.* 20 (2021).

12 Habermas, Jürgen, *Autonomy and Solidarity: Interviews with Jürgen Habermas* (Peter Daws, ed.) (London: Verso Books, 1992).

13 Kim Lane Scheppele, "Autocratic Legalism," 85 University of Chicago L. Rev. at 582–583.

14 Linda C. McClain, *The Place of Families: Fostering Capacity, Equality and Responsibility* (Cambridge: Harvard University Press, 2006), 50–84.

15 John Dewey, *Democracy and Education* (New York: Macmillan), at 99 (1916).

Index